Kaye and Kern Holoman

TRAVELS

AND OTHER JOURNALS IN THEIR ARCHIVE

EDITED BY

D. Kern Holoman

au Vieux Logis

Méricourt — Raleigh — Davis

FRONT COVER: Kaye Holoman's scrapbook: The Grand Tour, Europe 1956

BACK COVER: Kern and Kaye Holoman, house of Claude Monet, Giverny, 1991

Travels © copyright 2023 by D. Kern Holoman

AU VIEUX LOGIS

sites.google.com/view/dkholoman

ISBN: 978-1-7356907-1-1 (print)
978-1-7356907-3-5 (ebook)

Cover and book design by Mayfly Design

Library of Congress Catalog Number: 2023903113

CONTENTS

Foreword v

Dramatis Personae ix

Eugenia Herring: European Grand Tour (1928) 3

William Kern Holoman: Stuttgart Journal (1946) 43

Kaye & Kern Holoman: European Grand Tour (1956) 81

Kern Holoman: India (1982) 99

Kaye & Kern Holoman: France (1982) 119

Kaye & Kern Holoman: Australia and New Zealand (1992) 127

Kaye & Kern Holoman: Scotland (1994) 147

Kaye & Kern Holoman: The American West (1994) 155

Kaye & Kern Holoman: California (1995) 171

Kaye & Kern Holoman: France (1995) 177

Kaye & Kern Holoman: Nova Scotia (1996) 189

Kaye & Kern Holoman: Asia (1997) 199

Kern Holoman & Jackie Harper: The American West (2001) 209

Kern Holoman & Jackie Harper: Portugal and Spain (2002) 221

Kern Holoman & Jackie Harper: South America (2002) 229

Kern Holoman & Jackie Harper: The Adriatic (2005) 247

FOREWORD

As Grand Tour-ists have done since the beginning, my parents Kaye and Kern Holoman recorded the details of their European journey of 1956 as they went: in a gold-tooled, red leather diary embossed "TRAVELS." It rested for many years on a coffee table alongside the big scrapbook of the journey Kaye compiled after they got back. The red diary, and the trip it described, had a special place in our household.

Kern, who'd edited his high-school newspaper and had meant to become a journalist or an English professor, was a natural chronicler. From England, France, and Germany in wartime he wrote near-daily letters home, some of them published in the local press; after he retired he compiled a volume's worth of essays I enjoyed collecting and publishing as *Kern Holoman: Memoirs* on the occasion of his 90th birthday in 2010. It was only later that we discovered his diary from West Germany in 1946, transcribed here.

Our parents were always keen to travel. There were frequent car trips with the children, ranging from weekends or full weeks in and around North Carolina and Virginia to expeditions as far as Canada (1953) and Florida (1957) and the New York World's Fair (1964). Once I'd left home, the family trips began to go further and further afield, including to Disneyland (about which I'm still jealous) and—partly to visit Betty and me during the very first weeks of our dissertation year in Paris—to France, Switzerland, and Italy. Meanwhile Kaye and Kern had discovered that they liked cruises, and began to invite family members to join them in exploring the Caribbean, the Panama Canal, Mexico, and Alaska.

In fact they retired at age 60 largely in order to indulge their passion for travelling. In the "Family Chronology (1943–1993)" that Kaye prepared on the occasion of their 50th wedding anniversary, she writes:

A Turning Point. On his 60th birthday, August 10th, 1980, Kern became eligible for his military retirement, and he had been planning to be able to retire from his civilian work, Boylan-Pearce, at this time, as well. ... High on the list of activities which were now possible was TRAVEL, and the subsequent years attest to our success in this endeavor.

From then on they were away almost as much as they were home. In 1982, Kern led a six-week Rotary exchange to India, Bangladesh, and Nepal, taking with him a travel diary almost identical to the red one from Europe in 1956: both must have come from Boylan-Pearce, and I'm guessing that the green one had sat empty on the bookshelf for the 25-plus years that had ensued. Other diaries of the same general look and feel accompanied Kaye and Kern to Australia and New Zealand in 1992, on their long, long "Western Loop" by car in 1994, various shorter trips, and the big cruise from Japan to Alaska in 1997. After my mother's death that year, Dad traveled far and wide with Jackie Harper, diligently writing in diaries she had given him—but less successful every year in terms of legibility.

Altogether there are ten bound diaries in the archive of Kaye and Kern Holoman, now housed at Olivia Raney Local History Library, Raleigh, North Carolina. They document some sixteen journeys, ranging from Great-Aunt Eugenia Herring's Grand Tour in 1928 to Kern and Jackie's coach tour of Croatia and its environs in 2005.

But these volumes represent only a fraction of the trips we know something about. In the Family Chronology, Kaye writes:

> From the standpoint of traveling, 1986 was outstanding. This was the year when Kaye and Kern had Eastern Airlines "Fly Anywhere For A Year" tickets, and they were put to good use. The flights were combined with car rentals and made it possible to complete the list of all 48 contiguous states visited since retiring in 1980.

She goes on to list trips that year to New York City in January, Disneyland in February, Chicago ("via Key West," she says, "to view Haley's Comet") in March, New Mexico in April, California in July, Tennessee in

September, New England in late September, Chicago again and Northern California again in October and November.

In 1979 they took their first Leisure Ministries trip with Edenton Street Methodist Church and soon became the principal organizers of those tours. In 1986, for instance, they led trips to Charleston, Pennsylvania Dutch Country, and the Great Smokies. In 1993 they brought a group to Northern California, and we drove over to historic Sonoma to be with the group as they encountered—some of them warily—Mexican food.

What makes it possible to reconstruct most of Kern and Kaye's travel history, then Kern and Jackie's, is the large collection of color slides in the family archive. My father had bought an Argus C3 camera from the pawnshop before embarking on the Grand Tour in 1956, and for more than four decades scrupulously labeled and boxed hundreds of slides taken with that camera and its successors. The Argus C3, called "the brick," was the leading consumer 35mm camera of its generation (1930s to 1960s); that very camera went with me on both my summers in Siena, 1967 and 1968. The slides gradually gave way to prints, taken with lesser cameras and developed cheaply at K-Mart. But it's possible to develop a comfortably reliable list of the family travels from a combination of the diaries and the photographs. I've done so on the website associated with this book.

I have lightly edited these texts for consistency of format and obvious misspellings, but retained most of the place-name spellings then in use (Calcutta, Dacca) as well as the diarist's orthography of most of the proper names. Deciphering the handwriting toward the end demanded a good deal of guesswork.

Thanks are due, as always, to my wife Elizabeth Holoman, for proofreading and factual corrections. I am grateful to Julie Scheife, Ryan Scheife, and Mike Corrao at Mayfly Design in Minneapolis for guiding the production of this book. My brothers and I are grateful to Hannah Cox and the Olivia Raney Local History Library in Raleigh, now custodians of the diaries.

Corrections, additions, and links to the photographic sources are found at sites.google.com/view/dkholoman.

— DKH

DRAMATIS PERSONAE

Katherine Herring Highsmith (1922–97) married William Kern Holoman (1920–2015) in 1943. They were the parents of four sons: D. Kern (Mike), Dick (Dickie), Christopher (Chris), and David.

Allie = Alair Currier Holoman Fritz (b. 1986), elder daughter of Chris and Connie

Bessie Gray = Bessie Gray Gill Holoman (1907–95), wife of Dallas Holoman, Jr.

Belle = Mary Belle Herring, *see* Mary Belle

Betsy and Ralph = Elizabeth "Betsy" Battle Powell and her husband Ralph Baird Seymour (1922–2006), longtime Raleigh friends of Kaye and Kern

Betty = Elizabeth Ann Rock Holoman (b. 1947), wife of D. Kern

Boyce = Boyce Holoman (1915–72), brother of Kern

Chreston = George Chreston Holoman (1909–68), brother of Kern

Chris = Christopher Louis Holoman (b. 1957), third son of Kaye and Kern

Connie = Constance Leigh Currier Holoman (b. 1955), wife of Chris

D. Kern (DKH) = Dallas Kern Holoman (b. 1947), first son of Kaye and Kern

Dad (in WKH writings) = Dallas Holoman, Sr. (1884–1958), father of Dallas, Jr., Chreston, Boyce, and Kern

Dallas, Dal = Dallas Holoman, Jr. (1908–2008), brother of Kern

Dan and Tempy = Daniel Marshall Hodges (1921–2002) and Frances Templeton Hodges (1921–2002), high school friends of Kern and Kaye

David = David William Holoman (b. 1960), fourth son of Kaye and Kern

Debbie = Deborah Ann Mitchell Holoman (b. 1966), wife of David

Dick, Dickie = Richard Highsmith Holoman (b. 1949), second son of Kaye and Kern

Edna = Edna Lockwood Holoman (b. 1938), daughter of Chreston, niece of Kern

Eugenia, Jean = Eugenia Pherobe Herring (1888–1967), aunt of Kaye

Frances = Frances Highsmith Holoman (b. 1988), called Fran, younger daughter of Chris and Connie

Gerry = Kenneth Gerard Bello (1951–2013), son of Jackie Harper

Heather = Heather Carol Shelton (b. 1986), granddaughter of Louise

Mrs. Highsmith = Kate Maude Herring Highsmith (1880–1966), mother of Kaye and mother-in-law of Kern

Hodges, *see* Dan and Tempy

Jackie = Jacqueline Hutzler Bello Harper (1926–2014), Kern's companion from 1998

Jay and Ken = Jane Herring Wooten, MD (1918–2018), a cousin of Kaye, and her husband Kenneth F. Wooten, Jr. (1925–2009)

Jeff = Jeffrey Scott Holoman (b. 1978), second son of Dick and Sandy

Jordan = Jordan Belle Holoman (b. 1995), elder daughter of David and Debbie

Judy = Judy Bello (Mrs. Thomas), daughter-in-law of Jackie Harper

Kate = Kate Elizabeth Holoman (b. 1980), first child of D. Kern and Betty

Kaye = Katherine Herring Highsmith Holoman

Ken, *see* Jay and Ken

Kern (WKH) = William Kern Holoman

Laura = Laura MacDonald Holoman Murphy (1932–2020), elder daughter of Dallas and Bessie Gray

Louis = Louis Reams Wilkerson (1925–2001), husband of Louise

Louise = Louise Westbrook Highsmith Wilkerson (1924–2019), sister of Kaye

Lula Belle = Lula Belle Highsmith Rich (1912–66), sister of Kaye

Luna = Luna Crawford Byrd Holoman (1909–95), wife of Chreston

Lynn = Lillian Hales Didenhover Holoman (1918–2000), wife of Boyce

Mark = Mark Chreston Holoman (b. 1975), elder son of Dick and Sandy

Mary Belle = Mary Belle Herring (1897–1987), aunt of Kaye

Michael = Michael Kern Holoman (b. 1987), second child of D. Kern and Betty

Mike = family nickname for D. Kern

Pauline and Jim = Pauline Herring Sloo (1886–1966), aunt of Kaye, and her husband James Rearden Sloo (1889–1954)

Sandy = Sandra Kay Little Holoman, now Lear (b. 1948), wife of Dick

Susan = Susan Elizabeth Bello (1952–2008), daughter of Jackie Harper

Tempy, *see* Dan and Tempy, above

Va. = Virginia Barber Holoman (1920–91), second wife of Dallas Holoman, Sr.

Vara = Vara Herring (1879–1962), aunt of Kaye

EUROPEAN GRAND TOUR

June 14 – August 11, 1928

Eugenia Herring

*Eugenia Herring (far right) with friends,
likely on the* S. S. Caledonia, *June 1928*

SOURCE: Diary 1 (1928). Dark olive leather album with gold tooling, titled *My Travels Abroad*, roughly 3½ x 5¾ inches, with pencil holder. Gilt-edged lined paper, including alphabetized address tabs at end. Printed title page "A Record of the Travels of" inscribed:

*Eugenia Herring
604 North Blount St.
Raleigh, N.C.*

Printed itinerary for "Tour 416—62 Days—$650" pasted in at front.

European Grand Tour

June 14 – August 11, 1928

Eugenia Herring

Great-Aunt Jean, formally Eugenia Pherobe Herring (1888–1967), traveled abroad June 14–August 11, 1928. The News and Observer *of June 16 notes: "Miss Margaret Habel and Miss Eugenia Herring will leave New York today for Europe on the S. S. Caledonia, to be gone during the summer months." On August 16 the paper reported that "Misses Eugenia Herring and Margaret Habel have returned from a two months' trip abroad. They reached New York Sunday aboard the S. S. Carmania. While away they visited England, Scotland and other European countries." She has pasted the published itinerary at the front of her diary, included here on pp. 35–37.*

It seems reasonable to imagine that Aunt Jean was rewarding herself for having passed the North Carolina Bar the previous February. The newspaper reports on February 4, 1928: "Two of the three women who took the examination yesterday were granted licenses, the successful being Miss Eugenia Herring, secretary to Associate Justice W. J. Adams of the Supreme Court and long a prominent figure in the local and State organization of the Business and Professional Women's Clubs, and Mrs. Evelyn Messick Nimmoks, prominent widow of Fayetteville." She was admitted to practice before the Supreme Court on February 21.

She was 39 years old at the time of her voyage. I don't remember her talking about her European journey, nor Grandmother Highsmith talking about hers, but there was frequent mention of Aunt Mary Belle's summer stints as a maid on commercial freighters.

June 14, 1928 — Raleigh, N.C.

I left Raleigh at 9:10 p.m. for New York, where I sail on Saturday, June 16, for a two months trip. We were quite excited as so many of our friends came down to see us off and wish us "bon voyage." Margaret Habel is my traveling companion. Those who saw us off were Vara, Pauline and Jim, Mrs. Habel, Fred, Lola Yancey, Foy Lester, Epsie Headen, Dessie Clark, Mary Knight, Fannie Thomas, and Miss Poyntz and Annie Crews.[1] We had a very comfortable trip up. John Evans was on the train on his way to New York. We asked him when he sailed and where he landed. He said Saturday and at Glasgow, Scotland. We were surprised, as all the others going over this year have gone on other boats and most of them have landed in France. He is with the Carleton Tours and takes practically the same trip as we do. He returns on the same boat with us—the *Carmania*. We arrived in New York at 10:30, but 11:30 Daylight Saving Time.

June 15, 1928 — New York

We took a taxi up to the Prince George Hotel where the Allen people had engaged a room for us. We got settled in our rooms and then left for a shopping, or "just looking" tour. We went to Gimbels where we had engaged tickets to see Jane Cowl in "The Road to Rome." I called up Mary Shotwell[2] and we agreed on a place and time to meet. We had lunch at the Golden Pheasant and had some good clam chowder. At 2:30 we walked about 15 blocks to Roxy's Theatre for the matinee. The picture was "bum" but the musical program was fine. The theatre is gorgeous and we walked up and down steps on those beautiful plush carpets. Wonderful pictures were on the walls, and marble columns filled the atrium. Mary met us on the outside at 4:00 p.m. and took us to the Hotel Bristol for dinner. We sat and talked until 7:30. She had a date and had to leave and we went to The Playhouse to see Jane Cowl. We enjoyed the play immensely. It is quite risqué but very fine. After the show we started home on foot for the exercise, went several blocks out of the way, but finally reached there quite tired and exhausted. We had a very good night.

---

1. Annie Crews was a close friend of the Herring sisters and for a long time their housemate at 604 North Blount Street in Raleigh.
2. Mary Shotwell was a close friend of the Herring sisters, especially Kate Herring Highsmith. Like Kate, she was a graduate of Littleton College and Trinity College (later Duke University); they worked in similar capacities in public health.

When we got to the Hotel we found that Mr. Allen of the Allen Tours was there, also Mr. Lane, our tour manager.

He told us to be ready to go to the pier about 9:30 so as to have plenty of time to get on board and get our bags in the stateroom.

June 16, 1928 — New York

We got up at 7:00 a.m., which meant 6 standard time, dressed and had breakfast in the hotel by nine o'clock. We saw Mrs. Kate Burr Johnson in the restaurant perched up on one of those little round stools eating breakfast. We did the same thing as that was the quickest way to get served.

I rushed down to Saks on Broadway and 34 to get a few last-minute items while Margaret looked after the bags and that I did not get left. We took a taxi to the Cunard Pier at W. 14th Street, Pier 56. The charge was only 55 cents each, and it took us quite a long time to go.

The boat left at 12:00 noon sharp. Margaret had friends down to see her off but only saw them for a few minutes as they came on the boat by a different way than where we were standing. She brought her flowers and a box of nuts. When the whistle blew for the guests to depart, I thought everybody was going to get off.

When we got started Margaret and I went down to our stateroom and found the flowers and nuts which her friend had left. We unpacked our bags, hung up our clothes and got straight for a week's stay on board. It was lunch time by then and we found the dining room and sat just any place for that meal. The dining steward asked us to come down at 4:30 to get our permanent place at the table. Mr. Lance did that for all on his tour, so that we could all sit together and become acquainted better. We go down to the first table: breakfast at 7:30; lunch at 12:00; and dinner at 6:00. We have to be on time as the other table has to be fixed after we leave. I was glad to be at the first, even tho' it gets us up early. We like the fresh air on deck anyway.

I slept good last night tho' the ventilation didn't work well and it was quite stuffy and hot. We have a nice fan, but I'm not keen on having a fan on all night. However we did it, by pushing it up so that it did not blow on us. We have a nice stateroom and it is very comfortable for two. Four could get in it in a pinch, but I'd hate the push. We stayed out on deck all the time. It took us a little time to get our deck chairs, rugs and places.

After we got them we forgot to move until the dinner bell rang. We have good meals and good appetites. I try not to eat too much.

We are due to arrive in Boston at 1:00 p.m. on the 17th. After dinner we came back on deck and played bridge until it got too dark to see. Two young men joined us, Mr. Bradford and Mr. Gordon. They are from New York, where they work and now are on their way to England on their vacation of two months. They are originally from Liverpool. Margaret says she bets they are waiters in New York. They seem to be very nice and play a good game of bridge.

June 17, 1928 — On Board

We are not in sight of land at this time but we are traveling along the coast. We stay in sight most of the time. It is a beautiful day—not a cloud in the sky. It was beautiful on board all day yesterday. The water is so smooth—not a ripple in it anywhere. Feeling fine.

We had lunch before getting into Boston at 11:00 a.m. 433 passengers were taken on in Boston. We were due to leave at 4:00 but did not leave until after five.

June 17, 1928 — Boston Harbor

While the boat was in the harbor, Margaret and I and a young man explored the decks *on high*. It is perfectly lovely on first deck. The tea room, writing room and all kinds of cozy places and salons are so very lovely. I wondered if I should see Belle Cameron[3] anywhere up there, or find her chair. About the second chair I looked at was hers but she was not in it. She had a bundle of letters on it, so I wrote her a note. Before I left she came up to her chair and we had a little chat. She invited us up to have tea with her at 4:00. We went up at that time and were served tea and sandwiches and cookies. I don't know that I balanced the tea cup like an Englishman but I enjoyed it just the same. She took us over the first-class (only) deck and then down to her room to show us what she got. Her room was filled with flowers, a big basket of fruit,

---

3. Belle Cameron (Isabelle Mayo Cameron, later Mrs. Eric van Lennep, 1899–1983) of Raleigh was the daughter of the wealthy Bennehan and Sallie Mayo Cameron. She had recovered from polio contracted in the summer of 1916, later marrying into European aristocracy. She and her sister had attended St. Mary's School on Hillsboro Street in Raleigh, the land for which had been donated by her father.

books and magazines by the dozen(?), and just lots of candy. She made us take a box of candy, which turned out to be assorted nuts. We then went up on the highest place we could find to have a good view as we left Boston. Before we got very far out, our bell down below rang and we had to leave. I enjoyed it every much up there. It was wonderful to see how the pilot could guide this big boat out of the harbor between the little islands etc.

June 17, 1928 — On Board

After dinner we sat on deck and read the Boston papers (Sunday) for awhile and at 9:00 p.m. went to church in the Second Class dining room. Margaret guessed when the preacher got up that he was a Methodist but after the service she said he was a Baptist. I don't know who or what he was. It was a very nice service. The collection was for the sailors' wives and orphans.

After that to bed and dreamland. Still feeling fine.

June 18, 1928 — Out on Ocean

It is a perfectly grand day—not a cloud in the sky. The air is cool and the sun is hot. Margaret is reading a book that Belle loaned us, "Two Flights Up" by Mary Roberts Rinehart, while I am writing my diary. I have one too which she loaned us, "Daughters of Folly" by Cosmo Hamilton. I can guess it is "spicy" by the lines of dedication: "Dedicated, with respect, to fainting women, the defunct bustle, the stuffed canary in a glass case and the regular bottle of port."

Margaret and I and scores of others are sun burned. My nose is red—oh, horrors. I hate a red nose above all things. I cold creamed around it last night but it is still red. I forgot to tell what I received on board. Linda sent me a box of wash cloths (3) and Mr. Hamsted sent me a box of nuts and a box of candy in one package. I received a telegram from State Convention of BPW [Business and Professional Womens'] Club in session at Fayetteville. Letters from Mrs. Dennis, Carrie Phillips Hubbard, Annie Lewis Bledsoe, and Mr. Hamsted.

I walked around the deck 12 times this morning with Miss King of Hagerstown, Md. She eats in front of me.

I was real excited when a radiogram was handed me. I could not imagine who it could be from. I opened it and read "Won Stunt Prize.

Gurganus."[4] Isn't that just like her—always doing something unusual and nice. I am so glad we won the stunt at the State Convention of B. & P. W. Club which met at Fayetteville, even if I could not be there to help put it across.

Mr. Lane asked the "Allen Tour" people to meet him at 3 p.m. in the dining room. He wanted us to know everyone on the trip and to plan for stunt on stunt night, also find out what we could do in the way of entertainment. I have no parlor accomplishments, however, so I shall be a spectator.

There was dancing from 4–5:30 with the orchestra on C-Deck, forward. Tea was served out there.

JUNE 18, 1928 [CONT'D.] — OFF NEWFOUNDLAND

After dinner we sat on deck for awhile, then went inside and played bridge until 10:00 with two girls from Penn.

There was dancing on the upper deck but we were sleepy, so we decided to turn in.

It is lovely weather. Margaret, John Evans, and I played Deck Tennis for awhile. It is lots of fun but I hurt my finger and had to stop. Margaret's fingers are stiff this morning too.

JUNE 19, 1928 — OFF BANKS OF NEWFOUNDLAND

It is much colder this morning as we are off the Banks of Newfoundland and the icebergs are near us. We have not sighted any yet but it is C.O.L.D. I have my rug wrapped around me real snug and tight. The sea is rougher this morning and the ship rocks some. The sun goes and comes, and it is cloudy. I still feel good!

We got the news this morning of the first woman to cross the Atlantic [Amelia Earhart]. Isn't that wonderful? She will always be proud of her feat.

The most interesting thing we did today was to have a bridge tournament. Prizes are awarded on Friday night. After the tournament, we

---

4. Dess M. Gurganus was chair of the publicity committee of the Raleigh Business and Professional Women's Club and staged the stunt in question, winning first prize for the best stunt given by any club at the state convention. The winning stunt is described in the *News and Observer* of June 18. Annie Lewis Bledsoe, mentioned in the previous paragraph, was president of the Raleigh club. Elsewhere in 1928 there is reference to Eugenia Herring and Dess Gugarnus presenting joint addresses on behalf of the B&PW.

were requested to put on our life belts and go up on deck for instructions. We *did* and they *did*.

A dance on C Deck ended that day.

I am still feeling fine.

June 20, 1928 — Middle of Atlantic

We passed a huge iceberg about 5:30. The boat slowed up but we didn't know why. In fact I didn't know it. I'm sorry I didn't see it. After breakfast we sighted two ships about two miles away—going in the same direction. We soon passed them.

This is the worst day we've had. Lots of empty places at table at breakfast. The boat rocks terribly. It is very cold as we are in the iceberg region off the coast of Newfoundland. We sighted a lighthouse last night before going to bed. It was at St. Johns, Newfoundland. Miss Small and I walked the deck for half an hour and then sat on deck until I got so cold I had to come in. Miss Small is from Salem, Mass.

Belle Cameron same down to see us in the afternoon. It took her one and a half hours to find our location. We were out but she left a note. She knows some other girls on here from Richmond, Va.

We had a gala affair at dinner! It was carnival night. There were caps and favors at each plate—horns, balloons and lots of noise-making souvenirs. It was too bad that so many were sick, and couldn't enjoy the fun. A masquerade ball ended the day. Belle came down to look on for awhile and we saw her. The costumes were very effective. Several Japanese costumes brightened it up.

June 21, 1928 — Still amid ocean

The sun peeks out occasionally. I was sitting on deck, wrapped in my robe and fixed for the morning when it began to rain without any warning. There was scrambling to get under cover. It didn't rain long, and the sun came out again.

In the afternoon there was horse-racing up on B Deck, and there was lots of betting and lots of fun. There were other games, too. I moved my watch up an hour today.

June 22, 1928

The same old thing over again: breakfast at 7:30 (if you could make it), lunch at 12 noon, and dinner at 6:00. There were two sittings and I happened to get at the first one.

We went up on the bridge where the Captain stays and saw everything that it takes to make a boat go. It was quite interesting and the view from there lovely. I would like a job up there.

Miss Cameron asked us up to have tea and sit with her. It was a lovely afternoon and the day was so lovely. The deck steward brought each of us a tray of tea with several little cakes. I enjoyed it very much, and she is lovely to be with. I think I was very lucky to have a friend on "A" Deck as we could go up most any time and feel alright about it.

We had a lovely concert in the evening sponsored by Tourist Third but there were artists from first and second. Two members of our party performed—one on the violin and one sang. I forgot to say that on Thursday we had "Stunt Night." There were some of cutest stunts I nearly ever saw. One young girl who teaches in Pittsburgh and [is] going over to London to teach this summer, wrote a cute little stunt very much like "That Old Sweetheart of Mine" called "Reveries of a Bachelor." She wrote it at one sitting, and there was every kind of girl in it.

June 23, 1928

I didn't get up this morning for breakfast. I was so sleepy, but our berth is so hot that I couldn't stay in very long. I took a good salt shower bath and a few other things and then beat it for the deck. I read, slept and sat on deck until lunch.

After lunch there was a treasure hunt which took us all over the ship. It was lots of fun, but I got awfully hot and tired and gave up the hunt before the treasure was found.

The most beautiful sunset so far was last night, but after eleven o'clock it was so lovely and bright that we wondered if it could be from the sun. We asked one of the ship men and he told us that was the gloaming. It was a soft glow after the sun had gone down but it lasts so long and is so bright. In the summer there is only about an hour of darkness and the sun rises about 4:00 a.m. We stayed up until after twelve, and hated to go in then.

June 24, 1928

We should have landed today, but we will not land until early morn.

Everyone has been quite excited all day expecting to sight land. We did not sight land until about 2:30. It looked good to me. It was an island and as we passed it a wire to N.Y. said that we had arrived.

I am so thrilled over Ireland! I never dreamed it could be so pretty or that we would get a glimpse of it. It has been a beautiful day and someone told us that it was an unusual day, because as a usual thing the sea is so rough and it is rainy so that you can't see anything. The boat does not land, but a barge or boat from Londonderry comes out to meet this boat and takes the passengers ashore.

The land is intensively cultivated in something green. It looked like a patched work quilt. There were patches for grazing and others planted in something, yellows, greens and brown. It was worth everything just to get this peep at Ireland.

Sunset

The most wonderful sight I've ever seen was the sunset tonight and the afterglow which lasted for hours. The sun did not set before 10:00 and the whole heaven was red and then changed to every color. No one could leave it, but gee it was cold. The rays from the sun shot up, with a wide ray from the top going up redder than the other rays. I've never seen one in America like it.

The inspectors came on board and looked at our passports and gave us a landing card. He told us not to lose it if we wanted to land. I got some money changed into English money. He gave me a pound note for a five-dollar bill. It is a funny looking little piece of paper and doesn't look like money to me. I have to take his word for it.

(My baggage was inspected immediately and we were taken up to the Grand Hotel.)

June 25, 1928

We did not get to bed until after twelve on the last night as everybody was so excited, and about 4:00 a.m. a little boy came into the berth next to ours and yelled to another to get up and see the sunrise. I was awake then so I had to get up to see it. It was a glorious one—the heaven was all aglow with this lovely rising sun. It was a beautiful morn, but before we got into Glasgow it was raining and was a typical Scotland weather day. We were a day late getting into Glasgow so we missed one trip—to Burns's country.

The Montreal people got in on Sunday and took this trip in on Sunday p.m.

We met the other part of our party at the Grand Hotel and left immediately for Edinburgh by way of the Trossachs.

Scotland is a beautiful country with everywhere a soft green carpet. Someone said it rained here 51 weeks out of 52. I hoped we would happen to be here on that rainless one but it is very cloudy and rained part of the day. We did not get to see Glasgow except the part we passed on our way to the Trossachs. We passed Dunbarton rock and Castle, Rob Roy's grave, and many other interesting places. Loch Lomond is a beautiful lake surrounded by mts. White clouds were between us and the mts. and it was a lovely sight. The lake is 20-miles long and we drove along the edge of it all the way. The road was narrow and winding. We saw lots of wild flowers and got out a time or two to pick some. While we were there a bagpipe player and his wife came up. He played and she took up the pennies. They get quite a few.

Lake Katrine is not so large as Lake Lomond but it is very pretty with its little islands in it. Ellen's Isle is the largest in the lake. *The Lady of the Lake* by Scott tells all about this lake and island.

We got to Edinburgh about 10:30 and it was still light. We ate after we got here. We had lunch at a cute little place, Lochearnhead Hotel. We stopped at Dumblaine to view a very old cathedral.

June 26, 1928 — Edinburgh

This has been a wonderful day even if it did rain all the morning. We visited Holyrood Castle and Abbey. We saw the bedroom of Mary Queen of Scotts and the hangings, coverings of bed and wall paper just as it was when she lived there. We saw John Knox' home and the church where he preached—St. Giles Cathedral. Part of this edifice dates back to the 12th century.

Another very interesting castle was Edinburgh Castle, built up on the rock overlooking the city. This used to be an old garrison. The barracks, erected in 1796, have been transformed into the magnificent and impressive Scottish National War Memorial, consisting of a Hall of Honour and a shrine, "To the Glory of God and in memory of the Scots who fell 1914–1918." It was opened July 1927 by Prince of Wales.

This afternoon we went window shopping. I bought two tam-o-shanter caps for Katherine and Louise.[5]

We were very tired so came home and rested and then ate dinner. After dinner I took a street car ride to Robert Louis Stevenson place and the George Heriot School [George Heriot's School], the founder of this school being the ancestor of Judge Heriot Clarkson.[6] I was anxious to see it as the judge asked me to find it.

June 27, 1928 — Windermere

We had breakfast at 8:00 and left at 8:30 for Melrose and Abbotsford, Scott's home. It is just *so* lovely as the pictures show. We had lunch at Melrose and then saw the abbey. It was built in the 11th century. Nothing but ruins, but it must have been a wonderful cathedral in its day. It is very near the borderland and many wars were fought along there. The guide at Abbotsford said that the owner, great, great grandson of Scott, had recently married a rich American and would bring here there in Oct. He offered her a name for her money and she took him up.[7]

The trip over the Cumberland mountains was the most beautiful drive we've had so far. The flowers are in bloom, and the grass is just like velvet. The mts have no trees on them but are covered in green grass. The houses are small whitewashed one and two stories and always a little flower garden somewhere around.

Melrose Abbey was built by David I [King David I of Scotland]. The heart of Bruce [Robert the Bruce] is supposed to be buried there.

The Library at Abbotsford contains 20,000 volumes.

At Penrith we viewed a very old church with what is said to be the most beautiful windows in it of the 12th century.

---

5. Katherine and Louise Highsmith, her nieces, later Katherine Holoman and Louise Wilkerson.
6. Heriot Clarkson (1863–1942), justice of the North Carolina Supreme Court, where Eugenia worked.
7. Indeed, Walter Constable-Maxwell Scott married Marie-Louise Logan, formerly Mme Calley Saint-Paul de Sinçay, on June 19, 1928. It was the second marriage for them both.

I must say something about the rhododendron. Since Loch Lomond we have seen every color in the world. I did not know there could be so many different colors of it. It reminded me of Magnolia Gardens in Charleston, S. C.

We passed the English Lake region. Lakes [space left], Grasmere, and Windermere.

We spent the night at Storr's Hall Hotel on Lake Windermere. This hotel was built over an old monk's abbey, and later used as a slave mart or hiding place for the slaves smuggled in. We ate lunch at Preston at the Bull and Royal Hotel.

June 28, 1928 — Chester

Today has been so rainy but we have traveled more than sightsee, so we didn't mind. We left at 10:00 and ate lunch at Preston at the Bull and Royal Hotel. We have the nicest coach to travel in and such a nice crowd to be with.

We arrived at Chester at 5 p.m. Just as soon as we could get down from our rooms we took a trip over the old Roman wall and the city. We saw the oldest church and oldest house in England. The wall is unusual and is 2¼ miles long. It went around the city at the time. The wall was built in 95 A.D. by the Romans. There are shops below the wall and shops above. Those above are more expensive, but they do have pretty things. We are stopping at the Blossom Hotel.

The most fun we have had was tonight all gathered in one room by a cozy fire and writing our diaries. It is still cold and rainy. That fire we sat by cost a shilling, so we found out next morning. These people are awfully tricky. They say: How would you like so and so, and if you do, you may be sure a shilling will be forthcoming. I can count the money just fine—until I pay for two or three people for theatre tickets out of a pound note and then try to collect. It doesn't seem to come out right and I think I'm always shortchanged. On the trams you pay for the distance. We paid a penny to go several blocks. That would be two cents in our country.

June 29, 1928 — Stratford

We left Chester in the rain and it rained the whole day. We arrived at Kidderminster about 1 p.m. and had lunch. We stopped at a little town in

Wales, Wrexham, where there is a fine church. One girl bought a lovely vase and I wanted its mate but it was too unhandy in the bus.

We visited Stratford, Shakespeare's birth place, Anne Hathaway's Cottage, Warwick Castle, and the little church where Shakespeares are buried. Leamington that night.

June 30, 1928 — Oxford and London

Oxford is quite a large city. The Duchess of York was there that day and was attending a garden party. We did not get to see her.

We visited some of the buildings of Oxford University. Christ Church is where the aristocracy go, and they are registered, to go there, at birth. We saw the kitchen and dining room. Wesley's (John) picture was on the wall as were lots of others who had attended school there and made a mark in the world. Magdalen College is where the Prince of Wales went to school. These were only two of the 26 colleges comprising the Oxford University. Ate dinner or lunch at The Wilberforce Hotel. We had the same food, beef or lamb, it never varies.

From Oxford to London we drove along the Thames Valley. We arrived at the Bonnington Hotel in London about 5:30 p.m. and immediately ate dinner. We went to the Gaiety-Theatre to see "Marjolane," a musical comedy, and it was lovely. Monday night we saw a revue, "Clowns and Clones." We have single rooms at this hotel, and it was very nice and clean.

July 1, 1928 — London

We had a sightseeing trip on Sunday p.m. over part of the city and to Kew Gardens. This is a lovely garden belonging to the King and he has given it over for experimental purposes. We were served tea here in the Gardens. Saw Prince of Wales home, Princess Mary's, and other royalty places. In the morning I attended services at St. Paul's church and heard Dean [William] Inge, considered the greatest minister of the Episcopal church. We saw "The Light of the World" here and an artist there painting a copy from original. After returning from Kew Gardens we went to Westminster Abbey for evening service. It was very inspiring and we enjoyed it fully. There was a procession after the service, which was impressive.

July 2, 1928 — London

Monday we were taken on a trip to Stoke Poges, the scene of Gray's "Elegy" and the elm tree under which it was written. We passed a picnic place called Burnham Beeches, a beautiful forest of nearly 400 acres. Wm. Penn's family are buried at Stoke Poges. There is a private entrance to this church for the Lord of the Manor. St. Burnham is the house in which Milton wrote "Paradise Lost." The most beautiful sight on this trip was Hampton Court Palace, home of the King & Queen (one of them). There was a room full of pictures of Rubens, also one of Van Dyke's pictures. The state bedroom was lovely, where Kings and Queens of other countries sleep while there. The audience room of the Queen was gorgeous in lovely draperies and wall coverings. The banquet hall seats 160 for state affairs. The throne room where the Order of Knights of the Garter is bestowed was also wonderful. We went to top of one of the towers and got a grand view of Eton and Windsor. Eton College is just across the Thames River and all the boys belong to the nobility. They have to wear high top hats and Prince Albert coats all the time, and they are real young.

July 3, 1928 — London

On Tuesday we took another tour of city and London Tower and the room where the royal jewels are kept when not worn. The largest diamond in the world is in a mace here in the Jewel House. The collection of armor is the largest in the kingdom. Old Curiosity Shop was very quaint among all the tall buildings around it. We shopped in the p.m. and went to London museum and saw very interesting dresses of the Queen's and other royalty. Liberty's Store was a dream with all the gorgeous silks, draperies, rugs, etc. It was too expensive for me. We had dinner early, took train for Harwich and then boat to Holland.

July 4, 1928 — The Hague

Arrived at Hook of Holland at 6:00 a.m. Took a bus to The Hague where we had breakfast at 8:30. We stopped at Hotel Galerie [Hotel des Galeries] at Scheveningen, a lovely resort of Holland called the Atlantic City of Holland. We visited the stores in the morning. Margaret's friend Mr. van Jenk met us in the Express office, took us to a cute place for coffee (11:00) and then to a museum and the state house. We were invited to his house for a real Dutch lunch, consisting of soup and a combination of rice with something in it, very good, after that strawberries on buttered bread and cherries. They were lovely to us and had a beautiful home. After lunch Mrs. van Jenk borrowed a Kodak and took pictures of us and his wife and himself. The maid took the pictures. He took us to the Peace Palace where we joined the party for a tour of city. Carnegie gave this building at a cost of $1,000,000(?) We saw the queen's palace, also her daughter's, the next queen. I like these people very much. They are so clean, and every house has the loveliest white curtains and hung perfectly at each window. Little canals run through the town in all directions. The most beautiful place in The Hague was the Palace in the Woods. We saw the lovely Chinese and Japanese rooms given by these countries before America was discovered.

The white dining room had remarkable paintings on the wall. They stood out like sculpture. The inlaid tables, etc., in the rooms were the loveliest I have seen. The whole of the main dining room walls and ceilings are covered in paintings and in the very top of the ceiling is the Queen's picture. We saw a mirror that was painted before quicksilver [was] put on. It is a lost art now. Chinese walls had silk embroidery wall coverings. It was all so lovely.

After dinner we went down on the boardwalk and out on a pier to a variety program that we could not understand. We felt out of place and very conspicuous when we ordered some ices.

July 5, 1928 — Isle of Marken

Left hotel at 7:00 a.m. for Volendam to take boat to the island. Passed Leyden [Leiden], a little town that held on longer than any other against the Spaniards and was given a university as a reward. John Robinson, the pastor of the Pilgrim fathers, is buried in St. Pieter's Kerk. At Amsterdam we crossed the Y on a barge and then traveled about 16 miles to the quay where we sailed by small steamer to the Isle of Marken. The customs and costumes of these island people are so fantastic. All the people are Protestants except one, and he goes to Volendam to worship. Boys and girls dress alike until they are six years old. The only way of telling a boy is by the little patch on the back of his cap. There are 7 villages on the island, and each have their own peculiar style of dress. They must live off the tourists in the summer as I could not see much farming land in cultivation. There are no fruit trees, except for pear trees in the pastor's yard, because of so much salt in the ground.

The busses met us in Volendam where we had lunch, served by young ladies in their native dress. The white caps are snowy white and stiff. They wear black caps until their work is over and then they don their white caps and aprons. The island is surrounded by the Zuider Zee and North Sea. The government is reclaiming the land of the Zee and in a few years it will be part of the mainland.

At Amsterdam we only had time to see the famous picture of Rembrandt, "The Night Watch." A lovely ride brought us back to Scheveningen. Tour 423 were there to greet us. After dinner we walked along boardwalk, window shopped for awhile and viewed the display of fireworks on the beach.

I like Holland, the people and especially the food.

July 6, 1928 — Brussels

We stopped at Palace Hotel here, very lovely with private bath, and had a ride over city in afternoon. Brussels was occupied by the Germans during the war, but the city was not damaged very much. We visited all the public places of interest. The Palace of Justice is one of the largest buildings in the world and is beautiful with its numberless columns. We saw where Edith Cavell[8] was shot, also the soldier who refused to shoot her. He was ordered to shoot her and when he refused, was shot on the spot. Miss Cavell was buried there, but two years ago was removed to England. We stopped at a lace factory where the Queen patronizes. Collars and lace 'kerchiefs were bought by the dozen.

The battlefield of Waterloo was very interesting, especially the panoramic view painted on canvas. We could not distinguish where the painting stopped and the real began. It was dome-shaped and contained the whole history of the battle in one painting. It took five years to paint it. Several of us climbed the 228 steps to the top of the pyramid. During this war there was a sunken road on one side built by Wellington and was a great factor in causing Napoleon to lose the battle, as so many of

---

8. Edith Cavell (1865–1915) was a British nurse executed by a German firing squad for helping 200 Allied soldiers escape from occupied Belgium in World War I.

his men were trapped in this sunken road. It is no longer there, as the earth on both sides was used to build the pyramid. Victor Hugo wrote part of *Les Misérables* in a little village on one side of the battlefield, Mont St.-Jean.

Margaret and several of our party flew by airplane from here to Cologne. It took them only two hours, whereas it took us five by train. They said it was fine and they want to do more of it. One or two got sick but it didn't last long.

July 7, 1928 — Cologne

We didn't stay in Cologne long enough to see the city. We did get a glimpse of the wonderful cathedral on Sunday morning, during early Mass service. Thousands of people were coming to the early service so that they could spend the rest of the day hiking or cycling it over the country. There was a press exposition on across the Rhine River. It was all lighted and viewed from the opposite side of the river was very beautiful. The lights on the Cathedral at night made an unforgettable picture. Another lovely sight was the lights on the houses with the window boxes filled with colored flowers, and the homes were painted different colors. It looked like a backdrop or scene for a play in a theatre. Some people were leaning out of the window and some children playing on the outside. It made a lovely setting.

July 8, 1928 — Rhine River

We left Cologne at 8:30 for a whole day trip up the Rhine River. It was a glorious day, and it seemed that the whole of Cologne was leaving for the day. Several boats left before ours and all well filled. We took an express that did not stop at every place. Lots of other American parties were on this boat. The trip up is more beautiful than one can imagine, with the mt. sides covered in vineyards and dotted here and there with historic castles and fortresses. All the castles are ruins now, but the legends about them are still thrilling. Some of the most wonderful mts. are the Druchenfels and Lorelei. There are several interesting towns along the Rhine: Coblenz, St. Gras, and Bengin with the Mouse Tower in the middle of the river on an island nearby. We reached Wiesbaden at 9:00 p.m., ate a grand dinner and went to bed.

The houses along the Rhine are typically German, and I really felt like I was in a foreign place. They are very narrow and many sharp points and turrets, and fancy work on them. The Germans do not like the Belgians any too well and would not take their money in exchange. The Belgian soldiers are stationed on the border and said they would be there until Germany paid up every cent she owed them. Germany looks prosperous as do most of the other countries visited. Lots of buildings are being put up everywhere, and the people seem to be happy and contented.

We arrived in Heidelberg before lunch and stopped at the Roter Hahn Hotel (Red Cock).

July 9, 1928 — Heidelberg

We were happy to be in Heidelberg, because of the world-renowned university and "Student Prince." The River Neckar runs through the town, and mountains surround the town. After lunch we had a ride over the city, the university, and the castle of Heidelberg. This castle is situated above the city on the side of the mountain and is reached by road, path, or cable from city. It is very picturesque, and the grounds around it are worth the trip up to see and linger in. The castle was half fortress and half castle and now contains a collection of pictures, coins, etc. Our guide was a young fellow 21 yrs old, a student at the university and had only been talking English for one year. He did it very well for that time. His accent was not broken, and he did not look like a German. He says he is coming to America as soon as he is through school and line; and that he wishes to marry an American as the girls are much prettier, dress better, and more charming. He was a fine little fellow. His name was Henreick Rohrer. After the tour we went shopping. The meals at the hotel were very good, and the lettuce was especially enjoyed. Ten of us went to a German beer garden after dinner, with our guide and Mr. Lane. We got a beautiful view of the city lighted at night. It was tame.

July 10, 1928 — Lucerne, Switzerland

We left Heidelberg about 9:30 with our little lunch bags and arrived at Lake Lucerne about 3:30. On our way down we passed the Black Forest. We could not see very much of it from the train, but the scenery was lovely. We stopped at a lovely hotel on the lakefront: Palace Hotel. Rooms in most of the hotels are large, several windows and single beds which are very comfortable. After dinner I went to find HenriEtta Owen[9] in Brownell tour, who was to be there at the same time. She left her hotel in search of me and of course [we] missed each other. We did see each other though for a few minutes about 11:30, and then she and one of the young men in her party walked with me to my hotel. I was locked out and would have been frantic had I been alone. We found a bell and someone came to my rescue.

We loved Lucerne and hotel. I hated to leave so soon. The shops were tempting with lovely hand-worked 'kerchiefs, dresses, scarves and every other thing imaginable. All the girls wanted the little ball watches to hang on a chain. I bought two, one for Vara and one for [Mary] Belle [her sisters]. It has been gorgeous weather all the time since we left Scotland. It has rained a little in the morning, but cleared off by noon.

July 11, 1928 — Interlaken, Switzerland

We left Lucerne at 8:30 in busses for the wonderful trip across the Alps, by way of the St. Gotthard pass. The Alpentrasse highway, some parts of which have been hewn from the rocks, on to the Rhone glacier, and then over the Furka pass to Interlaken. It will always remain one of the high spots in my life. We stopped about 5 minutes at Altdorf and saw a statue of William Tell and a fountain to mark the spot where the boy was bound to a tree and the spot where William Tell stood when he shot the apple off his son's head. We went thru tunnels in the bus, by lakes on one side and high mountains on the other. We ate lunch at the highest point and snowballed each other in the snow. With opera glasses we found a little lake away up in the mountains "a million miles away," so it looked. Later we passed it on our way to [the] glacier. The glacier is between two mountains which completely fills it [the valley] up. A cave [the Eisgrotte Rhonegletscher] has been cut in it and the color of the ice was so blue and pretty. While standing there we saw a huge piece of the glacier fall and it made a loud noise. We saw numerous waterfalls, streams from snow and gorgeous scenery all the way up and down. I got a sunburned nose on that trip but it was worth it. We reached Interlaken about dinner time and after dinner walked out to

---

9. A friend of the Herring sisters through the B&PW Club and Edenton Street Church.

view the Jungfrau. I was so tired I did not stay up very long. I did my week's washing and had a good night's rest.

July 12, 1928 — Interlaken

Shopping is one of the things all of us like to do, and the minute we are free, off we go to "look." At Lucerne all bought watches; at Interlaken we bought musical trays. We went into the Kursaal, a beautiful place, with a flower clock, beautiful shrubs and flowers. I saw the largest begonia flowers there—larger than my hand. After dinner we dressed in evening dresses and went to the Casino. At all of these places are tables with chairs around. If you sit down you are supposed to have something to eat or drink. There is always a concert, and after you buy something you can stay as long as you like.

July 13, 1928 — Montreux

With reluctance we left Interlaken for Montreux, another fashionable resort of Switz. We got there early in the afternoon and went immediately to see the Castle of Chillon. It was in good repair, and we got a glorious view of the lake from the windows. I saw where Byron carved his name on one of the columns in the castle, and where the prisoner that he wrote about ["The Prisoner of Chillon," 1816], was chained. We went swimming in the lake afterwards, and it was just great.

We had a lovely dinner overlooking the lake, and then had a long ride on a motorboat. We were quite cooled off and slept fine. Next morning all rushed out to get cards, etchings, paper etc. before leaving for Stresa on Lake Maggiore, the largest of the Italian lakes.

July 14, 1928 — Stresa, Italy

To get to Stresa, we crossed the Alps between Switzerland and Italy, passing thru 20 tunnels in all on that trip. The largest one was twenty-five minutes long and distance 12 miles. It is the St. Gotthard's Pass. The customs officers met us just as we got thru this tunnel, inspected our passports and baggage and we went into another long tunnel. This was a very pretty trip—the Rhone River on one side, mountains on the other covered with grape vines full of grapes. The earth is terraced all the way up to keep the dirt from washing away. When we got into the Lake district in Italy it began to get hot and by the time we got to our destination we were awfully hot, dirty and tired.

The first thing we did was look for the bathing beach. We finally found it but it was full. The owner said he would send us with suits over to a small island. Imagine our surprise when we got there and found only bushes and reeds for dressing rooms. Did we roar? Anyway we had our swim and then a boat ride to our hotels. After dinner we went to ride in a carriage and had lots of fun. The poor old horse jiggled us for an hour.

July 15, 1928 — Milan and Venice

On our way to Venice we stopped between trains at Milan to see the cathedral. It is a beautiful cathedral and I think the prettiest from an architectural standpoint of all we've seen. It has a great many spires and 2000 statues all over it. We got a good view of the city from the top of the highest tower.

It was terribly hot on train and also after we got to Milan. Everyone wanted something cool at every stop. When we heard "Gelati! Gelati!" we rushed to the window to get ice cream.

Arrived in Venice about 5:00 p.m. Of course it was the most unusual city we had seen.

July 16, 1928 — Venice

The only streets in the city connecting one part with another are canals, a network of small ones leading into the Grand Canal. Their means of conveyance are gondolas, motor launches and big boats. The big ones run on schedules and stop at designated stations. They are always full.

After dinner we went for a ride in the gondola. The gondolier stands at the back and guides his boat. The canals are always full but they never even hit another but the small canals are so narrow and crooked that we expected a collision often. On the Grand Canal were serenading parties in dressed-up gondolas lighted in Chinese-lantern effect. There were 6, 8, or 10 in the party and a small orchestra. They took their turn in singing. Hundreds of gondolas with tourists as well as of natives gathered around them. After a concert they would take a collection going from one boat to another until he had visited all.

We spent the morning in the shops in and around St. Mark's Place. I never saw so many things, beads, shawls, jewelry and everything else as in the shops here. In the afternoon we took a motor launch to the Lido, a very popular resort, and had a nice swim in the Adriatic. On the way we stopped to see St. Mark's Cathedral, the square full of pigeons, and the Doge's palace. The cathedral is in the Byzantine style, with mosaics on the exterior and interior. It was very colorful inside and out. When the gun fired at 12 o'clock, as it does every day, all the pigeons flew all over the square.

After dinner we went on another gondola ride and enjoyed it very much.

Venice had lots of smells and we did not think things so clean, as I am told all the sewers empty into the canals.

We enjoyed seeing this famous place, but glad to leave for Florence.

July 16, 17, and 18, 1928 — Florence

Florence is a very delightful place, and I hated to leave it. We were lucky to get a room with bath and made for it the first thing. Baths are luxuries over here and you have to pay for them. The bath towels are as large as a sheet for a single bed and are hard to manage. I wrapped myself in one and it lies on the floor all around. After supper we went to the Ponte Vecchio, a very old bridge over the Arno River. There are jewelry shops on both sides of the bridge. Everybody bought rings here and silver cross pendants.

In the morning we went thru the square where Savanarola was burned, the Palazzo Vecchio, the old capitol built in 1298, and the Uffizi Art Gallery. Here we saw some of the finest paintings in the world, as well as tapestries and sculpture. We visited the Pitti Palace and saw the Royal Apartments.

In the afternoon we took a ride over the city and up to Fiesole, a very old town containing a monastery high up on a mountain. We got a grand view of the city from here. We saw the famous statue of David by Michelangelo. It is a masterpiece and looks it.

We visited the wonderful cathedral in Florence. The cathedrals in Italy are not so ornate as the other cathedrals we have seen. This one on the outside was of different colors of marble which gave it an unusual look. The campanile by Giotto is also made of many-colored marbles to match the church. It is 292 ft. high and is adorned with statues and reliefs by masters. The bronze doors of the Baptistry (12th century) are wonderful. Michelangelo said of them "They are worthy of being the gates of Paradise."

After dinner we shopped along the Ponte Vecchio and by the river. I bought my topaz ring here.

July 19–22, 1928 — Naples

Left Florence at 9 a.m. and were on train all day to Naples. However we stopped in Rome for about two hours in between trains. We got our mail at the hotel and everybody was happy for the rest of our hot, dirty train ride to Naples. We ate dinner at 11:30 p.m. and went to bed awfully tired. My room was very noisy and I did not sleep well—terrible for the next day's strenuous trip.

Called at 7:00 a.m. as usual, had bread and jam and were ready by nine for our trip to Pompeii. It is 16½ miles from Naples over cobblestones and through the heart of the slum section. It seemed 27 mi. on our return trip over those cobblestones, and same smells.

Pompeii was destroyed in 79 A.D. by the eruption of Vesuvius and was rediscovered in 1748. Systematic excavations have been conducted since 1860. Only half of the ancient city has been uncovered. There is a museum near the entrance which contains lots of interesting things found, but most statues and everything of importance is in the Naples museum. There are lots of temples, houses of the rich, villas, bakery shops, forums, public baths, etc. It was very interesting and we had a good guide, one who could talk "good old English" so we can understand it.

We were in very comfortable cabs. We left Pompeii for Amalfi for lunch. We crossed a mountain or two to get there. It is situated on a lofty promontory with the Bay of Salerno in the foreground. It was in a very picturesque setting. We ate lunch at the hotel, the dining room or porch on 3rd floor overlooking the bay. We saw lots of sights while eating: people in swimming below us and using boats, some none, for dressing rooms. One old man was such an expert at the business, that no one was shocked, but all amused. After leaving Amalfi we took the far-famed drive to Sorrento called the Amalfi Drive.

July 20, 1928 — Sorrento and Amalfi

In most places we were hundreds of feet above the bay below; sometimes we had to pass through tunnels and one curve after another all the way down. We were thrilled over the grandeur of the scenery. The towns of white and colored stucco and plaster or cement glistened in the hot Italian sun and it was a pretty sight. Sorrento is a resort for tourists. They had the most beautiful things to sell, as shawls, lace hand-embroidered work etc. We went crazy over it but did not buy very much. I bought a Roman striped scarf and tie.

We ate a lemon squash and went swimming to cool off. Every place in Italy big enough is planted in something, mostly grapevines. I never saw so many bunches of grapes in my life. This is the section for lemons and oranges. Lemon trees are trained to spread out instead of grow tall, and the lemons hang underside like grapes from an arbour.

This was a long, but beautiful ride, one not to be forgotten. We were so tired that we did nothing after dinner but go to bed.

I was disappointed not to see Vesuvius at close range. We could see the smoke at all times and flames at night, but did not have time to go up.

July 21, 1928 — Capri and Blue Grotto

We left at 8:30 sharp for the boat which took us to Capri and Blue Grotto. We had heard that more people got seasick on this trip than did crossing the ocean. I was surprised to find it was very calm and no one even thinking of getting sick. That was a lovely trip as we had to eat no dust from the boat in front. Eaten more than my share of Italian dirt.

We had lots of fun going to the grotto. The big boat parked a good distance away and small rowboats came to take us in two in small ones and three in the larger ones. Margaret, Sara Montrose and I went together. The water was the most gorgeous blue before we got into the grotto, and when we got inside everybody said oh! oh! oh! it was such a lovely sight. It seemed that there were lights below the water shining on lovely blue stones. It was not dark nor very light. We had to get into the bottom of the boat as he went through the opening. One boy lost his Kodak as he went to get up after getting into the cove. It got caught on side of boat. It belonged to one of the girls. The cove is quite a large place and we rode around it, up into little grooves and around for a while. The dome of the cave was very high and of a pretty grayish blue color like it might be of lapis lazuli stone.

We ate lunch in Capri under a vine covered place. Three Italian musicians gave a concert during the meal and took up a collection for it. The singer had a good voice and sang *O sole mio* with great feeling.

We went up a funicular railway to the top of mt. to get a view of the city, and surrounding country. We saw century plants in bloom. After they bloom they die.

This was a wonderfully enjoyable day. The boat ride back cooled us off and we were ready for a good dinner which we got and enjoyed.

We took a buggy ride after dinner over the city: Margaret, Bill and Dutch Ludwig and I. We happened to have good luck in picking out one that could speak English. Before getting the ride we walked to the business square and I never saw so many men in my life. The place and streets were swarming with men, and only a few women. We decided to take a ride so hailed a carriage. It took us all over the old and part of the new Naples. We got a lot of thrills out of it. But we went through some smelly joints where 5, 6, 7 and 8 in a family live in one room.

Sunday morning we slept late and rested. About 10:30 some of us went to the national museum and saw all the statues, vases etc. taken from Pompeii excavations. A cute little Italian boy told us something about the things in there. We took the streetcar home, ate lunch and left for Rome at 2:30.

July 22, 1928 — Rome

We felt that we were returning to a place we were familiar with, as we stopped for our mail here on the way to Naples. Rome does not seem to me to be just an Italian city but a place and nationality of its own. It is a much cleaner city than Naples and I like it better.

We left Naples about 3:00 p.m., and it was terribly hot on the train. On the way we saw the ruins of the old aqueduct and other ruins.

Monday morning we were called at 8, breakfasted on honey, bread and coffee and left on a tour to St. Peter's cathedral and the Vatican.

July 23, 1928 — Rome

On the site of this church it is said that St. Peter was buried after his crucifixion. It is an immense church. Michelangelo built most of the building, or designed it, when he was 72 years of age. The approach to the church, in the form of an ellipse bounded by imposing colonnades, consisting of four rows of massive Doric columns, 284 in all, is the most beautiful in the world. We saw several masterpieces of art and sculpture by Michelangelo, Canova, Bernini, etc. "Pieta" by Michelangelo is so lovely. The church is so large in every way that the people walking inside look like pygmies beside the statuary and lofty ceilings. All the pictures on the wall are copied from the famous pictures all over the world, but are in mosaics. There are 37000 [pieces] in some of the larger pictures. One chapel is made of solid gold. There is much gold used in the church, especially the dome. People come from all over the world to see this marvelous dome by Michelangelo. A mosaic picture of St. Peter walking on the water and many others depicting Bible scenes were here. The original bronze statue of Peter holding the key is in this church. His toe has been kissed so much that it has been covered in bronze, which has worn off considerably since being covered.

The Vatican, residence of the Popes, contains 11,000 rooms filled with original Gobelins tapestries, pictures, statuary, alabaster and other precious vases, and gifts from other kings and countries, etc. "The Last Judgment" by Michelangelo is in the Sistine Chapel. I saw the largest and smallest Bible in the world in the library. The Canova gallery of Greek statues contains the Laocoon group, Discus Thrower, Venus, Apollo, Minerva etc.

In the p.m. went to the Colosseum, an amphitheater begun in A. D. 72 with a seating capacity of 50,000. Only a third of the building remains. We also saw it by moonlight, as also the Forum and Temple of Vesta. It was a lovely sight.

The Appian Way took us to the Catacombs, burial places of the Christians. We saw a Quo Vadis chapel, the spot where Jesus appeared to Peter. We next visited St. Paul's Outside the Walls, where St. Paul is said to have been buried. On the inside were 6 alabaster columns which belonged to an earlier church. The cloister is very beautiful, all columns being different.

July 24, 1928 — Rome

We had this day free to see the rest of Rome. Imagine our doing it in one day! We went first to the Forum, which was the heart and center of the ancient city. There are many ruins here of temples, arches, shrines etc. Our guidebook helped us to visualize the setting of the ancient city. We could only spend a little time at each place as we had so much to see and do. Next we visited the Palatine Hill, the most interesting of the seven hills of Rome. That is where the nobility lived and was the scene of great magnificence during the period of the late Republic.

There are many more cathedrals in Rome dating from the medieval times, than modern ones. St. Peter in Chains contains the chains which bound him in prison. We saw them. We saw the famous statue of "Moses," Leah and Rachel by Michelangelo.

Quite an interesting and beautiful Church is St. John's. It takes the precedence even of St. Peter's in that is the church of the Pope as Bishop of Rome. The cloisters are beautiful works of 12th century. Nearby in a small building is the sacred stairs, a flight of 28 marble steps, said to be from the house of Pilate and to have been trodden by the feet of Jesus. We saw three old women going up on their knees and saying prayers that each step. When they got to the top they kissed the floor. Each person going up gets nine of years off of their stay in Purgatory. Children going up kiss each step. I did a little shopping after this, taking a carriage to the shopping district. The driver could not understand English, but I had an address which I showed him. We had a nice room at Continental Hotel. The manager on our last night gave us a souvenir of that hotel—an address book for ladies; a matchbook for gentlemen.

July 25, 1928 — Rome to Genoa

Before leaving for Genoa at 10:30 we went shopping for last-minute articles. On our return we took a streetcar for the station which took us all over the city and to outskirts before taking us to the station. We began to get anxious, and we kept saying in our best Italian *"stazione."* He understood and assured us we would get there. We did at last.

We hated all train travel in Italy. It was so dirty and hot. The scenery was lovely along the Italian Riviera when we were not in a tunnel. The mountains and sea meet and we went through endless tunnels. We had our first lunch on the train about 3:00 p.m. We were starved by that time and ate what was left. We had to buy water thru Italy. At each station along the way when we heard "Gelati, Gelati," all heads popped out calling for it—a poor form of ice cream. It was cold and hit the spot. The glass in doors and windows could be lowered, and we hung out of them all the time.

We arrived at Genoa in time for dinner. Then we went window shopping for a while and also to see statue of Columbus. We were *tired* and re*tired* early, but it was too hot to fall off right away. The maid brought us ice water which cooled us so that we slept. We stopped at Hotel Britannia near station.

July 26, 1928 — Genoa to Nice

After breakfast Alex got two carriages and eight of us went for a ride over the city—four to each carriage. We visited several churches, and Columbus's home. The driver then took us up to the highest part of the city to give us a good view. We had to go up a hill of cobblestones. I had just said I wondered if the horse would make it—that some of us had better walk. Alex said that reminded him of a joke and started to tell it when the horse stumbled and fell in the street and could not get up. We teased him about his joke toppling the horse over.

I had quite an exciting experience just before leaving. I had seen a small Tower of Pisa in one of the stores and decided that I must have it, as we had passed the leaning tower of Pisa the day before but did not stop. I went after it, and the bunch went on to the station. I followed afterwards but could not locate them. No one it seemed could understand me. Finally I got a man that did and he took me up stairs, then down stairs and around corners until I met another man looking for me. All the girls were frantic and Alex was a little worried, but after all I had plenty of time. I knew it but not being able to make them understand is a little confusing and quite exciting if you are left alone.

More tunnels and more beautiful mountains and sea scenery brought us to Nice. But on the borderland we had to get off the train and huddled in one hot stuffy room to go thru the customs. It took over an hour to get through and we felt that we could not stand much more of such treatment. We had such a nice hotel at Nice that we soon forgot the inconvenience we had just gone through. Hotel Ruhl is on the waterfront overlooking the Casino. We had a suite of rooms with bath. We dressed in our evening togs and after dinner went to the casino. There was a very poorly acted operetta being performed, as well as dancing, gambling and eating and drinking at small tables.

July 27, 1928 — Nice

We had several good swims in the sea. It was very rough one day and the rocky bottoms made it worse. We visited the shops in the morning, and in p.m. took the famous Grande Corniche ride to Monte Carlo. It is indeed lovely, and the views of the sea from the top of the mountain was grand. We stopped for an hour at the Casino in Monte Carlo. Most of the party tried their luck at roulette—some lost and some won. I did not try! The drive back by the waterfront was very beautiful and enjoyable at that time of day—late p.m.

We enjoyed the hotel lobby and sat around in it for a long time, writing letters or talking. They have the outside tea tables, and after-dinner dancing in between drinks.

July 28, 1928 — Nice to Avignon

When we reached station on way to Avignon, one of the girls missed her bag of money which she carried around her waist. It was quite exciting for awhile, hearing her frantically crying she had left it in the hotel and stopping and feeling all over her person for it. We felt sorry for her, and I asked her to look in her bag. She was too excited to get her bag open or to find it at first. It was there, though, and we all calmed down after affording a lot of amusement to hundreds of travelers at the station.

It was a long, hot and tiresome trip, but we finally reached Avignon about 3:30. We had a good lunch on train, 7 courses: 1. cantaloupe, 2. egg on lettuce, 3. chicken patties, 4. main course, 5. pastry, 6. cheese, 7. fruit. Avignon is quite an old palace—the residence of the popes in 14th century. We visited the papal palace and gardens. The city is surrounded by a wall which is in perfect preservation. You enter the city through gates. We saw the ancient bridge of St. Bénézet over the Rhone river. He was a young boy, and had a dream that he must build this bridge. We had a lovely buggy ride around, and in the city. We stayed at Hotel d'Europe. We had good meals here, and wonder of wonders plenty of jam for breakfast *free*.

Alex was to leave us at this place, and we were ready to weep over his leaving us before getting to Paris. He put us on the train early in the morning for our day's ride to Paris.

July 29, 1928 — Paris!!!

We dreaded it but it turned much cooler and was a gorgeous day. We loved it all the way. That section of France was lovely. We had a bridge tournament, a good dinner at 11:00 a.m. and tea at 4:30. We were in good humor on arriving in Paris. Hotel Paris Etoile near Arc de Triomphe.

Paris came up to all expectations in every way. We had a sightseeing trip to the New and Old Paris one day; the Louvre gallery, Eiffel Tower, unknown soldier's grave another day; and to Fontainebleau Castle, the home of French kings, Marie Antoinette's home and later the home of Napoleon. It is in a very beautiful part of France. The American Conservatory of Music is there.

On one afternoon we drove to Versailles and saw the castle and beautiful grounds with the lovely fountains and flowers. We saw the table on which the peace treaty was drawn, the room and the marks of Woodrow Wilson made with his knife, beating unconsciously on the table.

The most interesting trip was to battlefields at Belleau Woods, to Chateau Thierry, Rheims, and Soissons. Our guide gave us the positions of the different armies and how the Americans took Belleau Woods inch by inch from the Germans. We saw one little village which had changed hands six times. The holes just large enough for one man and his machine gun are still there, as are shell holes, relics of guns, etc. The woods are of new growth but no trees. We saw the cemetery of American boys—white stone crosses, row after row—stone star for Jews. A huge American flag flies above all the time. At Chateau Thierry we saw the Methodist Community House, museum, social center used by the town. It is also a nursery where the poor leave their children while at work. It has been running 9 years and is kept up by the tourists who visit it. We had a good lunch and then visited Rheims. It made us sad to see the beautiful cathedral in ruins. Part has been restored and they are working on it every day. It will take 50 years to finish it. Rockefeller has given 40 million to replace it.

The wine cellars at Rheims were interesting. There are 12 miles of underground passageway where the wine is kept. It takes 8 years to make a bottle of champagne. Rheims was bombarded every day for four years, and out of the city of 14,000 buildings only 60 remained inhabitable after the war. We had tea at Soissons and saw the ruined cathedral there. We passed Le Bourget Field on our way home. We reached Paris at 10:30 and had our dinner and went to bed tired out.

We saw several good shows: Raquel Miller at the palace, *Madame Butterfly* at the Opera Comique, and *Samson and Delilah* and *Salome* at the Grand Opera. They were all very fine—the first one very risqué as to dress or look of it. We went to Moulin Rouge, a night club, after the show and saw a bit of night life in Paris.

August 4, 1928

We left Paris at 7:30 for Havre for the *Carmania* to take us to the good U.S.A. We got on boat about 1:00 a.m. and to bed at 2:30. We did not get up for breakfast, but were ready for first sitting of dinner or lunch at 12:30.

August 5, 1928

Sunday August 5th was a lovely calm day. We were tired out though, and did not move out of our deck chairs when once in them. It began to get a little rough at night and by morning it was terrible rough and continued so all day Monday and Tuesday. I did not feel at all comfortable but went to all meals.

August 8, 1928

Wednesday was much better and also my feelings. Margaret and I played some deck tennis. I read "Constant Nymph" all that day with bridge in between. I stayed on deck most of the time, too lazy to leave when once down.

August 9, 1928

Thursday was better still and I felt excellent. Margaret and I walked around the ship five or six times—several miles it seemed. That night we had a bridge tournament and one of our party won first prize. She also won two others—one for potato race and the other for best dressed lady at Fancy Dress Ball.

August 10, 1928

Friday was very calm in the morning but in p.m. it was rougher and the wind was stronger. It rained some and cleared away the fog that we were getting into. We have passed several ships. Friday night we had a concert. Mr. Bennett, an English cinema star, appeared in person on the program. He is making his first trip to America. There is a good college orchestra on board, and they play for each meal.

August 11, 1928

Saturday it was so calm we could not see a ripple on the ocean. It was as smooth as a lake. We played deck sports for quite a while and then I had to leave and write in my diary. It took me nearly all the morning to catch up. There are lots of people on here who were with us on the *Caledonia*. Only 13 of our party are returning on *Carmania*. Others leave on the 11th a week later, and others Sept. 1st.

In the afternoon I played bridge with two ladies of Nebraska and one from Mass. I had real good luck, so they liked to play with me. (?)

We had a real good dinner there were individual souvenir menu cards at each place. It was our farewell dinner on board. After dinner we had to pack our bags and figure out our purchases.—I could just squeeze under my allowance.

August 12, 1928

I had my bath at 7:00 a.m. and breakfast at 7:30. We then finished packing, filled out our declaration cards, tipped our stewards, walked around the deck several times and spent the rest of morning on deck. About noon the ship began to dip terribly.

After lunch we had our last chat with friends we had met on boat and said "goodbyes" to those on our tour who were leaving immediately after landing.

We reached port about 6:00 p.m., and it took us about two hours to go through the customs. We got by without any trouble and went from there to Prince George Hotel for the night.

I was thrilled to have my friend Linda Rodenbeck of Chicago meet me at the boat. I was glad to be back in the good old U.S.A. and *very* happy to be one of her citizens.

Izzie took me to Roxy's theater that night and it was so crowded we could hardly get in.

Next morning we shopped at Saks, Best's etc. I bought a dress and hat. Ate lunch at Schrafft's. I left Margaret and Isabel and met Linda at station about 5:00 p.m. We bought our tickets and left at 6:40 reaching Raleigh next day [Tuesday, August 14, 1928] at 12:00 noon, *broke* but *happy*. Great trip.

Tour 416[10]

62 Days $650
Cabin Class $750

SCOTLAND, ENGLISH LAKES, NORTH WALES, ENGLAND, HOLLAND, BELGIUM, GERMANY, RHINE, BLACK FOREST, SWITZERLAND, ITALY, THE RIVIERA, FRANCE

Features

Scotland by Motor
England by Motor
Wales by Motor
Holland by Motor
Switzerland by Motor

JUNE

14	Montreal	Room with bath provided at Queen's Hotel.
15	New York	Room with bath at Prince George Hotel.
15	SS. Athenia	Sailing from Montreal.
16	SS. Caledonia	Sailing from New York.
17	Boston	Members may embark on Caledonia.
24	Glasgow	
25	Trossachs	By motor, rail and boat.
26	Edinburgh	Motor tour of the city.
27	English lakes	By motor.
28	North Wales	By motor.
29	Shakespeare Country	By motor.
30	Thames Valley	By motor. Windsor, etc.

---

10. Allen's Tours, Inc. of 154 Boylston Street ("Piano Row") in Boston was owned by Ben Franklin Allen. His classified ads in major papers were headed: "EUROPE: $7 A DAY."

JULY

1	London	Motor tour of the city.
2	London	Motor tour of the city.
3	London	
4	The Hague	Grand Holland Motor Tour, Hook of Holland to The Hague, Scheveningen, Leyden, Haarlem, Amsterdam, Isles of Marken Excursion.
5	Amsterdam	Motor tour of the city.
6	Brussels	
7	Cologne	
8	Heidelberg	By Rhine Steamer. Motor tour of the city.
9	Black Forest	To Lucerne.
10	Lucerne	
11	Interlaken	Grand Alpine Motor Tour, Furka Pass, Rhone Glacier, etc.
12	Montreux	
113	Furka Pass	
14	Italian Lakes	
15	Venice	Stopover at Milan.
16	Venice	Gondola tour of the city.
17	Florence	Drive of the city.
18	Florence	Drive to Fiesole.
19	Naples	
20	Capri	Blue Grotto and Sorrento by boat.
21	Amalfi	Drive and Pompeii by motor.
22	Rome	
23	Rome	Motor tour of the city. Motor tour Appian Way, catacombs, etc.
24	Rome	
25	Genoa	
26	Nice	Corniche Drive, Monte Carlo, etc.
27	Nice	
28	Avignon	Papal Palace and Gardens.

29	Paris	Two motor tours of the city. Rural France drives to Barbizon, Fontainebleau, The Chateau, Melun, St. Assise, Millet's home, Malmaison, Versailles, The Trianon, Wood of Fausses Reposes, etc.
30	Paris	
31	Paris	
1	Paris	
2	Paris	
3	Paris	
4	Paris	Sail from Havre S.S. Carmania.
14	New York	

Allen Tour "416"

J. Alex. Love (manager)
Dadeville, Ala.
Allen Tours, 154 Boylston Street
Boston, Mass.

Izzy–Mommer–or anything you want to call me. Ever.
Maybe Mrs. Allen A. Davis
406 Ridge Ave.
Troy, Ohio

Minnie Kate Rogers
331 North Church St.
Tupelo, Mississippi

Rosa Rogers
345 Church St.
Tupelo, Miss.

Mrs. F. C. Montross (Sara)
Troy, Ohio

Nadine Runyan
112 South Porter
Norman, Oklahoma

Dorine Guthrie
706 Jenkins
Norman, Oklahoma (by Nadine)

Corinne Kelso
260 Wis. Ave.
Oshkosh, Wis.

Elizabeth Knox
804 Main Street
Fort Morgan, Colo.

Jessica Reed
413 N. Naches Ave.
Yakima, Wash.

Wilma Ludwig (Bill)
1201 South Main St.
Findlay, Ohio

Naomi Ludwig (Dutch)
1201 South Main St.
Findlay, Ohio

Caroline Wingo
Martin, Tennessee

Elizabeth Crisler
Hazlehurst, Miss.

(Mrs.) Florence E. Glazier (Boston)
798 Centre St.
Jamaica Plains, Mass.

Mary Jewell Kimbell
1920 Highland
Shreveport, La.

Debra Pearl Munday
Dalyell
Shreveport, La.

Cleveland W. Humble
Hereford, Texas

Margaret Habel

Mr. and Mrs. O. K. Cummings
Fairhope, Ala. (Tour 423)

Mary E. Deering (Tour 423)
500 W. 20th St.
Wilmington, Del.

Mrs. Kitty Cox
Investigatory Police Dpt.
101 South 29th Street
Omaha, Nebraska

A. Ruth Kelley
Reedsville
Mifflin Co., Penna.

Laura C. King (No. 423)
39 E. Franklin St.
Hagerstown, Md.

Helen Clark Martin (student, No. 45)
156 Wentworth St.
Charleston, S.C.

Bess K. Martin (No. 423)
29 E. Franklin St.
Hagerstown, Md.

Mrs. H. D. McLaughlin (No. 423)
Oak Hill Ave
Hagerstown, Md.

Mary G. Radcliffe (No. 45)
36 Meeting Street
Charleston, S.C.

Rafael Ruiz y Ruiz
Madrid — Jorge Juan 8

Nadine Runyan
115 South Porter
Norman, Oklahoma

Esther L. Small (No. 423)
Salem, Mass.

Caroline Wingo
316 Main St.
Martin, Tennessee

Louise Naber
331 N. First Ave
Phoenix, Ariz.
Home: Wabash, Ind.

Stuttgart Journal

June–December 1946
William Kern Holoman

Nice, 1946

SOURCE: Brown leather album with gold tooling, oblong 8½ x 7¾ inches high. Gilt-edged fine paper. About 100 leaves, of which 30 are used, recto only. flyleaf inscribed:

William Kern Holoman
1st Mil[itary] Gov[ernmen]t B[attalion]
2123 Woodland Avenue[1]
Raleigh, NC

---

1. 2123 Woodland Avenue was the address of Kern's father, Dallas Holoman, Sr., and still his legal home address, since Kaye and Kern had not yet acquired their first home in Raleigh.

STUTTGART JOURNAL

JUNE–DECEMBER 1946
WILLIAM KERN HOLOMAN

This journal covers my father's return to Germany from a post-War leave in North Carolina in the spring of 1946. It begins on June 15, 1946, as Kaye and Kern drive to Fort Bragg to collect his redeployment orders, and concludes with the entry of December 29, 1946, written in their new apartment on West Park Drive in Raleigh. I was born the following September, 1947.

This is the period of my father's residence in Stuttgart, which wound down with a rest-and-relaxation leave to Italy and Switzerland (October 12–23) and a short trip to Berchtesgaden to see the remains of Hitler's compound there (November 9–11).

Since the wartime portion of his Memoirs *stops abruptly with the end of his time in Weinheim (May–December 1945), it seems likely that he meant to build one more narrative chapter, based on this text. Or perhaps he did write one, and the manuscript has been lost.*

The full chronology of my father's activities during World War II can be reconstructed from the preserved sources—his Memoirs *and the sources on which they were based, this diary, a scrapbook kept by Kaye and containing photographs and telegrams, and the chronology compiled by Kaye on the occasion of their 50th wedding anniversary in 1993. In brief:*

Kern graduated from UNC in June 1942 and was drafted immediately into the United States Army. He reported on August 8 to Fort Bragg, then underwent basic training at Camp Wheeler (Macon, Georgia) and Fort Gordon (Savannah, Georgia). Kaye graduated from Duke on May 22, 1943. Kern, meanwhile, had been assigned for immersion training in French at Rutgers. He got a short furlough to go home to Raleigh to get married. The wedding was on June 22, 1943, following which Kaye and Kern established their first household in New Brunswick, New Jersey.

Kern sailed for Manchester, England, on March 23, 1944. Kaye returned to Raleigh and lived at 832 Wake Forest Road, the Highsmith residence, working at WRAL Radio. With Eisenhower's headquarters, Kern travelled from London to Paris, arriving in August 1944, shortly after the Liberation. He was commissioned as an officer on April 9, 1945, and after two weeks of officer training near Troyes in France was assigned to a small Military Government detachment in Weinheim. Victory in Europe was achieved on May 7 and in Japan on August 15, 1945. Franklin D. Roosevelt, the president, had died the previous April 12. Kern says he served roughly eight months in Weinheim, which would have been May–December 1945.

In Spring 1946 Kern was given a 90-day leave to return to the United States. On March 16, Kaye's father, J. Henry Highsmith, wired her at Woman's College, Greensboro, where she was visiting her sister Louise: "Kern says will arrive Raleigh first week April." But on March 26 he wired that he was stalled at Le Havre and might not leave until Friday, March 29. On the 29th he wired "Leaving Saturday, slow ship." The crossing probably took about 10 days, perhaps less. Thus the happy couple had something like two months, mid-April to mid-June 1946, to enjoy time together.

"We made several short trips," writes Kaye: "with Kern's father to Florida; to New York, and to the mountains. We also had an apartment on White Oak Road for one month."[2]

My father hoped that the time until his final discharge from the Army would be of short duration. He wrote a line or two every single day. On shipboard he logs the number of miles traveled each day as well as the weather and sea conditions—practices he continues in his later travel journals as well. He notes all the films he saw—there were movies every day for military personnel—and the books he was reading. Many of the books were in the Armed Services Editions[3] *paperbacks that lay around the officers' clubs and mess halls for the taking. He began to read the Old Testament in order and*

---

2. "Kern and Kaye Holoman: Family Chronology, 1943–1993."
3. There were more than a thousand titles in the series, listed in *Wikipedia*. See also *Books in Action: The Armed Services Editions*, ed. John Y. Cole (Washington, 1984).

had reached I Chronicles *by the time he was packing for home in early November. He notes correspondence received and sent, primarily with his wife, his father, and his best friend Dan Hodges. Nearly every entry concludes with "Kaye," meaning he'd written her a letter that day. She wrote him every day, too. (This was in keeping with a family tradition of writing a letter or a postcard every day one is apart from loved ones. We continue to keep that tradition, though postcards have yielded to electronic media.)*

Several of my father's life-long habits are to be noted from his diary: counting the days and weeks since or until milepost events ("left Kaye 2 months ago today," "in Army four years today"). He notes, at the beginning, that his third anniversary, June 22, 1946, was the first spent with Kaye. He records the name of every hotel and restaurant he visited. (Later journals include what was consumed and a rating of how it went.) Many, perhaps most, of his evening meals in Stuttgart were taken at the Graf Zeppelin Hotel directly across the street from the Hauptbahnhof. Whereas in Weinheim the officers of his small detachment enjoyed a requisitioned house with gardens, pool, and domestic staff who provided the meals, in Stuttgart he was billeted in an apartment without a cook, and officers were responsible for their own meals.

He also diligently records the sights he has seen—most of the Berlin landmarks in a single day, via hired taxi; Rome's treasures, one by one. He doesn't seem to have missed much. Many of the souvenirs he writes of acquiring (Pinocchio, a Swiss music box, a map of the US Sector) are familiar to his children, who grew up with them at 2912 Hostetler Street.

But this particular diary also reveals a number of facts that have missed transmission in the family lore. One is the plan, eventually abandoned, for Kaye to have joined Kern in Germany until his discharge. There are multiple references to horseback riding, though I'm certain I never saw my father near a horse. He was clearly disappointed not to be promoted to Captain as he left the Army, and declined the opportunity to join the ORC (Organized Reserve Corps), though he enlisted in the North Carolina National Guard at the rank of Captain the following September 1947. From other correspondence we learn that he declined an offer of employment with the Foreign Service to return to home and hearth (with firewood supplied by Aunt Bessie Gray)—and to Boylan-Pearce, the business his father was anxious to leave to all four sons.

The overriding theme here, not surprisingly, is the depth of his agony at being away from Kaye. There's also evidence of his life-long workaholism, streaks of what he calls being "blue" and what we would now call depression, and his unquenchable Wanderlust.

The longtime home of these sources—and what was left of the Highsmith manuscripts—was the attic at 2912 Hostetler. I so wish that my fading memory could come up with what else there was besides these things that have ended up in what has become the boxed archive of Kaye and Kern Holoman's papers. Surely my parents kept their daily wartime correspondence, and I can't imagine there weren't other diaries. I know I remember at least one other diary, kept by my father in his teens, where he wrote something like "I haven't been so blue since Mother died" (in 1935, when he was 15).

I couldn't connect all the proper names with real people, in part because I couldn't always decipher the handwriting. Some of the names I knew already from the Memoirs; *some showed up in other documents, like a printed banquet menu for Christmas 1945 that included a photograph of the Military Government staff in the region—several dozen men—along with their printed names. Here I identified my dad's all-important cribbage-playing, jeep-driving buddy, whose name he usually spells as Bazinksy. In fact he was Capt. Alexis S. Basinski, emerging as an important judge and magistrate in post-War legal actions involving Germans and Americans.*

At the front of the diary, before the first chronological entry, my father has listed central place names, officials, and businesses in Weinheim, then left several blank pages as though he meant to summarize that period as an introduction to the journal of the Stuttgart period. Or perhaps this was merely an aide-mémoire *compiled during his early weeks in Weinheim, the album then left aside for more than a year, until June 1946. I've placed these lists at the end of this transcription, pp. 75–77.*

15 June 1946 – Saturday

Drove to Fort Bragg with Kaye. Picked up orders.

17 June 1946 – Monday

Left Raleigh for New Brunswick on Silver Meteor.

18 June 1946 – Tuesday

Arrived New Brunswick. Registered Rutgers House. Reported Camp Kilmer. Dinner at Roger Smith [New Brunswick hotel]. *Diary of A Chambermaid* [1946 film].

19 June 1946 – Wednesday

Went to Camp Kilmer with Kaye requesting information on Kaye's status in going overseas. Referred to Brooklyn Army base. Kaye and I took train to NYC. Brooklyn base referred me to Washington. Cocktails at Martinique [New York hotel]. *Cluny Brown* [1946 film]. Dinner at Caruso's. Frank Fay in *Harvey* [Broadway play].

20 June 1946 – Thursday

Reported Camp Kilmer.[4] Got 48-hr. pass to go to Washington. Bought white coat for Kaye's anniversary. Visited Princeton.

21 June 1946 – Friday

Went to Washington with Kaye. At Pentagon found no chance to get Kaye overseas without upgrading category.[5] Also no chance for discharge. Visited sessions of Senate and House. Dinner at Burt's [Burt's Trans-Lux Restaurant, 14th St.].

22 June 1946 – Saturday

3rd anniversary. First one spent with Kaye. Corsage of sweet peas. *Hurricane* [1937 film] and *Kismet* [1944 film with Marlene Dietrich] at Highland Park. Dinner at Elks Club.

23 June 1946 – Sunday

So Goes My Love [1946 film]. Dinner at Howard Johnson.

---

4. Camp Kilmer, just north of New Brunswick, New Jersey, was the assembly site for troops leaving for and returning from the European Theatre of Operations. It was named for Joyce Kilmer, the poet killed in World War I, who had lived nearby.
5. That is, presumably, extending commitment time in Europe.

24 June 1946 – Monday

Reported to Camp. No news. Went to New York with Kaye. Cocktails at Rockefeller Center. Dinner at American-Hungarian [restaurant on W. 31st Street]. Grace Moore and Jan Peerce in *La Bohème* in Lewisohn Stadium.

25 June 1946 – Tuesday

Reported to Camp. No news. Picnic in Banleagh[?] Park. Dinner at Howard Johnson. *Gilda* [1946 film] in Sayreville.

26 June 1946 – Wednesday

Scheduled to sail 28 June on *Frederick Victory*. *Janie Gets Married* [1946 film]. Dinner at Roger Smith [New Brunswick hotel].

27 June 1946 – Thursday

Reported loss of duffel bag. Expect to be removed from shipment. Brought Kaye to Camp Kilmer. Officers' Club. *Night and Day* [1946 film] at post theatre. First night away from Kaye since I came home.

28 June 1946 – Friday

Scratched from shipment because of loss of duffel bag. *Badman's Territory* [1946 film].

29 June 1946 – Saturday

Marco Polo [1938 film *Adventures of...*] and *Topper* [1937 film]

30 June 1946 – Sunday

Took bus to South Amboy and back. Dinner at Rutgers House. *Spiral Staircase* [1946 film]. Atom bomb dropped [at Bikini Atoll].

1 July 1946 – Monday

Went to New York with Kaye. *Smoky* [1946 film] at Roxy. Dinner at American-Hungarian. Rode bus to 175 Street and took subway back.

2 July 1946 – Tuesday

Duty officer at beer hall at Camp Kilmer. Saw Kaye at 10:30 p.m.

3 July 1946 – Wednesday

48-hour pass. Bought shoes. Took bus to Princeton. Dinner at Lahière.[6]

4 July 1946 – Thursday

Slept late. *Without Reservations* [1946 film]. Went to Highland Park.

5 July 1946 – Friday

Am scheduled to sail on *Sedalia Victory* 8 July. Wired Dad. Took bus to Roxbury and Perth Amboy. *Call of the Wild* [1935 film].

6 July 1946 – Saturday

Forever and a Day [1943 film]. Dinner at Colonial [New Brunswick restaurant]. Bus to Dunellen.

7 July 1946 – Sunday

Kaye came out to camp to meet me. Sandwiches at Victory Room [at officers' PX]. *A Night in Casablanca* [1946 Marx Brothers film]. Went back into New Brunswick with Kaye. Left her at midnight. Now I am alone.

8 July 1946 – Monday

Left Camp Kilmer at 11:30. Boarded *Sedalia Victory* Staten Island, Pier 11 at 3:15. Am much more blue than I had expected to be. Kaye is in New York, just a few miles away. She will go to Raleigh tonight. Sailed at 5:45. Out of sight of land at 8:30. Kaye.

9 July 1946 – Tuesday

260 miles from NYC at 1200. Average 15.5 knots. Mason: *Budapest Parade Murders* [1935 novel], Kelland: *Dreamland* [Armed Services Editions[7] 1025, 1946]. Kaye.

---

6. Lahière was an upscale French restaurant on Witherspoon Street in Princeton, a favorite place for romantic meals in the period Kaye and Kern lived in New Brunswick.
7. Hereafter ASE.

10 July 1946 – Wednesday

672 miles from NYC at 1200. Average 15.5 knots. Slightly seasick. Sea very calm. Dad.

11 July 1946 – Thursday

1002 miles from NYC at 1200. Average 16.1 knots. No longer seasick. Sea very calm. Wister: *The Virginian* [ASE 887, 1945]. John Womble[?] (80 S. Main St., Homer, NY).

12 July 1946 – Friday

1346 miles from NYC at 1200. Average 14.3 knots. Sea very calm and temperature warm. Chandler: *Farewell, My Lovely* [1940 novel]. Kaye.

13 July 1946 – Saturday

1780 miles from NYC at 1:00. Average 15.4 knots. Sea fairly calm. Temperature cold. Jim Kelly (274 Dillon Hall, Notre Dame).

14 July 1946 – Sunday

2093 miles from NYC at 1200. Average 16.1 knots. Sea choppy. Temperature cool. Huxley: *The Gioconda Smile* [ASE 926, 1945]. Kaye. Dad.

15 July 1946 – Monday

2457 miles from NYC at 1200. Average 15.8 knots. Sea rough. Foggy and cold. Gardner: [*Case of the*] *Half-Wakened Wife* [Perry Mason novel, ASE 1039, 1946]. Mac Crellich[?] (22 Lowell Road, Wellesley, Mass.).

16 July 1946 – Tuesday

2823 miles from NYC at 12:00. Average 15.5. Sea rough. Overcast and cold. Van Druten: *Voice of the Turtle* [ASE 815, 1945]. Glenn Sawyer (Peter Bent Brigham Hosp., Boston, or 1618 Spencer Ave., New Bern). Later: Raised Land's End at 2230. Moon is one day past full. Very beautiful. Am beginning to dread returning to work.

17 July 1946 – Wednesday

3210 miles from NYC at 1200. Average 16.56 knots. Sea calm. Weather sunny. Raised Beachy Head at 1300. Dropped anchor at Dover 1700. Kaye.

18 July 1946 – Thursday

3313 miles from NYC at 1200. Average 15.5 knots. Sea choppy. Weather overcast. Left Dover at 0700. Am blue. Lewis: *Cass Timberlane* [ASE 971, 1945]. Dad.

19 July 1946 – Friday

Docked at Bremerhaven 0845. Weather warm. Am still very blue. Mrs. Highsmith.

20 July 1946 – Saturday

Left ship at 0645. Time here is seven hours ahead of Raleigh. Departed 0900. Bremerhaven to Bremen to Hanover to Giesen [near Hildesheim] to Göttingen to Kassel. Did not sleep. Bell: *All Brides Are Beautiful* [ASE 1007, 1946].

21 July 1946 – Sunday

Arrived Marburg 0545. 159th Reinforcement Depot. Will be able to leave tomorrow. Walked into Marburg. Visited Elizabeth Church and Marburg Schloss (12th century; site of meeting between Luther and Zwingli). Church is oldest Gothic cathedral on continent. Arranged for transportation to Frankfurt tomorrow. Sabatini: *Mistress Wilding* [1924 novel]. Kaye.

22 July 1946 – Monday

Left Marburg in jeep 0900. To Alsfeld, to Bad Nauheim. Dinner with OIC [officer in charge]. To Frankfurt. Baselerhof Hotel. Info on Kaye. Am eligible to return home after 30 months overseas despite category. [Seton:] *Dragonwyck* [ASE 489, 1944]. Kaye, Dad.

23 July 1946 – Tuesday

In Frankfurt. Partial payment $100.00. Bought overcoat. Kaye. Cable to Kaye and Dad.

24 JULY 1946 – WEDNESDAY

Left Frankfurt 0940. Darmstadt, Weinheim, Heidelberg, Bruchsal, Bretten. Arrived Stuttgart 1410. Registered Graf Zeppelin Hotel. Reported 1st MG BN [Military Government Battalion] (Larson). Can get Kaye here by signing category IA (to remain year after Kaye arrives). Can get home in November or December. Will probably be assigned to Stuttgart. Booked transatlantic phone call to Kaye for Friday night. Doris Ritz is dead. Dinner at Graf Zeppelin with Lt. Arliss. *My Sister Eileen* [1942 film]. Kaye, Dad. Feeling very encouraged.

25 JULY 1946 – THURSDAY

In army four years today. Moved into billet at 40a Neuweinsteigerweg [Neue Weinsteige]. Will be assistant adjutant to Bn [battalion]. Received letters from Kaye (June 15, 16, 17, 19). Kaye can get here in November. Dinner at Graf Zeppelin with Captain Basinski.[8] (Lunch with Lt. and Mrs. Mayer). Went to Solitude [castle near Stuttgart]. Kaye. Have almost decided not to have Kaye come, but to go home as soon as possible. Mostly depends on what Kaye says on the phone tomorrow.

26 JULY 1946 – FRIDAY

Began work. Talked on telephone to Kaye. Reception *very* clear. She wants me to come home instead of her coming over here. Am very pleased with this decision. Very much in love with Kaye. Kaye.

27 JULY 1946 – SATURDAY

Went to Heidelberg. Bought clothes. Lunch at Victorian Hotel. Return to Stuttgart. Lonely. *Leave Her to Heaven* [1945 film]. Dan, Kaye.

28 JULY 1946 – SUNDAY

Sept late. *The Sailor Takes a Wife* [1945 film]. Dad. Kaye.

---

8. Alexis S. Basinski (1911–83) was a lawyer from Chicago who became a magistrate in the American sector of occupied Germany, adjudicating cases between German nationals and US citizens. He was still serving in this capacity, from Heidelberg and Mannheim, in the 1950s.

29 July 1946 – Monday

Four letters from Kaye (July 18, 19, 20, 22). Cribbage with Basinski. Irish: *After Dinner Story* [ASE 594, 1945]. Kaye.

30 July 1946 – Tuesday

Letter from Kaye (July 24). Cribbage with Basinski. Kaye. Dad.

31 July 1946 – Wednesday

PX Inventory Office. Went to Pforzheim. Cribbage with Basinski. Guy Wharton (13413½ Harding Ave., San Fernando, Cal.). Kaye.

1 August 1946 – Thursday

Holiday (Army Air Force Day). Horseback riding. Cribbage with Basinski. Dinner at Graf Zeppelin. *The Madonna's Secret* [1946 film]. Kaye. *Exodus*.

2 August 1946 – Friday

Organization chart and meeting on T/O [Theater of Operations] allocations. Cribbage with Basinski. Horseback riding. Dad, Kaye.

3 August 1946 – Saturday

Beginning to worry about my job. *Gilda* [1946 film]. Am discouraged and very blue. Took walk up to Sonnenberg and back. Thackeray: *Henry Esmond* [ASE 609, 1945]. Kaye.

4 August 1946 – Sunday

Slept late. Did virtually nothing. Charlie Morrow (USS *Los Angeles*, CA 135, FPO SF Cal). Kaye.

5 August 1946 – Monday

Four letters from Kaye (July 24, 25, 26, 27). Cribbage with Basinski. Kaye, Dad.

6 August 1946 – Tuesday

Three letters from Kaye (July 28, 29, 30). One beautiful letter. Shelley, M. W.: *Frankenstein* [ASE 909, 1945]. Kaye.

7 August 1946 – Wednesday

Dinner at Graf Zeppelin with Arliss. Horseback riding. Kaye.

8 August 1946 – Thursday

Left Kaye and US one month ago. Dinner with Basinski at Graf Zeppelin. *House of Dracula* [1945 film]. Kaye.

9 August 1946 – Friday

Letters Kaye (July 31, Aug. 1, 2, 3), Dad, Jim Kelly. Dad, Kaye.

10 August 1946 – Saturday

26th Birthday. Letter from Kaye (Aug 4). Was alone in office today. Cribbage with Basinski. Kaye, Jim Kelly (2122 Capitol Way, Olympia). *Leviticus*.

11 August 1946 – Sunday

Slept until noon. Plüderhausen with Basinski. Dinner at Graf Zeppelin. *Jessie James* [1939 film]. Champagne. Kaye.

12 August 1946 – Monday

Cribbage with Basinski. Dad. Kaye.

13 August 1946 – Tuesday

Mr. Larson says that I may have to serve in Europe until six months after left the states (until 8 Jan. 1946). He intimates, however, that I'll go home in November. Letter from Kaye (5 Aug.) and Dad. Birthday telegram from Kaye. Cribbage with Basinski. Kaye.

14 August 1946 – Wednesday

Argued Larson into agreeing to report me as eligible for return in December. Letters from Kaye (Aug. 6, 7). Dinner at Graf Zeppelin. *Well-Groomed Bride* [1946 film]. Kaye.

15 August 1946 – Thursday

Very trying day at work (telephone directory, memorandum, etc.). Letter from Dan. Ambler: *A Coffin for Dimitrios* [1935 novel]. Kaye, Dad.

16 August 1946 – Friday

Capt. Giunta says no one will be held past date on which they became eligible to return to US. Will to go Berlin for three days next week to inspect OMGUS [Office of Military Government, US] files. *Tarzan and the Leopard Woman*. [1946 film]. Kaye. Dan.

17 August 1946 – Saturday

Received orders to go to Berlin on Monday. *Road to Utopia* [1946 Bing Crosby / Bob Hope film]. Gardner: *Case of the Lucky Legs* [1934 Perry Mason novel]. Kaye.

18 August 1946 – Sunday

Slept late. *Abilene Town* [1946 film]. Made arrangements to call Kaye at 1000 Thursday night. Kaye. Dad.

19 August 1946 – Monday

Very hard rain cancelled air flights. Couldn't go to Berlin. Hope to go tomorrow. Arranged to call Kaye from Berlin if necessary. Three letters from Dad and three from Kaye (Aug. 8, 9, 10). Canby: *Walt Whitman* [ASE 324, 1944]. Kaye.

20 August 1946 – Tuesday

Left Stuttgart with Alex Thelen at 1:15. Arrived Frankfurt 1:44. Left Frankfurt 2:20. Arrived Berlin 3:52.[9] Stayed as Gossler Hotel. Dinner with Thelen at Truman Hall [new Consolidated Mess Hall in Berlin]. Drinks at Harnack House [Officers' Mess at the time; soon returned to Max Planck Institute]. Kaye.

21 August 1946 – Wednesday

Finished up all work before noon. Think I know about OMGUS file system. After dinner hired taxi, and went to see Radio Tower, Under den Linden, Tiergarten, Reichstag, Russian memorial, Berlin Dome, Brandenburg

---

9. The three days in Berlin, August 20–22, 1946, were Kern's only visit there. Concerning accommodations in Berlin, and Military Government in general, see Pat McMann Gilchrist, *It's Midnight in Berlin: A True Story of an American Girl in War Torn Berlin, 1946–47* (2013).

Gate, Hindenburg Palace, Propaganda Ministry, Reichskanzlerei, Wertheim's [department store], Wannsee. Dinner at Truman Hall. Dad, Kaye.

22 August 1946 – Thursday

Four months from today I'll be eligible to go home after 30 months overseas. Left Templehof at 8:15. Arrived Frankfurt 10:12. Plane to Stuttgart cancelled. Bad weather. Col. Cooke arranged for me to come back in car that brought Thielen. Rode back with Bill Daniels. Arrived Stuttgart 10:15. Talked to Kaye. Connection was bad. She is blue, and I am disappointed in phone call. Love her dearly. Kaye. *Numbers*.

23 August 1946 – Friday

Back to work. Began study on files. Ten letters. Six from Kaye (Aug. 11, 12, 13, 14, 15, 16), Dan, Dad, Wharton, Charlie Morrow. Bought cigarette lighter and photograph album. Helen Twelvetrees in *The Man Who Came to Dinner* [traveling USO production]. Kaye.

24 August 1946 – Saturday

Birthday card from Kaye. Bad Wimpfen with Basinski. Supper at Red Cross. Cribbage with Basinski. Gardner: *Case of the Curious Bride* [1934 Perry Mason novel]. Dad. Kaye.

25 August 1946 – Sunday

Slept until noon. Dinner with Basinski at Graf Zeppelin. Drove to Heidelberg. Supper at Hotel Wagner. Kaye.

26 August 1946 – Monday

Cribbage with Basinski. Two letters from Kaye (Aug. 17, 18). Kaye.

27 August 1946 – Tuesday

Larson says I may be kept until six months after date of reporting back to this organization. Also says, however, that I have to leave 15 days before eligibility date. One letter from Dad, two from Kaye (Aug. 19, 20). Won radio in PX lottery. Bought music box. Dad, Kaye.

28 August 1946 – Wednesday

Larson wrote out a sheet on me today listing 15 December as my expected date to arrive in the US. Dan, Kaye.

29 August 1946 – Thursday

Hughes: *The Fallen Sparrow* [ASE 409, 1944]. Kaye.

30 August 1946 – Friday

Arranged for trip to Garmisch with Basinski and Guthman. No reservations, but we will go anyway. Letter from Dad and two from Kaye (Aug. 21, 22). Dad. Kaye. [Added:] Birthday telegram to Dad. Dinner at Graf Zeppelin.

31 August 1946 – Saturday

Stuttgart to Ulm to Dachau to Munich. Dinner at Excelsior Hotel. Arrived Garmisch at 9:30.[10] Stayed at Markplatz Hotel. Went with Basinski, Henry Guthman, Clair Wynkowski.

1 September 1946 – Sunday

Breakfast at Post Hotel. Walked around town. Dinner. Went to Eibsee [nearby lake]. Went to Oberammergau. Ordered madonna and chessmen.

2 September 1946 – Monday

Got up late. Left Garmisch 2 p.m. Oberammergau. Bought wooden toys and toy dwarf. Bought limburger cheese. Landsberg, Augsburg, Ulm, Stuttgart. Supper at Red Cross. Kaye.

3 September 1946 – Tuesday

Six letters from Kaye (Aug. 23, 24, 25, 26, 27, 28), two from Dad. Two snapshots of Kaye. Bought radio and music box. Kay, Dad. *Deuteronomy*.

4 September 1946 – Wednesday

Letter from Kaye (Aug. 29). Am arranging for work to be done at Secy.

---

10. This was presumably the occasion of a visit to call on Richard Strauss at his villa in Garmisch-Partenkirchen. The maid would not receive the "occupiers." We children heard the story often.

[James F.] Byrnes's speech here on Friday. Kaye, Eddie Baczewski (Chove[?] Hall, D-37, Soldiers Field [Harvard Univ. housing] Boston 63, Mass.).

5 SEPTEMBER 1946 – THURSDAY

Worked until 2200 preparing [for] visit of Secretary of State Byrnes. Bought alarm clock. Kaye. Charlie Morrow (USS LA [*Los Angeles*], CA 135, FPO, San Francisco, Cal.).

6 SEPTEMBER 1946 – FRIDAY

Saw Secretary Byrnes make address at Century Theatre in Stuttgart. Also present were MacNerney, Connelly, Vandenberg, Murphy. Got letter from Kaye (Aug. 30) including two snapshots. Bought photograph album and Swiss doily. Kaye, Dad.

7 SEPTEMBER 1946 – SATURDAY

Stuttgart to Ulm to Memmingen to Kempten to Oberstdorf. Dinner with Constabulary. Stayed at Bergblick Pension. Drinks at Luitpold Hotel. Kaye.

8 SEPTEMBER 1946 – SUNDAY

Slept until ten. Breakfast of ham, eggs, cheese, coffee. Climbed Nebelhorn in cable-car and to top on foot. Tiring but fun. Saw Austria and Switzerland. Dinner at Snack Bar. Returned to Stuttgart. Left Kaye 2 months ago today. Kaye.

9 SEPTEMBER 1946 – MONDAY

Duty officer. Slept in Col. Dawson's office. Inspected PX, motor pool, garage, buildings etc. Two letters from Kaye (Sept. 1, 2), Wilson: *Ruggles of Red Gap* [ASE 884, 1945]. Dad. Kaye.

10 SEPTEMBER 1946 – TUESDAY

Letter from Kaye (Sept. 5). Dan, Dad. Cribbage with Fitzgerald. Kaye. *Joshua*.

11 September 1946 – Wednesday

Col. Cooke went to Berlin. I managed the office by myself. Did all right. Two letters from Kaye (Sept. 3, 4). *Return of Frank James* [1940 film]. Kaye.

12 September 1946 – Thursday

Worked hard alone all day today. Was exhausted and exhilarated at the end of the day. Letter from Kaye (Aug. 31) with 2 snapshots, letter from Dad. *A Walk in the Sun* [1945 film]. Dad. Kaye.

13 September 1946 – Friday

Worked until 9 o'clock on Top Secret Instruction. Letter from Kaye (6 Sept.). Kaye, Dan.

14 September 1946 – Saturday

Got out instructions on converting marks into scrip. Will work Monday on actual conversion. Baseball game. *Perilous Holiday* [1946 film]. Graf Zeppelin, Club. Kaye.

15 September 1946 – Sunday

Slept until noon. Have bad cold and sore throat. Gardner: *Case of the Sulky Girl* [1933 Perry Mason novel]. Went to Karlsruhe and brought Basinski back. Ate cheese and drank cognac with Basinski. Kaye.

16 September 1946 – Monday

Worked all day until 4 a.m. (17 Sept.) taking in Allied marks. Took in over $42,000 worth. Checked in $4 short. Four letters from Kaye. Very very tired.

17 September 1946 – Tuesday

Worked all day paying out new scrip currency. It will check in fairly close, but I'm worried that I should be short. One letter from Kaye (11 Sept.) Dad, Kaye. *Judges*.

18 September 1946 – Wednesday

Paid out all the rest of the money. It came within 5¢ of being right. Started in on my old job again. Letter from Kaye (Sept. 12). Kaye. *Ruth*.

19 September 1946 – Thursday

Worked hard all day catching up with my work. Dinner at Graf Zeppelin. Bought a bag of Swiss handkerchiefs. Cribbage with Fitzgerald. Letter from Kaye (Sept. 13). Kaye.

20 September 1946 – Friday

Placed telephone call to Kaye for 10 Sunday night. Kaye, Dad.

21 September 1946 – Saturday

First day of Fall. It turned cold and very windy during the night. My cold is better, but have crick in neck. *Easy to Wed* [1946 film]. Letter from Kaye (14 Sept.). Kaye.

22 September 1946 – Sunday

Will have 30 months overseas in three more months. Slept until noon. Went to see last half of *Spellbound* [1945 film]. Worked for an hour. Still have crick in neck. No connections to America so could not call Kaye. Sent her a telegram. Kaye.

23 September 1946 – Monday

Arrangements made for my replacement to come on 15 Nov. Kaye, Dad.

24 September 1946 – Tuesday

Fitzgerald promoted to Capt. today. Letter from Kaye (15 Sept.). Cribbage with Basinski. Kaye.

25 September 1946 – Wednesday

Worked hard again all day. Took overcoat to tailor for alterations. Kaye.

26 September 1946 – Thursday

Another hard day at work. Letters from Dad and two from Kaye (Sept. 17, 19). Lunch at Graf Zeppelin. Kaye.

27 September 1946 – Friday

Hard at work again. Until 9 tonight. Two letters from Kaye (Sept. 16, 18), one from Dad. Deferred phone call to Kaye until Monday. Kaye.

28 September 1946 – Saturday

Another hard day at work. Went to Heidelberg in jeep. Dinner at Wagner Hotel. Returned to Stuttgart. Kaye. *I Samuel.*

29 September 1946 – Sunday

Slept until noon. Went for a ride with Basinski: Daimler Benz. Polo game. Drinks at Graf Zeppelin. Stage show *Diamond Horseshoe.* Drinks at Officers' Club. Kaye.

30 September 1946 – Monday

Letter from Dan. Five from Kaye (Sept. 20, 21, 22, 23, 24). Larson hinted that I might go home in October. Talked to Kaye on phone. Excellent connection. Am very much in love with her. Dad. Kaye.

1 October 1946 – Tuesday

Letters from Dad and from Kaye (Sept. 25). Pay Day $1.19. Kaye.

2 October 1946 – Wednesday

Letter from Kaye (Sept. 26). Kaye, Guy Wharton 13413½ Harding Ave., San Fernando).

3 October 1946 – Thursday

Spring: *Fame is the Spur* [1940 novel]. Dad. Kaye.

4 October 1946 – Friday

Hughes: *The So Blue Marble* [ASE 785, 1945]. Worked late. Kaye.

5 October 1946 – Saturday

Chreston's Birthday. Letter from Dad and Kaye (27 Sept.). Worked hard all morning. Cribbage with Basinski. *The Virginian* [1946 film]. May be able to go home 15 November. Kaye.

6 October 1946 – Sunday

Slept until noon. Gardner: *Case of the Velvet Claws* [the first Perry Mason novel, 1933]. Dan (224 West 79th St., NYC, telephone Schuyler 49853). *II Samuel*.

7 October 1946 – Monday

New orders make it seem virtually certain that I'll go home in November and will be discharged soon after arriving in US. Col. Cooke approved a leave to Switzerland and Rome for me. It is planned that I'll leave on Friday. Played cribbage with Basinski. Kaye. Am very thrilled and cheerful.

8 October 1946 – Tuesday

Very cold weather. Hectic day at work. Ticklish situation with TWX [TeletypeWriter eXchange Service, i.e. early Telex] machine. Four letters from Kaye (Sept. 29, 30, Oct. 1, 2). Kaye.

9 October 1946 – Wednesday

Still cold. Submitted letters to Larson requesting release on or before November 15. Feel very ineffectual at work. Kaye.

10 October 1946 – Thursday

Expect to leave for Switzerland tomorrow. Kaye.

11 October 1946 – Friday

Slept until 8. Picked up my orders, and made arrangements to go to Mulhouse by train. Ate dinner. Read and slept all afternoon. Forester: *To the Indies* (ASE 709, 1945). Went to club. Basinski offered to take me to Mulhouse. Missed train. Drank too much. Dad. Kaye.

12 October 1946 – Saturday

Had headache. Got up late. Gassed up Basinski's jeep. To Calw, to Baden-Baden, to Strasbourg, to Saverne. Went to see "Katy" who lives in a little village near Phalsbourg. Good supper. To Strasbourg, to Colmar, to Mulhouse. Reported in at Leave Center.

13 October 1946 – Sunday

Met Joe O'Brien. Spent day processing and reading. *Heartbeat* [1946 film]. Kaye.

14 October 1946 – Monday

Left Mulhouse 0730. Arrived Basle [Basel] 8:15. Sightseeing tour in Basle. Corner of 3 countries. Dinner in Basle. To Lucerne, through St. Gotthard tunnel, to Bellinzona, to Lugano. Am staying at hotel called Schmid's Paradiso. Dinner. Walked around looking at Lugano. *Frenchman's Creek* [1944 film]. Casino Cécile. Kaye.

15 October 1946 – Tuesday

Early breakfast. Took funicular railroad up Mt. San Salvatore. Could see Monte Rosa, Italy, Matterhorn, Po Valley. Ice-capped mountains, Lago Maggiore. Left Lugano 1400. Crossed into Italy at Chiasso. Como Lake. Milan. Detrained for 3 hours. Excellent dinner at Hotel Savoia. Genoa, Rapallo, spent night on train.

16 October 1946 – Wednesday

Breakfast and lunch on train. Beside Mediterranean. Arrived at Rome 1500. Staying at Nuova Roma Hotel. Good dinner. Walked through the city. Very pleased and thrilled. Drinks at Ambassador Hotel. Kaye.

17 October 1946 – Thursday

Vatican and Vatican art galleries and museum. Sistine Chapel. Pantheon. St. Paul's. St. John's. Coliseum. Tomb of unknown soldier. Romulus and Remus. Dinner at Passetto's. Kaye.

18 October 1946 – Friday

Colosseum, Caracalla, Arch of Germanius, Appian Way, Church of Domine Quo Vadis, Catacombs, Church of St. Peter, Pietà. Shopping. Bought sweaters and skirt for Kaye. Dinner at Passetto's. Kaye.

19 October 1946 – Saturday

Walked through Forum, arches, Castor and Pollux, Sacred Way, etc.

visited Church of St. Pietro in Vincoli. Michelangelo's Moses. Bought Pinocchio. Visited Borghese Galleries, Holbein's Henry VIII, Titian's Sacred and Profane Love, Bellini's [Bernini's] Aeneas, Raphael's Descent ["The Deposition"], Pauline Bonaparte Borghese. Bought gloves for Kaye. Dinner at Passetto's. Kaye.

20 October 1946 – Sunday

O'Brien is sick and will not return with us. Rome toward Milan via Leghorn and Pisa. Lunch and dinner on train.

21 October 1946 – Monday

Arrived Milan 0600. Breakfast at Hotel Savoia. Saw square where Mussolini hung. Church of St. Ambrose. Leonardo's "Last Supper." Sforza palace. Cathedral of Milan. Read John Hersey's *Hiroshima* in *New Yorker* [August 31, 1946]. Milan to Chiasso, to Lugano, to Lucerne. Stopping at Hotel Continental. A dump. Kaye.

22 October 1946 – Tuesday

In Lucerne. Went shopping. Bought music box, bear, candy, and breadplate.[11] Went up Mr. Pilatus (2133 meters). Very lovely. Complete 28 months overseas today. Kaye. *Hangmen Also Die* [1943 film].

23 October 1946 – Wednesday

Left Lucerne at 7:30. To Basel, to Mulhouse. Lunch. To Strasbourg to Karslruhe. (Dinner.) Arrived Stuttgart 2300. Kaye.

24 October 1946 – Thursday

Went back to work. Larson and Col. Richardson say I am supposed to leave here 31 October. Am very pleased and excited. 14 letters from Kaye (Oct. 4–17), two from Dad, one from Dan. Kaye says she has an apartment for us to live in. Booked telephone call to Kaye for Saturday night. Kaye, Dad.

---

11. This carved wooden plate was inscribed "Unser tägliches Brot gib uns heute" ("Give us this day our daily bread") and hung in the kitchen at 2912 Hostetler Street. The Swiss music box was one of Kaye's treasured possessions. I suspect the bear was a straw-filled brown teddy bear I grew up with. The wooden Pinocchio mentioned just above now lives in Davis, California, in several pieces. It was among my father's favorite souvenirs from the journey to Switzerland and Italy.

25 October 1946 – Friday

Two months until Christmas. There seem no obstacles at all between me and departure on 31 Oct. Bought two cigarette lighters at PX. Kaye. Dan. *1st Kings*.

26 October 1946 – Saturday

OMGUS [Office of Military Government, U. S.] orders postpone my departure until 9 November (to be in Bremerhaven). Bryan to teach Zak my job today. Very bad day at work with trouble with classified TWX's [Telex]. Letter from Kaye (Oct. 14). Cribbage with Basinski. Cancelled phone call to Kaye because of bad connections. Kaye.

27 October 1946 – Sunday

Slept late. Steak for dinner. *Do You Love Me* [1946 film]. Adams: *Education of Henry Adams* [ASE 534, 1945]. Gardner: *Case of the Caretaker's Cat* [1935 Perry Mason novel]. Club. Kaye.

28 October 1946 – Monday

A hard day at work. Could not get connection to talk with Kaye. Deferred call until Wednesday. Two letters from Kaye (Oct. 20, 21). One from Dad. Kaye, Dad.

29 October 1946 – Tuesday

Fitzgerald went to hosp. with infected hand. Zak says he won't be able to relieve me and do his job. Col. Cooke is going to try to keep me in that job until the end of November. I am very disappointed, dejected and blue. Kaye.

30 October 1946 – Wednesday

My shipping date remains unchanged. I'm scheduled to leave here on 8 November. Two letters from Kaye (Oct. 22, 23). She says she has bought a DeSoto sedan for us. Talked to Kaye on telephone this afternoon. She is fine, and happy that I'm coming home. Have a promise for an apartment. Told her to expect me home in a month. Hallow'e'en party at Club. Kaye. Ullman: *The White Tower* [ASE 1053, 1946].

31 October 1946 – Thursday

Hallow'e'en. Four letters from Kaye (Oct. 17, 18, 19, 24). Orders came out today sending me to Bremerhaven on Nov. 9th. Cribbage with Basinski. Kaye.

1 November 1946 – Friday

Worked hard again today. My shipping date has been postponed until 14 Nov. Am disappointed. Letter from Kaye (Oct. 25) and Dad. Kaye.

2 November 1946 – Saturday

Pay Day. $123.50. Played cribbage with Basinski all afternoon. Planned trip to Berchtesgaden next weekend if I'm still here. *II Kings*. Kaye.

3 November 1946 – Sunday

Slept late. Went to Bad Wimpfen with Basinski. Supper at Red Cross. Cribbage. Irish: *Phantom Lady* [1942 novel; Irish was pseud. of Cornell Woolrich]. Kaye.

4 November 1946 – Monday

Tried to get reservations at Berchtesgaden for weekend. No luck. Lt. Zak on orders as Asst. Adj. Went to Ludwigsburg with Col. Cooke. Bought model house. Dad, Kaye.

5 November 1946 – Tuesday

Zak working full-time at my old job. Got typhoid shot at 387 hospital in Bad Cannstatt. Three letters from Kaye (Oct. 26, 27, 28). Hammett: *The Maltese Falcon* [1930 novel]. Dad. Kay.

6 November 1946 – Wednesday

Went to work late. Didn't do much at office. Made reservations for Berchtesgaden. Cribbage with Basinski. Hammett: *The Glass Key* [1931 novel]. Kaye.

7 November 1946 – Thursday

Have decided that I enjoyed my old job. No reservations available at Berchtesgaden, but we are going anyway. Dinner and cribbage with Bob Mayer and wife. Kaye.

8 November 1946 – Friday

Got Basinski's jeep out of the shop for him. Bought map of W/B[12] at PX. Packed a box of my stuff to send home. Cribbage with Basinski. Kaye. Left Kaye 4 months ago today.

9 November 1946 – Saturday

Did last work for MG [military government]. With Basinski went to Ulm, Augsburg, Munich. Dinner at Hotel Excelsior. Rosenheim. Berchtesgaden. Staying at Geissler Haus.

10 November 1946 – Sunday

Got up at 1000. Breakfast. Went to Koenigsee. Took road toward Eagle's Nest. Visited Hitler House. Street: *The Gauntlet* [1945 novel]. Kaye.

11 November 1946 – Monday

Breakfast in bed. Salt mines. Left Berchtesgaden 1230. Snack at Hofbraukeller in Munich. Arrived Stuttgart at 2000. Kaye, Dad.

12 November 1946 – Tuesday

Processed out. Colonel Cooke gave me an efficiency rating of 5.8. Don't feel very good. Made arrangements to leave on 1205 train tomorrow. Letter from Dad, three from Kaye (Oct. 30, 31, Nov. 1) including her last letter. Sold my radio, whiskey, and surplus rations to Basinski. Said goodbye to Basinski. Don't feel much emotion of any kind about leaving. *I Chronicles.* Packed.

13 November 1946 – Wednesday

I said goodbye to Fitz, Mayer, Lawson, Daugherty, Zak, Col. Cooke. Left Stuttgart on train at 1205. Accompanied by Captain Fadley. Bretten, Bruchsal, Heidelberg, Weinheim, Darmstadt. Arrived Frankfurt 1630. Got coach tickets. Left Frankfurt 1900. Bad Nauheim, Giessen, Marburg, Kassel. Spent night on train.

---

12. A color poster-map of the US Zone, Wurtemberg-Baden, published by the Army Exchange Service and subsequently hanging in the living room at 2912 Hostetler Street.

14 November 1946 – Thursday

Hanover, Bremen. Arrived Bremerhaven 1030, three hours late. Billeted in caserne. Accommodations are quite satisfactory. Expect to be here between 6 and 20 days. Expect to be assigned to a packet of troops. Gardner: *Case of the Stuttering Bishop* [Perry Mason novel, 1936]. *Faithful In My Fashion* [1946 film]. Kaye. Am very impatient to get home.

15 November 1946 – Friday

Muster of Army. Thurber: *Is Sex Necessary?* [ASE 368, 1944] Bridge. Am detailed to Provost Marshal tomorrow. Kaye.

16 November 1946 – Saturday

Unimportant detail with Provost Marshal. Miers: *Big Ben* [ASE 1027, 1946]. *Rendezvous with Annie* [1946 film]. No packet yet. Kaye.

17 November 1946 – Sunday

Left Raleigh five months ago. *The Green Years* [1936 film]. Kaye.

18 November 1946 – Monday

Kaye.

19 November 1946 – Tuesday

Cronin: *The Keys of the Kingdom* [ASE 113, 1943]. *Badman's Territory* [1946 film]. Kaye.

20 November 1946 – Wednesday

Wodehouse: *Psmith, Journalist* [1915 novel]. Didn't get posted on list to sail. Very disappointed and blue. Kaye.

21 November 1946 – Thursday

Assigned to packet RE-9348, scheduled to leave 27 Nov. Am Currency Exchange Officer for packet. Meeting of Currency Exchange Officers. Began to reread *War & Peace*. Went by bus into Bremerhaven-Wesermünde with Captain Kerr. Red Cross. Dinner at transient mess. *Cluny Brown* [1946 film].

22 November 1946 – Friday

Meeting packet officers. Prepared for Currency Exchange. *Somewhere in the Night* [1946 film].

23 November 1946 – Saturday

Clothing inspection of Enlisted Men. *Our Hearts Were Growing Up* [1946 film].

24 November 1946 – Sunday

Began collecting currency. May load on ship on Tuesday. Kaye.

25 November 1946 – Monday

Collect currency for packet. Over $13,000. Six dollars short.

26 November 1946 – Tuesday

Ship will not leave on 27 November. Perhaps 28. Counted U. S. currency. It checks. Obtained clearance for my packet. Went into Bremerhaven-Wesermünde with Captain Kerr. Dinner at transient mess. *Of Human Bondage* [1946 film.]

27 November 1946 – Wednesday

Met Kaye six years ago tonight. My packet will sail on *General Muir* Friday. As advance party I will board ship tomorrow night. Capt. Kerr left tonight. Kaye.

28 November 1946 – Thursday

Thanksgiving. Had physical exam. Thanksgiving Dinner was exceptionally good (tomato juice, consommé, turkey dressing, potatoes, carrots, asparagus, onions, olives, celery, pickle, small potatoes, cranberry sauce, pumpkin pie, ice cream). Only two meals today. Left caserne at 1900. Went in boxcar to Bremerhaven docks.

Boarded *General Muir* at 2000. Have a fine stateroom to be shared with 3 other men. Ship is amazingly good. The crew says it rolls badly. Scheduled to sail at 1200 tomorrow. Am very thrilled, happy and encouraged.

29 November 1946 – Friday

Received packet money. *General Muir* sailed at 1220. Out of sight of land at 1400. I must serve as PX officer for two compartments of EM [enlisted men]. Food is excellent on board. Night is clear, cold, and windy. She is moderately choppy, but boat is pitching. I am a little seasick.

30 November 1946 – Saturday

Was quite seasick just before going to bed last night. The sea calmed down during the night and was fairly smoothed this morning. Distributed PX ration requisition blanks. We dropped our pilot at Dover about 1330. I paid off my packet in US money. All but a few paid. Money checks out exactly even. 338 miles from Bremerhaven at 1300. Average speed 15.5 knots. Night is dark, sea is choppy, and becoming more so.

1 December 1946 – Sunday

Ocean has been rough all day. Ship pitching badly. Have been quite seasick intermittently all day. Collected PX money and began to make consolidation. 670 miles from Bremerhaven at 1300.

2 December 1946 – Monday

Boat has been pitching badly all day. I have been slightly seasick all day, but not so bad as yesterday. Finished making PX consolidations, and turned in money. Will pick up goods tomorrow. 978 miles from Bremerhaven at 1300. 2422 miles from NYC.

3 December 1946 – [Tuesday]

Sea is still rough but I am hardly sick at all. Has calmed down considerably since this morning. Weather is fine and clear, a bright noon. Ship is not making very good time. I gave out PX rations today. Figures don't check at all, a very sloppy job. 1264 miles from Bremerhaven at 1300. 2136 from NYC.

4 December 1946 – Wednesday

Sea is phenomenally calm. Weather is sunny and mild. No longer seasick. 1643 miles from Bremerhaven at 1300. 1957 from NYC.

5 December 1946 – Thursday

Tolstoy: *War and Peace*. Weather overcast. Sea is moderate, with swells. Announcement that ship will probably reach NYC Monday. 2057 miles from Bremerhaven at 1300. 1543 from NYC.

6 December 1946 – Friday

Wallace: *Kid Galahad* [1936 non-fiction, just released in paperback]. Van Doren: *Shakespeare* [ASE 1142, 1946]. Weather overcast. Sea rough, especially after dark. 2479 miles from Bremerhaven. 1350 from NYC.

7 December 1946 – Saturday

Forester: *Payment Deferred* [ASE 213, 1944]. Exceptionally rough weather becoming milder after dark. Overcast. 2862 miles from Bremerhaven at 1300. 967 from NYC. Pearl Harbor was 5 years ago.

8 December 1946 – Sunday

Five months today since I have seen Kaye. Debarkation is scheduled for Tuesday morning. Meeting to discuss the debarkation. Captain's dinner. Sea calm. Beautiful sunshiny day. Moon at night. 3355 miles from Bremerhaven at 1300. 550 from NYC.

9 December 1946 – Monday

Burns: *Saga of Billy the Kid* [ASE 1108, 1946]. Rehearsal for debarkation. At 13:30 a seaplane landed and took off a burst appendix case. Weather is cool and a little overcast. Sea is very calm. Ship traveling very slowly all day. 3704 miles from Bremerhaven at 1300. 200 from NYC.

10 December 1946 – Tuesday

Off Ambrose Lightship 0530. Docked at Brooklyn Army Base 0815. Ferry to Jersey City. Boarded PRR [Pennsylvania Railroad] train at 1210. Arrived Camp Kilmer 1240. Telephoned Kaye at 1500. She has apartment for us. Will be discharged at Fort Dix [NJ] rather than Fort Bragg. Hope to be discharged by Saturday. *The Bells of St. Mary's* [1945 film].

11 December 1946 – Wednesday

Gave passes to EM [enlisted men]. Duty officer for packet. Bought underwear, gloves, silver dish. Called Dad. Tried to call Mme Richards. Tried to call Dan. *Betty Co-Ed* [1946 film].

12 December 1946 – Thursday

Left Camp Kilmer 1535. Arrived Fort Dix 1815. Expect to be discharged by Saturday. *Cross My Heart* [1946 film]. Called Kaye.

13 December 1946 – Friday

Began discharge processing. Am not eligible for terminal discharge and not eligible for terminal promotion. Decided not to join ORC [Organized Reserve Corps]. Will have completed discharge by 1600 Saturday. No train reservations to Raleigh.

14 December 1946 – Saturday

Took final physical exam. Passed. Signed final papers and received service button. Not promoted. My terminal leave expires 21 January 1947. Was paid $337. Took bus to Trenton. Dinner at Lorenzo's [Pete Lorenzo's Cafe, across from Trenton station]. Wired Kaye. Pullman. Trenton to Philadelphia to Baltimore to Washington.

15 December 1946 – Sunday

Arrived Raleigh 1005. Met Kaye at station. Went to new apartment at 313 W. Park Drive. Went to visit Dad. Dinner with Kaye's parents. Visit to brothers. Supper with Dad, Va., Bob and Bobby T. at Club Bon Air.

16 December 1946 – Monday

Bought kitchen equipment. Lunch at S&W. Ordered telephone.

17 December 1946 – Tuesday

Moved wedding presents into apartment. Bought more household gadgets. Visited Betsy & Ralph S[eymour].

18 December 1946 – Wednesday

Cleaned and repaired bookcase. Picked up books from Dad's house and arranged them. Unwrapped wedding presents.

19 December 1946 – Thursday

Went shopping. Bought pants. Tried to find presents for Kaye and Dad. Dinner at S&W. Looked for coffee table. Had Betsy and Ralph for dinner.

20 December 1946 – Friday

Went shopping. Got fire wood from Bessie Gray. Had W. T. Martin and Lula Belle for dinner.

21 December 1946 – Saturday

Bought new suit at Honeycutt's. Bought new shoes. Dad and Va. visited us after dinner.

22 December 1946 – Sunday

Went to Winston-Salem to get Louise. Took Mrs. [Mollie] Harrell to G'boro. Lula Belle went with us. Moravian *putz* and church. Trimmed Christmas tree. Mailed cards.

23 December 1946 – Monday

Dinner with Dad at Rotary Club. Got dress suit at Teague's. Picked up new suit. Ken and Jay Wooten visited us after dinner. Dan Hodges came over.

24 December 1946 – Tuesday

Christmas Eve. First at home in five years. Finished Christmas shopping. Lunch at Avon Grill. Dinner with Betsy and Ralph. Visited all three brothers and delivered presents. Arranged Christmas presents and filled stockings.

25 December 1946 – Wednesday

Christmas. Up at 0900. Opened Christmas presents. Visited Dad and Va. Went to Kaye's parents' home. Opened more Christmas presents. Excellent dinner with Highsmiths. Visited Chreston and Luna, Dad and Va. Held open house for all immediate family.

26 December 1946 – Thursday

Up at noon. Cleaned dishes and wedding presents. Louise visited us. Fine dinner at home. Went to Woman's Club. Visited Ken and Jay Wooten. Visited Boyce and Lynn.

27 December 1946 – Friday

Up about 1030. Went to dance at Woman's Club. Had hamburgers with Betsy and Ralph at Drive-In.

28 December 1946 – Saturday

Bought kitchen cabinet. Nice dinner at home. Dan and Louise Scott visited us. Priscilla [card game].

29 December 1946 – Sunday

Church. Dinner at home. Visited Kaye's parents and Dean Baldwin.[13] Supper at Dan's. Bridge at Beck Barnhill's. Hamburgers at Drive-In.

---

13. Alice Baldwin was dean of Woman's College at Duke and a good friend of Mrs. Highsmith, Kaye's mother.

Notes on Weinheim

These pages, at the front of the album, precede the daily diary and are followed by two blank folios.

Weinheim

Rathaus — 1847
Villa Freudenberg[14] — 24 Lützelsachsener Str.
Villa Wels   — 31   "
Burgermeister — Richard Freudenberg
    Wilhelm Brück
Landrat — Karl Geppert
Wohnungsamt — Seyler
Police — Langer
Food Office — Von Gienanth
Wine Merchant — Graf von Birkheim
Secretary — Graf von C[h]rustchoff
Kreisauhofrat[?] — Johann Mattheus Siehl
    Artur Kern
Reichsbank Direktor — Oscar Eugen Gütle
Administ[trator] of Jewish Property — Sernatinger
Dürre Schule — DPs [Displaced Persons], School
Bezirksgewerbe Schule [Trade School] — DPs, Lanratsamt
Pestalo[zzi] Schule — DPs, 84th DIV
Diesterweg Schule — DPs, 84th DIV
Bender Schule [Gymnasium] — VD Hospital
Friedrich Schule — Labor Company — School

Apollo Theater — 84th Div.
Modernis Theatre — Civilians

---

14. On Richard Freudenberg (1892–1975), his business, and his post-War leadership see Kern Holoman's *Memoirs,* chapter 10.

[manufacturing concerns:]
Firma Freudenberg — Leather
Badenia — Machine Parts
Naturin[15] — Sausage Skins
Leinenkugle Stuhlfabrik — Chairs
Gummifabrik — Rubber
Rita Schuhgrosshandlung — Shoes

Bergstrasse
Hauptstrasse
A. L. [Albert Ludwig] Grimmstrasse
Bismarckstrasse
Friedrichstrasse
Bahnhofstrasse
Birkenaustatstrasse
Rotturmstrasse [Rote Turmstraße]
Nibelungenstrasse
Brunhildstrasse
Kantstrasse — [Nazi:] Horst Wessel Strasse
Hegelstrasse — [Nazi:] Adolf Hitler Strasse

Wachenburg [castle]
Windeck [castle]

LANDKREIS MANNHEIM, 103,000

Landrat Karl Geppert
1. Laudenbach
2. Hemsbach
3. Sulzbach – Grunewald
4. Weinheim – Bruck
5. Lützelsachsen – Setzer
6. Hohensachsen – Leonhard
7. Großsachsen – Steinmetz (Haupt)
8. Leutershausen [an der Bergstraße] – Blum (Kunkel)
9. Schriesheim – Rufer
10. Laudenburg

---

15. Now Naturin Viscofan, world's leading supplier of sausage casings.

11. Heddesheim – Moos
12. Ursenbach
13. Rippenweier-Ritschweier
14. Oberflockenbach
15. Schwetzingen – [Valentin] Gaa
17. Plankstadt
18. Oftersheim
19. Ketsch
20. Brühl
21. Hockenheim
22. Altlussheim
23. Neulussheim
24. Reilingen
25. Edingen
26. Ilvesheim
27. Neckarhausen

Lustschloss (Schwetzingen [palace])
Havadora Cigars (Hohenheim)

Ladenburg – (Romans [i.e., Roman Lopodunum and antiquities at the Lobdengau-Museum])
Edingen – DP camp
Ketsch – Typhoid

Bergstrasse
Schriesheimer Tal [valley hiking trail]

Oberrheinische Eisenbahn Gesellschaft (OEG)
Starkenburg [castle] (Heppenheim)
Strahlenberg [castle] (Schriesheim)

Landwirtchaftsschule [agricultural school] – Ladenburg
Muderhaus [Deaconess Motherhouse] – Ladenburg

European Grand Tour

April 3 – May 12, 1956
Kaye & Kern Holoman

On board Queen Elizabeth, *1956*

Monaco

SOURCE: Diary 3 (1956). Red leather album with gold tooling, titled TRAVELS, roughly 4 x 6¾ inches. (Almost identical to green album from 1982.) Hands of both Kaye and Kern. Inscribed on flyleaf, hand of Kate Herring Highsmith:

To
Kern and Katherine
From
Mother —
Wishing you a
Most wonderful trip.

European Grand Tour

April 3 – May 12, 1956

Kaye & Kern Holoman

In April and May 1956 Kaye and Kern took a six-week grand tour of Europe, departing New York on the Queen Elizabeth *to Cherbourg and returning via BOAC airliner to Idlewild Airport, now JFK. My father had long wanted to show my mother some of the sights he had seen during the War, and they reckoned that we two children were old enough to survive the experience following the rather careful schedule they had set up. Pearl Hasty, the maid, would be with us during the school week and would cook dinners for us according to a large calendar posted on the refrigerator—where, also, we could cross off the days until they returned. Weekends were to be spent at the homes of family and friends. Dick was in the first grade; I was in the third. We didn't quite grasp how glamorous that kind of travel was in the 1950s. The newspapers carried pieces on their trip, including a photograph of their boarding the* Queen Elizabeth.

I write further about this episode in chapter 2 of my own memoir, forthcoming. Additionally a member of Kaye and Kern's tour party, Dr. A. E. Rodden, published his travel diary as "A Skowhegan Dentist Makes the 'Grand Tour'," The Somerset Reporter, *1956, transcribed at the website associated with this book (see Foreword).*

April 3, 1956 – Tuesday
Raleigh, NC – New York
Sunny and warm

Said goodbye to Pearl and children. Took Mike to school. Left town 8:45. Ate lunch at Howard Johnson, Petersburg. Visited cherry blossom bloom in Washington. Took picture. Supper at Aberdeen, Maryland. "Mayflower." Delicious crab cakes. Had a little battery trouble with car. Took wrong turn on parkway. Had to retrace steps. Arrived at Dan and Tempy's in Larchmont 11:15 p.m.

April 4, 1956 – Wednesday
New York, New York
Foggy!

Breakfast with Dan and Tempy. Train to NYC. On *Queen Elizabeth* at 9:30.

Champagne in cabin. Looked over ship. Dan and Tempy left.

Boat scheduled to leave at 1:30 p.m. Delayed by bad fog. Did not sail. Afternoon on deck in deck chair.

Meals are fine on board. Ship sailing posted at 1 a.m. Got leave and went in to Times Square. Looked around for two hours. Returned to ship.

In night (about 3 a.m.) ship departed. We did not go top. 200 miles at noon today.

April 5, 1956 – Thursday
At sea. 200 miles at noon
Sunny and fine. Breezy

Forgot to set clock forward. Missed breakfast. Steward gave us rolls and coffee. Dined with couple from Akron, Ohio, Lee and Dorothy Davis.

Went to sun deck. Bouillon on deck!!

Fine lunch. They feed us on every occasion on shipboard.

Went a meeting (in Cabin Class) of the other members of our tour. There will be 19 on our tour. 16 are on board. 3 will join us in Paris. Our guide is a young Austrian, Rudolph Kadenka. He will be with us until Switzerland.

Cocktails in bar. Party dinner with paper hats. Danced awhile in Wintergarden.

April 6, 1956 – Friday
At sea. 681 miles since noon 5th
Sunny and fine. A little rough

Neither of us are at all seasick. To the deckchairs after breakfast! Entered the ship's totalisator pool. Guessed we had been 669 mi. Did not win.

Game of shuffleboard before lunch. Kern entered table tennis tournament. Eliminated first round. Saltwater bath before dinner. Shish kebabs for dinner.

Saw movie "Backlash." Cocktails in bar. Dancing in Wintergarden. Bed about 1:30.

April 7, 1956 – Saturday
At sea. 675 miles since noon 6th
Sun and fine. Quite rough

Deck chairs after breakfast. Shuffleboard before lunch. Ocean got rough about noon. Went to a movie. "Miracle in Rain."

Kern got seasick after lunch. Kaye not so much.

Played bridge after supper. Bed about 11 o'clock.

April 8, 1956 – Sunday
At sea. 667 miles since noon 7th
Cloudy and windy. Sea calmer

No longer seasick.

Scheduled to land at Cherbourg 10:30 p.m. tomorrow. Disembark at 4 a.m. Tuesday.

Too windy for deck chairs in a.m. Went to church service. Very formal. Strolled around ship before lunch. Food is still fine.

Deck chairs after lunch.

Bottle of champagne with dinner. Went to birthday / cocktail party for Dorothy Lowe of our tour party in Cabin Class bar. Packed to have large bag ready by 9 a.m. tomorrow.

April 9, 1956 – Monday
At dock in Cherbourg
Sunny and windy

Meeting of our party in Cabin Class lounge for final instructions.

    Deck chairs until lunch.

    Shuffleboard after lunch.

    Went to cinema. Danny Kaye in "On the Riviera."

    Went to deck. Saw land. Island of Alderney and other Channel Islands. Ship docked at about 8 o'clock. Customs could not come aboard until next morning.

    Went to deck to look at Cherbourg. Went to bed early.

April 10, 1956 – Tuesday
Paris
Sunny and warm

Up at 2:30. Early breakfast. Passed customs. Boarded boat train for Paris.

    Beautiful cross-country ride to Paris. Arrived Gare St.-Lazare 11:45. Staying at Hotel Ambassador. Kaye and I lunched at a cafeteria, and strolled around. Went to Place de la Concorde and around.

    Nap until 5 o'clock. Dinner with group at Auberge Riquewihr. Alsatienne. Folies-Bergère. Benedictine at Cafe de la Paix.

    [Kaye adds:] Paris beds have large bolsters and thick comforters.

April 11, 1956 – Wednesday
Paris
Hazy but clear and warm

Café complet at hotel and with the group by bus to tour Paris. Modern Paris included Opera, Place de la Concorde, Church of the Madeleine, Arc de Triomphe, Bois de Boulogne, Palais de Chaillot, Tour Eiffel, Napoleon's Tomb. Lunched at a small cafe and bought perfume. Afternoon tour included Sacré-Coeur and Montmartre, Place de la Bastille, Notre-Dame, Pantheon, Sorbonne, Luxembourg Gardens, Latin Quarter, book stalls on the Seine and Louvre (exterior). Dinner at Le Helder was filet. Cafe and liquor on Blvd des Capucines and long walk up Champs-Elysées with Mrs. Wheeler and Miss Tozier. Lovely day!

April 12, 1956 – Thursday
Paris
Cloudy and rain

Kern and I started our morning at Les Halles, crossed to the Ile de la Cité and visited Sainte Chapelle to see the stained-glass windows, along the Left Bank with the book stalls, and very briefly to the Louvre to see a few high spots. Joined the group for boat ride on lovely excursion boat on the Seine. Long trip with lunch. Very nice in spite of rain. Stopped at Galeries Lafayette and shops. Ate a very lovely dinner at Les Noces de Jeannette. Very French and refined. Kern and I left the group and visited Montmartre. Had cognac and cafe and watched the crowd.

April 13, 1956 – Friday
Paris – Cannes
Rainy but clearing late

Tried to go up the Eiffel Tour but not open early enough. Visited the Louvre again. Left for Riviera from Gare de Lyon at 1:00. Snack lunch on train and tea with Helen Wheeler and Anne Tozier. Fine dinner on train with filet of sole and roast veal. Arrived at Cannes about 11:30 and, after checking in, walked along the waterfront park. All very beautifully lighted and lovely. On our train trip we saw wonderful orchards in bloom and hillsides filled with vineyards. Countryside very much like Van Gogh, etc. Beautiful country.

April 14, 1956 – Saturday
Cannes – Monaco – train to Rome
Rainy!

Lazed in room late when we saw rainy day. Breakfast in room. Kaye went shopping. Kern went walking. Both strolled around Cannes. Bought hats. Lovely seaside city. Town park very attractive.

Wonderful lunch at Hotel Majestic.

Left Cannes. Drove in bus to Juan-les-Pins, Antibes. Saw St. Paul—lovely medieval town. Narrow streets, church, White Pigeon Inn [La Colombe d'Or]. Saw Nice. Moyenne Corniche. Tea at Chateau Madrid. Èze.

Monaco. Decorated for wedding. Played roulette at Monte Carlo. Lost. Got on train for Rome. Dinner and bed on train.

April 15, 1956 – Sunday
Rome
Cloudy and wet

Slept poorly on train. Got up, had cafe expresso on train. Brrrrr! Train late arriving at Rome–9:30. Went to Hotel Flora. Very nice. Breakfast. Bus to St. Peter's. Noon in square. Pope appeared. Gave blessing. Went to St. Peter's church. Saw interior. Tour after lunch. Borghese Park, fountains, Quirinal Palace, Pantheon, Capitoline Hill, Forum, St. Paul's Outside Wall. Coliseum. Very nice tour, but cloudy and rainy.

Dinner at hotel. Walk with Rudi and group to Spanish Stairs and Trevi Fountain. Picture taken.

Hotel and bed.

April 16, 1956 – Monday
Rome
Sunny, cloudy, rainy

To Vatican museum after breakfast. Art treasures. Laocoon, Apollo, Discobolus, and many others.

Sistine Chapel. Most impressed by ceiling of Gallery of Maps, painted by Zuccari brothers. Return to St. Peter's. Pope and interior.

Visited Tivoli and Villa d'Este after lunch. Magnificent pleasure palace of Este family. 800 gorgeous fountains. A high spot of the trip.

Big dinner with group at Biblioteca Restaurant downstairs—with bottles on wall of fine drinks. Everyone had fine time.

Went to walk in Borghese gardens and shopping streets.

April 17, 1956 – Tuesday
Rome
Sunny, mild

Today was our "free day" in Rome. Helen, Doc, Ade Dietz and the two of us started out early by taxi for the Catacombs. We went shopping when we returned and had lunch at a small Italian place. We then walked to the Borghese Galleries in the park and saw the artworks there. Back for a short rest at the hotel and on to some shopping. After a lovely dinner in the hotel dining room, we went with Helen and Ann to see the Coliseum and Forum by moonlight. Back by 11:30 to pack.

April 18, 1956 – Wednesday
Rome – Naples, etc.
Sunny and clear

Rose early and took train to Naples. Arrived about 11:15 and Rudi met us with a small sight-seeing bus. We went to Pompeii and saw the ruins there. Lunch at Pompeii. Crossed over near Salerno and took the Amalfi drive. 1400 curves in mountain road overlooking the sea. Stopped at Ravello and visited Villa Cimbrone for gardens and sheer drop view. Long bus ride back to Naples along the coast. Absolutely marvelous trip with spectacular scenery. Late dinner and bed.

April 19, 1956 – Thursday
Naples and Capri
Sunny and warm

Left Naples at 9:07 for Capri. Boat takes 1½ hours to go. The sea was gorgeous—pure blue. As soon as we docked we went to the Blue Grotto. After this wonderful experience, we took cars to drive up the island to see Marina Piccola and Anacapri where we had lunch. Then to Capri (town) for shopping. Down the funicular to Marina Grande and back at 5:00 to Naples. Dinner at hotel and walk with part of the group. We walked more later around bay edge.

April 20, 1956 – Friday
Florence
Sunny and mild. Cooler at night

Rose a little later. Breakfast in room. Long train ride back to Rome and then to Florence.

Saw snow on mountains coming up. Scenery very green and lovely. Arrived Florence about 5:15. Took bus to Hotel Lucchesi. Small, homey, but very nice.

Walked along river bank. Arno river is light green. Walked across Ponte Vecchio. Wonderful old bridge with shops along walkway. Saw glimpses of campanile, baptistry, churches and palaces. Thrilling old city. Planned to go to concert in the square, but it was cool. Had coffee in lounge and went to bed.

April 21, 1956 – Saturday
Florence
Sunny and mild

Overslept. Rushed to join group at 9. Visited Medici chapel (Michelangelo). Visited baptistry and chapel of Santa Maria del Fiore (bronze doors by Ghiberti). Visited campanile and dome of church. Went to Uffizi Galleries (important paintings by Cimabue, Giotto, Leonardo, Fra Angelico, Filippo Lippi, Titian, del Sarto and others).

Visited church of Santa Croce. Tombs of Michelangelo, Galileo, Rossini and others. Mosaic factory and leather works. Went shopping in afternoon. Bought leather ties and a little jewelry. Pitti Palace silver collection. Found Dante's house.

After supper went with Dr. Rodden to concert in square.

April 22, 1956 – Sunday
Florence – Venice
Rainy

We had a leisurely start today since our train left at noon. We shopped for cheese and olives for Mrs. Wood before we left and added sandwiches and fruit on the train. The trip from Florence to Bologna is through many tunnels, one 4 miles long. We got to Venice about 5:00 and took gondolas to the hotel. After dinner we walked with Helen W. to St. Mark's square and visited the streets around there. Back at the hotel we wrote letters home.

April 23, 1956 – Monday
Venice
Cloudy with a little sunshine

Rose early and went on sightseeing tour. Saw St. Mark's square, church of St. Mark's. Elaborate clock. Doge's Palace (dominated by Tintoretto's paintings). Bridge of Sighs. Dungeons. Went to Salviati glass works.

The bells of Venice are wonderful. There are over 300 churches and some bells are ringing almost constantly. Our hotel is on Grand Canal (Hotel Europa). After nice lunch in a restaurant off the square, went to Lido and beach. Came back on vaporetto. Went up Grand Canal to Rialto Bridge. Walked back, shopping as we went. Drinks in square.

Birthday supper for one of group (Mrs. Hanney). Strolled after dinner. Saw Venice by moonlight.

April 24, 1956 – Tuesday
Venice to Innsbruck
Partly cloudy

We left Venice early—7:30 at the hotel—went by motorboat to the bus depot and boarded a Leoncino [coach]. We came through several small towns in Northern Italy, the "green-lake" country, and into the Dolomites to Cortina. We had lunch there and saw the Olympic ski jump and arena. We drove through much snow, some only three days old. We drove through the Brenner Pass and saw many fortifications from Franz Joseph as well as later wars. We entered Austria about 6:00 and came into Innsbruck. After dinner we walked around.

April 25, 1956 – Wednesday
Innsbruck – Garmisch – Oberammergau
Partly cloudy

After an hour for shopping, we left for a sight-seeing trip. We went over the Tyrolean Alps and to a little town called Mittenwald where we saw a delightful old man who made and played violins. Lunch at Garmisch-Partenkirchen. We shopped in Garmisch.

Visit to Oberammergau and Passion Play theater. Drove back past Tyrol, Zugspitz (highest mountain in Germany, 9,700), beautiful lake.

After supper we visited Keller of Maria Theresa Hotel. Sat and drank with Austrian people. Visited another night club. Danced.

Ate frankfurters on way home.

April 26, 1956 – Thursday
Innsbruck – Zell am See – Mittersill – Kitzbühel
Sunny and warm

All-day drive, through Austria and Tyrol. Left on bus. Drove east down Inn Valley. Rattenberg. Oldest town in Austria. Beautiful mountains — principally Wilder Kaiser. Lunch at Zell am See. Beautiful lake country in midst of snow-covered mountains. Grosglockner is Austria's highest mountain (14,000). Visited Mittersill Castle. Restored 9th-century castle.

Tea stop at Kitzbühel, ski and sport center. Lovely. Kitzbühlerhorn Mt. Gave farewell champagne party in bar of hotel for Rudi. Went to Stube of Hotel Goldener Adler for sitting and drinking. Frankfurters on way home.

APRIL 27, 1956 – FRIDAY
INNSBRUCK – LUCERNE
SUNNY AND QUITE WARM

Rose early and shopped in Innsbruck. Left Innsbruck on train. Rode to border and crossed into Switzerland. Met our new courier, a pretty Swiss woman named Eva Picard.

Drove by bus immediately to Liechtenstein and its capital at Vaduz. Independent country. 800 sq. mi. Had brief talk by a baroness of Liechtenstein, Baroness von Falz-Fein.[16] Drove back into Switzerland, through glorious mountain country. Stopped at lower end of Lake Zurich for a tea stop. Lovely spot on balcony. Drove on to Lucerne. Our hotel is the Lucerne Palace. Fine big one on lake. Strolled along the lake and over Chapel Bridge after dinner.

APRIL 28, 1956 – SATURDAY
LUCERNE – BERNE – INTERLAKEN – LUCERNE
COLD, RAINY AND RAW

Rose early and met group. Said goodbye to Rudi before we left for Bern. Went by bus to Bern. Visited a Swiss cheese factory on way. Stopped in Bern. Visited bear pits. Watched Zeitglockenturm strike 12. Lunch at Kornhauskeller. Lovely. Drove to Lake Thun. Weather very bad. Impossible to see high mountains of Bernese Oberland. Stopped for Swiss cheese and coffee snack. Visited Interlaken. Did not stop. Lake Brienz, Meiringen. Returned to Lucerne.

Met a new courier, William Dekker, a tall Netherlander who will go with us to Amsterdam. Went to bed after a late dinner.

---

16. Virginia von Falz-Fein was in fact English, daughter of the noted politician Sir Henry Curtis-Bennett. It was her idea to convince tour operators of the era to route tourist buses through Liechtenstein, where she built a successful souvenir shop at the main square. See Beverly Baxter, "Where Dreamers Pay No Income Tax," *Maclean's,* 29 October 1955.

April 29, 1956 – Sunday
Lucerne
Alternate sunny and cloudy. Cool

Rose at 9:00 a.m. Went to walk with Mrs. Ruegg, sister of our travel agent. Visited a cloister, climbed Kleine Rigi and Dietschiberg [referring to the railway Kleine Rigi Dietschibergbahn]. Lovely mountain walk. Had dinner of cheese fondue and apple strudel at a quaint place called Stadtkeller.

Visited famous Lion Monument. Very impressive. Took picture. Took street car to Kriens and from there took a cable car to Mt. Pilatus, 7,000 ft. high, landmark of Lucerne. View was superb. Mountain was snow covered, cloudy and cold at top, beautifully sunny at bottom. Had tea and sent cards from mountain top. Met Fowlers, people from Raleigh.

Early to bed.

April 30, 1956 – Monday
Lucerne
Very rainy

Day completely spoiled by hard rain all day. Rose late. Went shopping. Bought watches for children, music box for Pearl. Had lunch at Old Swiss House. Visited panorama painting, like cyclorama in Atlanta. Depicted French crossing into Switzerland at the end of Franco-Prussian war. Went back to hotel. Spent remainder of day there. Went to Lucerne casino after dinner. Saw Swiss evening of yodeling, dancing, flag twirling and Alpine horn blowing. Won ten francs at the roulette game.

May 1, 1956 – Tuesday
Lucerne – Rothenburg ob der Tauber
Partly cloudy

We left Lucerne by bus in sleet to go to Zurich. Then by train to Stuttgart with lunch on the train—picnic style. After driving around Stuttgart, we came through rural Germany to Schloss Langenburg, a castle, for tea, and on into Rothenburg. The Hotel Eisenhut is very picturesque and lovely. After dinner we went to Cafe Baumeister and had hot wine.

May 2, 1956 – Wednesday
Rothenburg ob der Tauber
Rainy

We had a leisurely breakfast and joined the group at 10:00 for sightseeing in the rain. The town is remarkably lovely in its very old way and very picturesque. We lunched at Reichküchenmeister's. We bought spirits, etc. and walked about the town more. After dinner, we visited another cafe.

May 3, 1956 – Thursday
Rothenburg – Heidelberg – Wiesbaden
Cloudy, clearing in afternoon

Rose early and left Rothenburg for Heidelberg. Drove through countryside of Franconia, Wurtemburg, and Baden. Old, old villages with regal houses and cobblestone streets. Arrived in Heidelberg about noon. Lunch at Red Ox Inn, old student hangout. Visited Heidelberg Castle, stately red brick structure partly ruined, on hill. Largest wine cask in the world, 55,000 gallons. Other sites in Heidelberg, Holy Ghost church, etc. Drove up Bergstrasse, visited Weinheim briefly. Autobahn and road to Wiesbaden. Stayed at Nassauer Hof in Wiesbaden. Stylish hotel. Shopped for awhile. Bought toys for children. Strolled after dinner in casino garden. Beautiful lighted fountains.

May 4, 1956 – Friday
Amsterdam
Beautifully sunny and warm

Wonderful steamer trip down Rhine River on boat *Rhinelander*. Beautiful terraced vineyards and castles on high banks on both sides. Mausturm [Mouse Tower, Mäuseturm], Watch on Rhine, Pfalz, Katz [Katz Castle / Burg Katz], Lorelei and many others. A real high spot. Fine dinner on board. Left boat at Remagen.

    Bus to Bonn. Saw German government buildings and Beethoven's House. Bus to Cologne. Drove around to look at destruction. Visited cathedral. Damaged, but being repaired well.

    Train to Amsterdam. Arrived late. Walked briefly and saw lights and shops near hotel.

May 5, 1956 – Saturday
Amsterdam
Beautifully sunny and warm

This was Liberation Day in Amsterdam, a holiday for the people, and gaily decorated with flowers (tulip time) and flags and bunting everywhere. Lots of celebration, color, excitement and movement. Rose late and took little sightseeing boat around canals and harbors of Amsterdam. Very old and picturesque.

Went shopping. Bought wooden shoes for children. After lunch went sightseeing on bus. Rijksmuseum. Hals, Ruysdael, Rembrandt, Vermeer, de Hooch. Very fine collection. Around city — Mint Tower, palace, oldest house. Lots of interesting old architecture. Strolled around city. Aperitif before dinner. Dekker went walking with us after dinner. Lots of interesting sights after dark, including ladies' home from 16th century. Farewell cocktails with Helen Wheeler.

May 6, 1956 – Sunday
Amsterdam – Hook of Holland – London
Sunny and warm

Rose early and left Amsterdam by bus. Drove through Haarlem and Leiden and through tulip country. Unbelievably colorful and gorgeous. Shopped at Roozen nurseries to see flowers (tulips, jonquils, hyacinths etc.) in full bloom. Tulip parade had been the day before. Saw many flower floats that had been in parade. Drove past Keukenhof park (formal garden maintained by tulip growers). Lots of people visiting it in full bloom. Took [ship from] Hook of Holland. Left continent at noon on steamer *Mecklenburg.* Arrived Harwich 6:30. Took train to London. Staying at Hotel Kensington Palace. Took bus to Piccadilly circus and strolled.

May 7, 1956 – Monday
London
Cloudy and mild

Went with group to see changing of guard at Buckingham Palace. Other sightseeing around London, especially Westminster Abbey. (Parliament, St. James, parks, Big Ben.) More sightseeing after lunch, especially St. Paul's, Tower of London and Old Curiosity Shop. After changing, to

Aldwych Theater by bus to see *Threepenny Opera.* Supper after show at Lyons in the Strand. Subway back to near hotel and walk home. (Our courier for London is named Barbara Clarke.)

MAY 8, 1956 – TUESDAY
LONDON – OXFORD – STRATFORD
SUNNY AND MILD

Rose early for coach trip with group to Shakespeare country. Through West London, Middlesex, Buckinghamshire, past Blenheim Castle to Oxford. Went through Magdalen College at Oxford and drove around rest of town. Drove on through Oxfordshire and Warwickshire to Stratford on Avon. Lunch at White Swan Inn. Visited Shakespeare's birthplace and Anne Hathaway's house. Drove on to Warwick Castle. Magnificent collection of paintings and relics. Back to London via Banbury, Northampton, Aylesford. Drinks with some of party in bar. Strolled around Trafalgar after late dinner.

MAY 9, 1956 – WEDNESDAY
LONDON
SUNNY; RAIN IN P.M.

After breakfast went to walk in Hyde Park and Kensington Gardens. Saw flowers, Albert Memorial, Peter Pan Statue, Serpentine Lake, etc. Went to old haunts around Marble Arch, Green St., Grosvenor Square. Went shopping in stores on Oxford Street and Bond Street. After lunch with group to Madame Tussaud's Wax Museum. Looked for Wimpole Street. Could not find it. Went shopping and back to hotel. After dinner went to see *Summer Song,* musical play based on music of Anton Dvorak. Drink in lounge with some of the group.

MAY 10, 1956 – THURSDAY
LONDON – EN ROUTE TO USA
SUNNY AND MILD

Rose early to bid goodbye to group, who left for Southampton and ship. After breakfast went shopping in dept. stores. Visited Fleet Street, Old Cheshire Cheese, and Samuel Johnson's house. Went to lunch at the Falstaff in Fleet Street. More shopping and then returned to hotel. After tea we strolled around Kensington, finally to the Gardens and watched play around the Round Pond. Took taxi to air terminal. Met Barbara Clarke and her mother. Had cocktails. Took bus to London airport. Boarded plane and took off. Flight 71 at 9:30.

MAY 11, 1956 – FRIDAY
EN ROUTE NEW YORK – PALMYRA
SUNNY AND WARM

Plane flew by way of Keflavik, Iceland to avoid high winds. Landed there briefly. No total darkness all night. Flew on via Labrador, mouth of St. Lawrence, Mt. Washington. Arrived Idlewild New York 7:30 a.m. Cleared customs. Called home and talked to Dallas. Went into New York. Lunch with Dan at Peter Cooper Hotel. Drove car back to airport. Met Mike and Dickie with Laura, arriving from Raleigh. Began driving back home across Triborough Bridge and George Washington Bridge. Down turnpike to Palmyra. Spent night in motor court.

MAY 12, 1956 – SATURDAY
EN ROUTE RALEIGH
SUNNY AND QUITE WARM

Rose and began drive back to Raleigh. Uneventful trip. Stops for breakfast, lunch, supper, etc. Arrived Raleigh about 11:00. Dallas Junior and Dad [Dallas, Sr.] and family waited for us. Brief welcome conversations. Return home. Kaye called Lula Belle and talked to her. Total trip covered just over 11,000 miles.

Highlights of the Trip

April 14 — St. Paul's; the Moyenne Corniche

April 16 — Villa d'Este, 800 fountains

April 17 — Coliseum and Roman forum by moonlight

April 18 — Amalfi Drive and Ravello

April 19 — Capri and Blue Grotto. View from Anacapri

April 24 — Dolomite mountains around Cortina d'Ampezzo

April 25–26 — All of Austria was such a high spot it is hard to separate any one thing — violin shop of Mittenwald, lakes in German Alps, Zell am See, singing in the Theresienkeller and the Goldener Adler

April 29 — Cable car up Mount Pilatus at Lucerne

May 2 — Walled city of Rothenburg. Hotel Eisenhut, Meistertrink clock, Baumeisters' houses

May 4 — Steamer trip down Rhine river. Wonderful castles

May 5 — Amsterdam on Liberation Day. The color, movement, excitement, bustle. Bicycles, flags, flowers

May 6 — Flower fields of Holland. Tulips, hyacinths, canals

May 7 — Changing of the guard at Buckingham Palace

May 8 — Oxford – Magdalen College. Stratford – White Swan. Shakespeare, thatched rooves. Warwick Castle – magnificent paintings and armor

May 10 — Flight to America. Farewells, Ireland, the plane

May 11 — Reunion with children

INDIA

February 4 – March 22, 1982

Kern Holoman

The delegation leaves Raleigh–Durham Airport, February 4, 1982.

L. to R.: Kern Holoman, Miller Sigmon, Eric Vernon, Jim Standaert, Steve Levin, Rob Fisher

SOURCE: Diary 4 (1982). Green leather album with gold tooling, titled TRAVELS, roughly 4 x 6¾ inches. (Almost identical to red album from 1956.) Spine crumbling. Hand of WKH. Inscribed on flyleaf:

> Kern Holoman
> 2912 Hostetler St.
> Raleigh, N.C. 27609
> USA

> Rotary International
> Group Study Exchange
> to India - Bangladesh - Nepal
> Feb–Mar, 1982

Continues with "Trip to France, Aug–Sept, 1982, Kaye and Kern." Both sections in Kern's hand.

INDIA

February 4 – March 22, 1982
Kern Holoman

In February and March 1982, Kern Holoman led five younger Rotarians to India, Bangladesh, and Nepal on a Group Study Exchange. It was by a considerable measure his most ambitious travel outside wartime. Six weeks was a long time for him to be gone so far away to places we could scarcely imagine, often with limited options for communication. The daily agendas were packed with visits to and from important delegations: heads of government, leaders of industry, Mother Teresa—and often long, arduous drives to reach their destinations. Kern spoke nearly every day, and the delegation often sang the American versions of the Rotary songs. The living arrangements varied from lavish to what he calls, politely, "sub-standard." He enjoyed the socializing at places like the Calcutta Club and the Punjab Club, was awed by the scenery, tolerated the music, and detested most of the food. He was relieved and very glad to get back to North Carolina, but I think was always proud of having done it. "Indian food"—which Betty and I learned to love from our London friends—became something of a family joke, the obvious reply to his wondering aloud what we'd be having for dinner.

FEBRUARY 4, 1982 – THURSDAY
RALEIGH
FAIR AND WARM

Spent a.m. packing. Day was *very* warm. Kaye took to RDU. All were there with families. Durant Bell, John Rice, and Earl Barnes met us. Kaye took pictures.

At JFK, a wait of about 4 hours. Not unpleasant. We sat in the English pub at British Airways and drank: martinis for me, beer for most of the others. Concorde aircraft on runway but we didn't get a very good look at it.

Plane was a 747. Every seat filled. Large number of Orthodox Jews on board, going I don't know where. Sumptuous meal of pork tenderloin served at 10:30 (3:30 London time). People admire our uniforms.

FEBRUARY 5, 1982 – FRIDAY
LONDON
CLOUDY AND FAIRLY WARM

Arrived at 7:30 a.m. after a 6-hour flight. Had breakfast on plane (3 hours after lunch). Cleared customs OK. Subway into London. Hotel Tavistock is OK. Beer and sandwiches. Stood in line in Leicester Square to buy ½-price ticket to play ([*The Beastly Beatitudes of*] *Balthazar B*). Then we split up and went our ways. I walked to National Galleries—magnificent Old Masters. Then to Trafalgar Square, Piccadilly Circus, Westminster Abbey. Taxi home. London prices are about like NY.

Play: *Beastly Beatitudes of Balthazar B. very* bawdy and vulgar. Not without merit though. Late supper at Swiss Center. Very good German food.

FEBRUARY 6, 1982 – SATURDAY
LONDON EN ROUTE TO CALCUTTA
CLOUDY, COOL

Slept until 8:45. (Steve went off with a friend yesterday. We didn't catch up with him until airport. We were worried.) Continental breakfast in hotel. Then a two-hour sightseeing tour around London. Usual places—very quick. Saw changing of horse guards. Also a *big* Hussar demonstration with artillery salutes in Hyde Park, honoring George VI's death 30 years ago today. Impressive. Lunch at a pub—The Friendly Hand. British food hasn't gotten any better. Subway back to Heathrow. On plane sat beside an interesting man from Calcutta. A man from Bangladesh was behind us. Afternoon tea served on the plane. We stopped at Rome to refuel and take on passengers.

FEBRUARY 7, 1982 – SUNDAY
CALCUTTA
WARM AND SUNNY

Arrived on time at 10:00 a.m. Rather lengthy customs. (Steve lost a bag.) *Big* delegation of Rotarians met us. Pictures, flowers, the works. Staying with Lal Davar, an elderly attorney. Fine home, though without some of the niceties. We talked for several hours. Sumptuous lunch and dinner—western style... not Indian. I slept for 3 hours this afternoon. Others are farmed out to other Rotarians. At 7:30 p.m. Shyam Kayal brought over our five team members plus Dr. and Mrs. Ajit Prasad for drinks and conversation. Very amicable. Good conversation. Mr. Davar has a pretty garden... five servants, seems well to do. His wife Sheila is not here but [in] Delhi. She is a big social worker.

FEBRUARY 8, 1982 – MONDAY
CALCUTTA
WARM AND SUNNY

Nice night sleep under a mosquito net. Woke to a rooster and bird calls—mostly crows, pigeons, and myna birds. Morning tea at 7:30 with Lal. Breakfast at 9:30. Utpal came to see me. Dinner at the Rotary Club in downtown Calcutta. First speaker OK, not great. Visited American Consulate of Calcutta (George Sherman), a career diplomat. Not impressive. Afternoon tea at the Calcutta Club—old, stuffy, very conservative and grand. Rotarians Kamal and Gosch and their wives. Dinner at home with Lal and guest. Very large usual Indian meal, lots of rice, chicken, and curry.

FEBRUARY 9, 1982 – TUESDAY
CALCUTTA
SUNNY, WARMER

After breakfast to Calcutta Club, there to meet the governor of West Bengal. Charming fellow. Impressive old British Empire-style buildings.

Turbaned guards. Then to Jain temple—fantastically ornate mosaics, mirrors, and statuary. Addressed Rotary Club at Oberoi Grand Hotel. Big wreathed garland. Afternoon met with Chamber of Commerce. Dreary unproductive coach trip to Birla Museum. (Calcutta has miles of unbelievable squalor.) Went to an Indian wedding. Gorgeous, very elaborate. Flowers. Music. Refreshments. Gorgeous saris, exotic women. Happy hour at Punjab Club. I drank too much. So did some others. Dinner and much conversation with Lal.

FEBRUARY 10, 1982 – WEDNESDAY
CALCUTTA
SUNNY, WARM (AS ALWAYS)

Left early. Miller, Jim, and I called on Mother Teresa. Very moving experience. Mother herself, food distribution, infant care. Heartwarming—heartbreaking. I gave her $20. Special show for us at Birla Plantation. Routine. Afterward a lovely drink and buffet lunch at Saturday Club. In late afternoon saw performance and lecture on classical Indian music. I found it long, repetitious, unharmonic, but not completely unpleasant. Later a cocktail party given by Parasuram and wife. OK. The shops of Calcutta doing business after dark by candle and lantern are eerie. Dinner with Lal and Sheila, who has come home.

FEBRUARY 11, 1982 – THURSDAY
CALCUTTA
SUNNY, WARM

A long day. Visit to Ramakrishna Institute. Met with Swami Lokeswarananda. His pitch is that all religions have equal validity if they seek to reach ultimate truth. Lunch at mission, then a trip to south to Cancer Center. Big facility—new 1976—for diagnosis and treatment of cancer. Visit to Management Institute. Visit to Children's Home (orphanage). Visit to India Handloom Fair. Dinner at Aston Hotel with Rotary Club of Beluth. Beautiful outdoor affair. I spoke briefly. DG Prasad was there and spoke. Later we went to Chatterjee's home for late drinks. Indian saris are *very* flattering!

INDIA

FEBRUARY 12, 1982 – FRIDAY
CALCUTTA
CLOUDY, WARM. IT RAINED HARD IN THE LATE AFTERNOON.

Midnight, and I'm very tired. We had a leisurely morning and arrived at Victorian Memorial at 11 a.m. Quick tour. Symbol of Empire. Afterward to Calcutta Club for lunch and a press conference. Relaxed, "sweetheart" questions. Then to a girls school where the college girls sang for us and danced in native dress—saris. After a rest we had an interesting session with a big movie maker, Satyajit Ray. Impressed. Drinks for all at Davars', then to New Alipore for a big dinner with [illegible] Rotary. Early rising tomorrow for departure.

FEBRUARY 13, 1982 – SATURDAY
DURGAPUR, WEST BENGAL
SUNNY, WARMEST YET

Rose very early and packed. Tea, breakfast and goodbyes to the Davars. Crossed Howrah Bridge. Took train to Durgapur, about a two-hour ride past villages and rice paddies. Staying with O. P. Malhotra, an exec of Phillips Carbon Black Co. He lives in a company-owned enclosure with all kinds of nice facilities and pretty flowers. Miller is staying with me. In the late afternoon we took a hair-raising ride to the river (dam) and past Durgapur's many factories. (It is a 20-year-old city with *much* heavy industry.)

Later we went to a Rotary Club meeting. We spoke there, then supper and home to bed.

FEBRUARY 14, 1982 – SUNDAY (VALENTINE'S DAY)
DURGAPUR, WEST BENGAL
SUNNY, WARM. [STEVE HAS A VIRUS AND STAYED HOME.]

Rose at 7:00 a.m. and had breakfast with host and hostess. (Her name is Bromitla.) After a long visit, we departed for Santiniketan, the university founded by Rabindranath Tagore. He is very honored, and his campus is a shrine and memorial to him. It is about 40 miles from here. When we returned we went to a Rotaract meeting at an engineering college here in Durgapur. It was nice and relaxed. We sang for them and they liked that. We went by to see Steve, who says he is feeling better. Then supper with our hosts, conversation, and now bed. It really is beautiful here and even has its own Hindu temple.

FEBRUARY 15, 1982 – MONDAY
ASANSOL, WEST BENGAL
SUNNY, WARM

This place is not good. Our host tries, but it is substandard. (Host is Lt. Col. A. K. Mitra.) Left Durgapur after a delay catching up. Via Raniganj, where we caught up with the others. Divided into groups of 2. Jim and I went together, but in separate homes. Visited Assembly of God school, then lunch at Asansol Club. (Primitive.) Rested at home until 7:30. Met with and addressed Rotary Club. After we went to a "turbaning" for the son of a wealthy Sikh. Big party with drinks, refreshments, supper, dancing. Jim was given a turban. Home late. This room is really "the pits." Better luck next time.

FEBRUARY 16, 1982 – TUESDAY
ASANSOL, WEST BENGAL
CLOUDY, NOT SO WARM

Sort of a washout of a day. Did not seem well planned for us. They said it was to let us rest, but I think they just didn't want to bother. After an Indian breakfast (yek) we went to a pretty little park nearby. Then we went to a school and care unit for handicapped children (Cheshire Home), then a long hiatus until lunch at the club (yek, yek). After lunch we went to St. Patrick's High School for an impromptu 15-minute talk by both Jim and me. That was 3 o'clock and all for the day. Luncheon and Indian supper with our hosts (yek, yek, yek). Nice little girl here named Sanchita.

FEBRUARY 17, 1982 – WEDNESDAY
KHARAGPUR, WEST BENGAL
CLOUDY, WARM. THUNDERSTORM IN P.M.

A very long tiring day. Rose at 4:00 a.m. took train (3 hours) to Howrah. Very crowded platform. Changed trains immediately for Kharagpur in south. Local, crowded. Met by Rotarians and whisked away to Madanpur. Insisted on wash and cold drink. Then had *enormous* Indian dinner, none of wish I liked. Bought stamps. Communist demonstration at PO. Sightseeing — girls college plus vista overlook onto plains of Bengal.

Addressed Rotary Club. Then supper with a local. Back to Kharagpur for two nights in an IIT [Indian Institute of Technology] dormitory. Very nice indeed. Late drink with team. Morale is high.

FEBRUARY 18, 1982 – THURSDAY
KHARAGPUR, WEST BENGAL
CLOUDY, WARM, HUMID

In many ways our best day yet. Our hosts are wonderfully considerate. Accommodations are top notch. After American-style breakfast visited IIT and Architecture School. (Host and guide is Rangit Banerji, club president). Then visited mayor of city. After fine vegetarian dinner at home of PDG Vijay Bharandi, visited railyard headquarters. Then inspected a ball-bearing factory (Metal Box Corp.). Then visited an authentic Indian village. Fascinating! Tea with a Rotarian. Then put on an excellent program with local Rotary Club. Beer with Banerji. Now back to our dorm.

FEBRUARY 19, 1982 – FRIDAY
SERAMPORE, WEST BENGAL
SUNNY, WARM

We are here where Ambassador cars are made by Hindustan Motors. *Big* facility. Living in a compound with G. C. Borsali, Quality Control Manager. Very comfortable. Took train from Kharagpur to Calcutta this a.m. (I had an AC first-class seat.) Shyam met us with a letter from Kaye! Oh, joy! After lunch visited girls school, put on a short program. Signed autographs. Tea and dinner with host families. Very nice. She is Satpriya. 17-year-old son is Vinit. Everyone feeds us too much. After dinner walked to Hindu temple built by the company.

FEBRUARY 20, 1982 – SATURDAY
SERAMPORE, WEST BENGAL
SUNNY, WARM

Our host Gerry, wife Satpriya and son Vinit are so kind to us. Their yard is a burst of colorful summer flowers. This morning the Rotarians took us to Hoogli [Hooghly], where we saw some mosques and churches. Then to a Don Bosco School, founded by the Portuguese in 1590. Then lunch and fellowship at a *gorgeous* villa beside the Hoogli (Ganges) River. Tea and sympathy with our hosts. Then a successful meeting with the Rotary Club of

Serampore. We sing and are informal. Folks seem to like it. We are *showered* with gifts. Gerry has a very nice home but salamanders on his wall.

FEBRUARY 21, 1982 – SUNDAY
SERAMPORE, WEST BENGAL
SUNNY, WARM

A rather leisurely day, but even so I go to bed tired. Today is our last day in India for awhile. This morning we toured the production facilities of Hindustan Motors Factory. Lunch with the execs in their B[oard] O[f] D[irectors] room. After a rest a local Rotary project—hospital and eye clinic—30 beds. Very depressing and needy. Nice, restful afternoon. We addressed the local Rotary Club and then had (another) big dinner. Later we walked to the Hindu temple in the compound.

FEBRUARY 22, 1982 – MONDAY
CHITTAGONG [CHATTOGRAM], BANGLADESH
WARM

A long day! Rose early, and after breakfast and good-byes to our hosts took the plane from Dum-Dum [Calcutta Airport, renamed Netaji Subhas Chandra Bose International Airport in 1995] to Dacca. Customs and immigration was tedious. Kahn and his Rotarians were on hand to meet us. Deluxe lunch at Dacca Club. Afternoon conversation, then back to Zia Airport [Dacca] and plane to Chittagong. Rotarians met us. My host is Ismail Haq. Supper (Bengali style) at home of Rotarian Kamal, then an evening of Bengali music. Nice but too long. I asked to be excused. Sorry! So far Bangladesh has been surprisingly better than India.

FEBRUARY 23, 1982 – TUESDAY
CHITTAGONG, BANGLADESH
SUNNY, WARM, HUMID

Chittagong is only 1½ miles from the Bay of Bengal. It's like the beach in July as far as temperature. Each of us is with a different host. Haq's is a lovely "bungalow" up on a hill overlooking the city. Heard a nightingale in the evening. Light breakfast with host. Her name is Silena. Toured a jute mill and carpet manufacturer. Saw where Pres Zia was killed.[17]

---

17. Ziaur Rahman, the seventh president of Bangladesh, was assassinated by Army officers on May 30, 1981.

Session with president of Chamber of Commerce. Informative lunch at Glaxo (British) Pharmaceutical. Then a quiet afternoon at home. Tea with Silena. A walk into town (first time). *Big*, joint Rotary Club dinner at Hotel Agrabad. U. S. Ambassador Joan Coon[18] was Guest of Honor. I spoke briefly. Did OK. Jim sang.

FEBRUARY 24, 1982 – WEDNESDAY
CHITTAGONG, BANGLADESH
NOT QUITE SO WARM

Nice day! Before breakfast I saw a mongoose. After assembling late at Chittagong Club we had a session with chairman of Chittagong Development Authority. Then a nice boat ride across the Karnaphuli River to the Marine Sciences Institute. (Learned all about fishing and boating.) Lunch with host at Burma East Oil. Silena and I went for a drive in the hills and to Chittagong University. After tea, a reception at Chittagong Club for Ambassador Coon. Very nice! Scotch and pretty women. Quiet supper at home with hosts. Then a drive along the river and coffee with a company executive. The stay here is very pleasant.

FEBRUARY 25, 1982 – THURSDAY
DACCA, BANGLADESH
SUNNY, NOT SO WARM

A long day, but not unpleasant. Early rise and farewell to hostess. On way to airport went to see the Bay of Bengal. ½-hour flight from Chittagong to Dacca. Met by host PDG Mahisan Rahman. His wife is Rashida. Assembled at luxurious Hotel Sonargaon. Trip to Adamjee Jute Mills. Largest industry in Bangladesh, largest jute mill in world (35,000 employees). Drinks, lunch and speech with Rotary Club of Narayanganj. Visit with U.S. Ambassador Jane Coon. Tea and meeting with Rotary Club of Ramna. Lovely dinner at home of ex-minister of culture Habibullah Khan. Beautiful art work in home. Then a trip across town for a long boring evening of sitar and flute.

---

18. Jane Bell Coon, b. 1929, ambassador 1981–84.

FEBRUARY 26, 1982 – FRIDAY
DACCA
SUNNY, COMFORTABLY WARM

Nice day. Treated well everywhere. Day started at *fabulous* Hotel Sonargaon, then a couple of hours with Chief Justice of Supreme Court Kamal Hossain. Very considerate and thoughtful lawyer. Then a trip to an ancient Moghul fortress and shrine, Lalbagh. Lunch with hosts and a quiet afternoon in my room. Then a visit (at the hotel) to Rotary Club of North Dacca. Well received. In the evening we went to a Muslim wedding. *Very* crowded. (The bride was not present when the vows were solemnized.) Nice saris and *much* gold jewelry. Dinner for 1500. We had ours in an upper room. Rice, mutton, and chicken (yek, yek). Home with our nice hosts.

FEBRUARY 27, 1982 – SATURDAY
DACCA
SUNNY, WARM IN DAYTIME, COOL AT NIGHT

Nice, restful day. Mahisar drove me around the city on way to Hotel Intercontinental. Rotarians of NW Dacca took us on a picnic to the National Park. A nice "rest house" by a lake (but nothing picturesque). Team played frisbee and attracted a crowd. Then a boat ride on the lake. Afterwards drinks and a *very nice* box lunch. (On the way to the forest I quarreled with my hosts, defending American foreign policy.) We came home about 3:30 p.m. and I spent the afternoon reading, writing, resting. Took a walk. In the evening went to a nice dinner at home of District Secretary. Beautiful Louis Kahn design with a *gorgeous* hanging stairway. Late coffee with Rotarian Mahmoud. Then home and bed.

FEBRUARY 28, 1982 – SUNDAY
DACCA
CLOUDY, NOT WARM. DACCA IS COOLER THAN CALCUTTA.

An early-rise morning — 5:30. Drove to Bangla Academy and participated in 4-mile walkathon. ... a snap, about 1,000 participants. (I was on the telly, walking.) Afterward we spoke to the local Rotary Clubs. (Shema Rahman is the new president.) Home for a shower, then a quiet morning at home. For lunch we went to a local Chinese restaurant for a very good meal. (Long wait though.) Napped in afternoon, then went to a reception and dinner in our house given by Dr. Khan. Lots of Indian music and a typical Bangladesh meal (yek to both). Packed a single bag for the steamer tomorrow. Our 4 days in Dacca were pleasant.

MARCH 1, 1982 – MONDAY
ON THE GANGES RIVER NEAR BARISAL [BARISHAL]
CLOUDY, COOL-ISH ON THE RIVER

There really isn't much to write, but it has been a delightful day. Mahisut took me to the steamer terminal through horrendously rickshaw-jammed streets and alleys. The river steamer doesn't look like much, the toilet is depressing, but the cabins are OK and the food *very* good. We spent most of the day on deck watching the wide, glassy Ganges unfold before us. Beautiful, exotic, tropical scenery like you see in picture books. Some of the men slept. We took many pictures. Left Dacca at 11. Arrived Chanpur at 3. Scheduled Barisal at 9, but we haven't arrived yet. This has been *my* most pleasant day.

MARCH 2, 1982 – TUESDAY
KHULNA, ON THE GANGES
BEAUTIFUL, WINDY ON THE RIVER

The cruise continued leisurely through the night and morning. A panorama of India beside the Ganges. The food was ample and well-served. Arrived in Khulna about 2:30 p.m. Met by Rotarians. My host is Nuruddin Ahmed, manager of the local ship terminals[?]. We live at the great house in the compound. After a (second) lunch we visited a paper mill. Then tea with the local Rotarians, including a program of Indian music. Then dinner at a Chinese restaurant. Afternoon tea with our host. We are fed and overfed on every occasion. It's really too much.

MARCH 3, 1982 – WEDNESDAY
DACCA, BANGLADESH
SUNNY, RATHER COOL

Back again in Dacca. It's just like coming home. It's our last night in Bangladesh, and I am a little wistful to leave, the people have been so nice to us here. We rose early, and after breakfast the Jessore [Jashore] Rotarians arrived to take us there in a minibus. Tea at Jessore. Then a visit to a school and handicraft shop for underprivileged. After lunch and a long wait, a hurried trip to the library. Then a flight to Dacca. A clean up at Rahma's house and then a lovely farewell dinner at the home of J. R. Khan, president of the Rotary Club of Dacca.

MARCH 4, 1982 – THURSDAY
KATHMANDU, NEPAL
CLEAR, CHILLY IN THE EVENING

It's magnificent here. The mountains are just as I had pictured them—great snow-covered peaks that hold[?] on the horizon and are a constant presence. Left Dacca by air and flew here. Saw *many* Himalayas from the air. (Mt. Everest?). My host is a hotel operator and travel agent named Darius Shrestha. He is warm and generous. After a *delicious* lunch and a rest, his chauffeur drove me into downtown Kathmandu. Saw temples and exotic camps[?] of all sorts. Nice cocktail party and dinner with Rotarian Lotti. It's chilly in this room.

MARCH 5, 1982 – FRIDAY
POKHARA, NEPAL
CLOUDY, RAINY, CHILLY

I am sick today. Woke up last night with nausea, diarrhea and stomach cramps. Very uncomfortable during the day. Have been taking Dr. Khan's medicine Adysin, and it seems to help. Very long (120 miles) bumpy ride in mini-bus to try to see tall Himalayas. So far, a dud, because the rain has socked everything in. We are staying at Hotel New Crystal, which is nice. We took a walk (in the rain) this afternoon. (I got a nap.) After a bath we all went out to the bar, which is like a ski lodge with fire in the center. Dinner was in the hotel dining room and was quite pleasant. The young men are playing poker.

MARCH 6, 1982 – SATURDAY
KATHMANDU
RAINY, CHILLY

The pills did their work, and by morning I was in good shape. We arose at daybreak to see the sun rise but no luck! We could get a fair glimpse of Annapurna and some others, but it soon closed in again. After breakfast we went to a lake and a waterfall, and then to a fascinating Hindu temple with "holy men." Brief shopping. Then Jim plowed a team of oxen. Ride back was long and bumpy but not so bad because I felt better. It's raining. I got off in downtown Kathmandu, took a rickshaw to Hotel Annapurna, had a light supper, then read a newspaper until 8:30. Then home and now to bed.

MARCH 7, 1982 – SUNDAY
KATHMANDU
WARM, BEAUTIFUL, CHILLY AT NIGHT

Rose at 7:30. Took a walk and then rode with Dwarika[19] into town. Walked around Durbar (Palace Square) then a long walk to Swayambhunath Temple. Long climb, but spectacular Buddhist monastery and view (with monkeys). Took taxi to Yak and Yeti Hotel. Bought Mike a tee shirt. Had a drink. Had light lunch at Swiss restaurant. Missed contact with team member at Durbar Square. Bought a souvenir prayer wheel, then a walk and taxi ride back to Dwarika's. After a short nap and bath, we spoke to the Rotary Club of Kathmandu. Not a strong club. We did fair. Had Nepalese dinner (yek!). Home with host and a chilly evening.

MARCH 8, 1982 – MONDAY
KATHMANDU
WARM, BEAUTIFUL

A *fine* day. Rose at 7:30 and rode into town with Dwarica. (He is strange. Polite and considerate, but obviously too busy to be much concerned with me.) We rode in mini-bus to Bhaktapur and Patan [now Lalitpur]. Saw *many* temples. Beautiful! Spectacular! Fascinating! Also saw pottery, woodworking, metalcraft, and (at Tibetan refugee camp) rug making. The Himalayas were more beautiful than ever today. Took *many* pictures. After a fabulous Tibetan and Nepalese lunch, went back to monkey temple. (Great.) Then went to see child "goddess." After a rest at home, went to another fine farewell dinner and party given by Rotarian Gopal. Everyone hates to leave Kathmandu.

---

19. Presumably Dwarika Das Shresta (1928–92), founder of the glamorous Dwarika's Hotel in Kathmandu

March 9, 1982 – Tuesday
Bagdogra, West Bengal, India
Cool and clear, full moon

We've traveled nearly 1,000 miles today. Morning flight from Kathmandu after long wait. Shyam met us in Calcutta. Letter from Kaye. Glory be! (He says he has our tickets to Delhi and home all arranged.) Flight to Bagdogra arrived on time at 2:00 p.m. Rotarians met us. President is S. K. Ghosh. Our host is R. P. Gupta, manager of a local tea plantation. Wife, two daughters. I have a small room. Restful afternoon. Tea. Then proceeded to local Rotary Club meeting. Spoke and sang. Traditional Indian dinner (yek). Our "bungalow" in is the middle of the tea plantation.

March 10, 1982 – Wednesday
Bagdogra, West Bengal
Sunny, pleasantly warm

What a day! We rose at 8 and our host took us on a tour of the tea plantation and factory. *Most* informative. After a heavy breakfast we went to the club and celebrated "Holi," eating, drinking, dancing, but mostly having colored paint and power thrown on us. I did not enjoy it, and it is *very* hard to get off. Wash-up, tea, and then to Siliguri where we addressed the Rotary Club there. Did OK. Had a typical Indian dinner (yek) and returned "home," some 21 miles.

March 11, 1982 – Thursday
Darjeeling, West Bengal, India
Cloudy, chilly in mountains

We are in Darjeeling now and it is uncomfortably cool. Rose at 8 a.m. Lovely breakfast with hosts. Left Siliguri about noon after several delays. Breathtakingly beautiful ride up and into hills (about 7,000 feet). Arrived in Darjeeling about 3:30. Staying in Ajit Mansions. Surprisingly primitive accommodation and quite cold. We had a good lunch, and a lot of good conversation with Maurice Banerjee, team leader of GSE [Group Study Exchange] to California. Then a late supper and so home. Beautiful view outside window. Now to bed.

March 12, 1982 – Friday
Darjeeling
Warm in daytime, cold at night

We rose at 4:30 and rode in a 4-wheel drive Land Rover 14 km to Tiger Hill. Hundreds were there. Very steep climb. Arrived just before sunrise. Saw sun rise (pink) on Kangchenjunga with Everest in the distance. Gorgeous. After breakfast we went to Himalaya Mountain Museum and Zoo. Leopard, yaks, and tigers. Then to Tibetan refugee camp and then to old market. Lunch with dignitaries at Ajit. Opening session of Conference was impressive, but *very* cold. We sang poorly. I made short impromptu speech that was well received. Cold, cold, cold.

March 13, 1982 – Saturday
Darjeeling
Mild in daytime, chilly at night

A good day. Slept well under covers. Rose and had good breakfast. Went to District Conference. Usual boring business meeting. Our team addressed conference and did *very* well. The meals and the Gymkhana [Club] are Indian style and not tasty (yek, yek). Had delightful cup of tea at outdoor cafe overlooking hills. Attended afternoon session. Boring. Had fire built in rooms and received letter from Kaye. Morale up 300%. Went to Indian-Nepalese song and dance show at conference hall. Very good. Best yet. Supper at Gymkhana (yek, yek). Home to a comfortable room.

March 14, 1982 – Sunday
Darjeeling
Mild in daytime, chilly at night

This was the last day of the District Conference. It was interminable and boring. Ajit kept his cool and did well. I spent most of the day in and out of the conference. Had early morning espresso at Dreamland. Socialized and politicked outside the auditorium. Took a couple of walks on mountain walkways. After dark we went to a talent show then Ajit and Manshul had us to a late-night supper. Indian food (yek). Fire not doing well in room.

March 15, 1982 – Monday
Darjeeling
Overcast, cloudy, cool

A great day. Conference is over. Rose at 8. After breakfast had warm donut at Dreamland, visit to Happy Valley Tea Garden and Factory. Nice. Scenic. Back at Darjeeling took long walk into hills. Lunch at Glenary's.[20] Went shopping with Kathy Bannerjee for souvenirs. Paid brief visit to Ajit and Mangoo. Another walk, then back to supervise the fire making. Stared at fire. Nice supper at Glenary's. Then home to bed.

(Shyam says he has made arrangements for me to leave Calcutta on March 19. Leave Delhi on March 22. Hope he has done well.)

March 16, 1982 – Tuesday
Agarpara, Kamarhati (suburbs of Calcutta)

We're staying in a company guest house on the banks of the Ganges (Hoogli). Rose early in Darjeeling and packed. Ajit and Mangoo joined a fine breakfast. Left at 10 a.m. and took cars down the mountain to Bagdogra. Light lunch and then plane to Dum-Dum. Rotarians were on hand to meet us. Whisked away to Jain temple, then to *big* tea at home of Rotarian Rahim Sahar. Visited models[?] and display, then Sahar and wife took me on a lovely boat ride on the Ganges. Indian-type dinner with Rotarians at home of president of the Calcutta Club Metro, then to the guest house of Agarapura Jute Mill. Accommodations fair. Miller is leaving in a.m.

March 17, 1092 – Wednesday
Kamarhati [Calcutta] guest house
Warm, sunny, humid

This guest house is not bad. Lack of hot water is main drawback. Bed tea at 7:00. Delicious large breakfast on lawn overlooking river. Then a long wait as Rotarians responsible failed to show. After noon we went to see Shyam. Then to the TV station for another long wait before taping. And went by to see Amiyo Roy who has had a heart attack. He looks like a sick man. Tea with him. Then over to Davar's for a final drink and pick up of my stuff. Back to Amir for a Chinese dinner. Watched ourselves on t.v. Not bad. Kirit Shah brought us back to the guest house.

---

20. Famous bakery and cake shop, est. 1915.

March 18, 1982 – Wednesday
Kamarhati Guest House
Overcast, hot, thundershower in p.m.

Last day in the district. Another nice breakfast in the river arbor. Afterwards Rotary of Barrackpore took us to Gandhi shrine and park. Tea and music with Rotarian Arup Roychoudhury. Then lunch at Pres. Mukherjee's. (He did not come.) After lunch and nap visited ceramic factory with Samir Ghosh. Meanwhile H. N. Ghosh finalized tickets in Calcutta. Meeting and farewell dinner with Kamarhati club. *Very* festive, *very* emotional. Ajit, Shyam, Jerry, Amiya Gupta, many others. We sang, and well. A little tearful. Utpal Choudury came in from Raniganj. He helped pack. Goodbye to team members. Bed about midnight.

March 19, 1982 – Thursday
Delhi, India
Sunny, pleasant

GSE [Group Study Exchange] tour is over. Rose at 4:00 a.m. H. N. Ghosh came by to pick up Rob and me. Took off from Dum-Dum at 6:20. Arrived in Delhi 8:30. Much nicer city than Calcutta. Wide streets, well controlled traffic. Cleaner. Staying with Rob at Hotel Rangit (235 rupees per day). Walk around. Lunch at hotel coffee shop. Then conducted tour of Delhi: Red Fort, Gandhi's bier [Gandhi Smriti], other historic mosques, temples, etc. Snake charmer. Dancing bear. Afterward beer at bar. Cleanup and nap, then back to Red Fort for sound and light show. Very nice. Dinner at night-clubby place in hotel. Pleasant. A good day and we like Delhi.

March 20, 1982
Dehli — Agra — Dehli
Sunny, comfortably warm

Today was the trip to Agra day which is the reason for stopover in Delhi. Rose early. Took tour bus. Time to Agra about 4 hours. Bought book about Agra. Stopped at tomb of Akbar. Tremendous bus trip. Muslim architecture in red sandstone. Then on to Taj Mahal. Incredibly beautiful! Large! Very white amidst other red buildings. Pretty gardens. Taj is all I had expected. Stopped by Akbar fortress and citadel on way back.

They were great builders. Lost camera somewhere on way back. Will try to find tomorrow, but am pessimistic.[21] Returned at 10:30 p.m. Supper at hotel. Satisfying but it was a [a long] day.

MARCH 21, 1982 – SUNDAY
DELHI
SUNNY, WARM

First day of spring, last day in India. A good one. Rose late (8:30). Had breakfast at American-type tourist cafe and snack bar. Then shopped all morning for homecoming gifts. (Got ripped off on a shoe repair.) Bought four evening bags for Kaye and daughters-in-law. Bought expensive gold-brocade sari for Kaye I found in hotel. Met Rob and relaxed. He is a good companion. We went to Nirula's[22] Chinese restaurant for an unusually nice dinner. Beer at bar beforehand. Then a three-wheel taxi back to hotel. Asked about check-out arrangements. Packing and bed.

MARCH 22, 1982 – MONDAY
EN ROUTE DELHI – LONDON – NEW YORK
VARIED, WARM TO COOL IN LONDON

Travel home day. Rose at 3:30. Checked out. Hotel bill for 3 days, 3 meals and beer was 440 rupees (about $50). Checked through Delhi with no troubles. Plane ride was long, boring, uneventful. Stopped at Dubai and Kuwait (Arab oil states). They feed us all the time. Too much. Arrived London at 3:30. Parted with Rob. Enjoyed his company. 3½-hour wait at Heathrow. Then 7½-hour flight to JFK. Uneventful. Not much sleep. Arrived 9:30. Called Kaye. She is OK and happy. Checked in at Midway (Best Western) Motel. ($61.50). Slept very poorly. Excited I guess. Now for airport and home.

---

21. There are plenty of slides from the day-trip to Agra, so he must have found his camera.
22. Nirula's, est. in the 1950s, was the oldest Chinese restaurant in Delhi. In the 1970s Nirula's was emerging as a fast-food empire.

France

August 1982

Kaye & Kern Holoman

D. Kern, Kate, Kaye, and Kern
Château de Sancy, near Meaux

SOURCE: Diary 4 (1982). Green leather album with gold tooling, titled TRAVELS, roughly 4 x 6¾ inches. (Almost identical to red album from 1956.) Spine crumbling. Inscribed on flyleaf:

Kern Holoman
2912 Hostetler St.
Raleigh, N.C. 27609
USA

Rotary International
Group Study Exchange
to India - Bangladesh - Nepal
Feb–Mar, 1982

Continues with "Trip to France, Aug–Sept, 1982, Kaye and Kern." Both sections entirely in Kern's hand.

France

August 1982
Kaye & Kern Holoman

In 1982 Kaye and Kern were still experimenting with "space available" military flights, and in this case arrived at Mildenhall AFB in England and made their way to us in Paris via the Channel ferry. We were lodged in a one-room flat on the top floor of 10, rue de Braque in the Marais, congenial as to neighborhood but very hot under the building's tin roof. It was our first summer in France en famille, *and the parents had come primarily to see Kate, giving us the opportunity to go off to Amsterdam for a few days to visit the Floriade, a once-a-decade flower exposition.*

After we got back to Paris we took Kate and the parents on a car trip in a big arc to the east and north of Paris: Meaux, Chantilly, Beauvais, lastly Compiègne where the World War I Armistice was signed. The high spots were a fancy dinner at a prestige manor-house hotel near Meaux, where Kate and I visited the stables between courses; and, the next night, taking snifters of 75-year-old Armagnac to our bedrooms. Kaye and Kern continued their trip via car to Normandy and the Loire chateaux, ending at Chartres cathedral. They were very nervous, toward the end, about how they were going to get back to the United States, made worse by my father's inability to grasp the concept of international telephoning by country code–city code–phone number. Starting about then and for three more decades, we nearly always dialed long-distance calls for him.

August 7, 1982 – Saturday
Raleigh, Pope Field, en route

August 8, 1982 – Sunday
En route – Azores, Mildenhall, Cambridge

August 9, 1982 – Monday
En route – Cambridge, London, Folkestone, Calais, Paris

August 10, 1982 – Tuesday
Paris

August 11, 1982 – Wednesday
Paris

August 12, 1982 – Thursday
Paris

August 13, 1982 – Friday
Paris – Sancy-les-Meaux

August 14, 1982 – Saturday
Meaux – Compiègne

August 15, 1982 – Sunday
Compiègne – Beauvais – Chantilly

August 16, 1982 – Monday
Chantilly – Paris

August 17, 1982 – Tuesday
Paris

August 18, 1982 – Wednesday
Paris

August 19, 1982 – Thursday
Paris

August 20, 1982 – Friday
Paris

August 21, 1982 – Saturday
Paris – Lisieux – Caen

Rose early and packed. Mike and Betty had brought sweet bread loaf from Holland. I went to Gare de Lyon to pick up rental car. (A Peugeot 104. Smallest available. We call it "Hinky-Dinky.") Got lost going back to apartment. Loaded car and took off. Got lost leaving Paris. Finally made it out via Versailles. Countryside is beautiful. On to Hotel Métropole in Caen. Chintzy. Nice walk in town. Pretty. Drinks at American Bar. Trouble finding place to eat. Finally at Le Bouchon. OK, but long wait. Caen is a nice town.

August 22, 1982 – Sunday
Caen – Normandy Coast – Bayeux
Sunny, cool

Bed was uncomfortable. Sank in middle. *Petit dejeuner* in hotel dining room. Saw castle of William the Conqueror. Went to Abbaye aux Hommes and Abbaye aux Dames, but did not see tombs. Drove to Normandy invasion beaches. Stopped at Arromanches where British landed in 1944. Cheerful beach town now, but full of sad memories. Lunch at a crêperie. Drove along invasion coast, several stops. Visited American Military Center near Omaha Beach. Into Bayeux. Historic old town. Stayed at delightful Lion d'Or Hotel. Great dinner at one-star restaurant. Inn is picturesque and comfortable. Short walk after dinner.

August 23, 1982 – Monday
Bayeux – Mont St.-Michel
Coolish, alternate sunny and cloudy

Rose at 7:30. Continental breakfast at hotel. Visit to Bayeux tapestry. Electro-guided tour. Fascinating embroidered account of Norman conquest of England. Well done / well displayed. Bought wall souvenir.

Motored across Normandy via St. Lô and Avranches. Crêpes and cider in Villedieu, a copper manufacturing center. On to Mont St.-Michel. Impressive in distance, overwhelming up close. A real high spot! Parked on causeway, registered at Hotel Mère Poulard. Room is good, look out toward causeway. Spent afternoon tramping around. Fascinating in every way. Saw St. Michael's chapel. *Big* dinner at Mère Poulard dining room. Very chi-chi. Afterward watched tide come in by moonlight. Bed about 11 p.m.

AUGUST 24, 1982 – TUESDAY
MONT ST.-MICHEL – DINAN – JOSSELIN
CLOUDY, COOL

Rose at 7:45. *Petit dejeuner* in room. (They don't charge extra for OJ.)
Called Mike in Paris. All okay.
Guided tour of old abbey. Very old ... parts of it to 8th century. Mixed Romanesque and Gothic architecture depending on time of building. Formerly Benedictine monastery, later state prison. Now just a tourist attraction. Very impressive! All we had imagined and more. Checked out of hotel, but stayed on causeway to watch tide come in. Motor to St. Malo. Reconstructed walled city—wish we could have stayed. On to Dinan. Interesting medieval city. Lots of crêpes and cider. Did not like original planned place for night. Stayed at *charming* Hotel du Chateau, near castle at Josselin. Dinner was fair.

AUGUST 25, 1982 – WEDNESDAY
JOSSELIN – TOURS – BLÉRÉ

Rose at 8. Breakfast in hotel dining room. Long drive across Brittany into Anjou–Touraine via Loire River and Angers into chateau country. Nice lunch beside Loire at Les Pieds dans l'Eau. Saw chateaux at Saumur and historic one on a hill in Chinon. Went into Azay le Rideau, but was disappointed. Not well kept. Then to Villandry with *beautiful* gardens—kitchen, herb garden, formal topiaries. Unexpectedly pretty. Through Tours, thoroughly lost. Finally arrived in Bléré, a little town on Cher river. Had trouble getting room. Found a minimum type one at Hotel du Cheval Blanc. Ample meal in dining room. Armagnac at a bar down the street. Quaint town.

August 26, 1982 – Thursday
Bléré – Blois
Misty, rainy in a.m., cool in p.m.

Rose at 8:00. Breakfast at Cheval Blanc lounge. Drove 4 miles to Chenonceaux. Beautiful chateau across Cher river. Historic. Diane de Poitiers and Catherine de Medici. Did complete tour. Coffee and tarte at Au Bon Gateau. Bought pitcher and chocolate. Drove 10 miles to Amboise. *Very* historic chateau. Partly in ruins. François Premier, Leonardo da Vinci buried here. Lunch at Grille de l'Hotel de Ville. Drove upriver to Blois. Registered at Hotel du Gare. OK. Walked around Blois chateau. Decided not to go in. Disappointing. No good view. Drove to Chambord, biggest, most beautiful. Pizza supper. Coffee at hotel. Toured castle in semi-darkness. Sound and light show. OK, but in French. Pretty lights.

Australia and New Zealand

October 18 – December 1, 1992

Kaye & Kern Holoman

Kaye, Jeff, and Dick, Kuranda Station, Queensland

SOURCE: Diary 5 (1992, 1994, 1997). Brown leather album with gold tooling, roughly 5½ x 8½ inches. (Almost identical to blue album from 1994.) Inscribed on flyleaf:

Travels — Oct. 18 – Dec. 1, 1992
[added:] *June 17 – July 1, 1994*
Katherine H. Holoman

Begun as the Australia diary, continues with Scotland (1994) and Asia (1997). All three sections in Kaye's hand.

Australia and New Zealand

October 18 – December 1, 1992

Kaye & Kern Holoman

Dick and Sandy and their sons Mark and Jeff lived in greater Sydney, Australia, for two school years: 1991–92 and 1992–93. Kaye and Kern's six-week journey to visit them was the longest and furthest of their ventures abroad. En route *they stopped in California to plan for a Leisure Ministries trip the next year—and to leave suitcases with us pending their return. They went to Sydney via Hawaii, then for a driving tour of New Zealand, then back—again via Hawaii—to us at Windhaven on the California coast for Thanksgiving.*

Sunday, October 18 – Thursday, October 22, 1992
San Francisco

We left Raleigh on Sunday morning. David and Debbie took us to the airport. American.

The flight was very pleasant. Short transfer times in DFW—used the "tram" because of my knee.

In San Francisco we rented a Budget Ford Mustang—two-door—fine. We are staying at the Fort Mason Officers Club. Very quiet and convenient. Redecorated "Victorian" bathroom.

We have spent our time on details of Leisure Ministries trip next May. Some items are bothersome, but most have worked out well.

Sunday night we ate in Ghirardelli Square at McCormick and Kuleto's with crab cocktail in soup bowls! We ate one evening at the Mexican restaurant—La Banca—where we had eaten on an earlier trip. Otherwise, just meals.

We went to Monterey early on Wednesday—found a good motel and most other details. Were happy to have the services of a local travel agent, Carol-Anne Hoover. Stayed overnight at Fort Ord and did the 17-mile drive, etc. the next day. Simply gorgeous.

Talked to Mike and to Connie and will call D. and D. and Louise again before leaving. We will have supper with Mike's family on Friday night in Fairfield before we leave.

Friday, October 23 – Monday, October 26, 1992

We finished up the tour plans including a brunch in Tiburon. The road to Muir Woods is too narrow, etc. for a big bus, so that will not be possible.

Met Mike's family at a new Mexican restaurant in Fairfield—Chevy's—where we had a big mixed grill to make fajitas. Very good. They are all well and they took our bags to go to Windhaven.

On Saturday we got up and out to the airport without any problems. The flight to Honolulu was uneventful. We had aisle seats in the center section.

We were met—with leis—by a representative of United Vacations, along with 10–12 others. We were taken to our hotel, the Coral Reef. Our room was large and quite satisfactory although the hotel overall is shabby. We walked around and had a teriyaki steak supper.

On Sunday, we went to an orientation breakfast—very nice. The weather was mixed all day. Had drinks by the pool at the Sheraton Moana, newly redecorated and lovely.

Took a glass-bottom boat ride along Waikiki—very enjoyable. Stopped off at Ala Moana shopping center for a quick "lunch," then took the Circle Island bus around Oahu. A little long but quite interesting. Had a snack supper back near the hotel.

We were picked up a little after 10:00 p.m. for the flight to Australia. No problems—had window and aisle seats. Took a sleeping pill (each) and slept until a couple of hours before arrival at Auckland. Went from Sunday to Tuesday.

Arrived at Sydney on schedule. No trouble with customs, etc., and

Sandy was there to meet us. Sydney is a beautiful city with a great deal of water frontage. The house is in a busy residential "suburb." It is high and looks out over one of the many bays. It is a two-story split-level on the hillside.

Everyone is fine. Jeff is taking his exams. We visited with Sandy and unpacked, then the four of us joined Dick in the city for a very nice dinner at the American Club. We had drinks first at a "dockside" pub at the harbor—the Sydney Harbour Oyster Bar.

Wednesday, October 28, 1992

After getting Jeff and Dick off, Sandy made an appointment for me to get my hair done—quite an interesting experience. One older lady had her shop—she said if I would let her cut my hair I wouldn't need to have it rolled up! While I was there, Sandy and Kern shopped for groceries.

We went into Sydney by ferry—the principal means of transportation here. We walked around the old renewed harbor area called the Rocks, had a pub lunch with Dick at the Lord Nelson, visited an "opal mine," and returned home. Very nice dinner here.

Did a load of clothes.

Thursday, October 29, 1992

We packed our bags to go to Port Douglas and the Great Barrier Reef and then went to the zoo. Very good zoo with Australian birds and animals as well as such others as giraffes, snow leopard, white tiger, etc. Ate a quick lunch there, took an aerial car up to the top and main entrance, where Sandy picked us up.

Went by cab into town to get info from New Zealand travel office with Dick. Then by cab to airport for flight (Ansett Airline) to Cairns, via Brisbane, then by rental car to Port Douglas, a beautiful resort area near the Great Barrier Reef. (Had to swap cars—noisy.)

Our accommodations are great! We have an apartment with 3 bedrooms—2 downstairs and 1 up where Kern and I are. Everything is white and new. It was a long flight and after a nightcap we all fell into bed.

Friday, October 30, 1992

We had breakfast on the waterfront of Port Douglas. It is a nice resort—not overly built-up, with a very nice harbor mall. Dick booked us into a day-long cruise to the Great Barrier Reef for tomorrow. We went grocery shopping, walked down to the beach and then had lunch. This is Four-Mile Beach, one of the best in Australia. They have kept it natural, with shrubbery, etc. on the ocean—no buildings to speak of.

Wrote cards to the boys, Louise, Alma, Jean,[23] Dal and BG, Luna, Lynn, and the Sunday School class (McGraw).

Jeff arrived in late afternoon—no problems. We ate at a seafood restaurant in town—simple but good fish.

The birds here are noisy at dawn and evening. The parrots—lorikeets—are very colorful and prevalent—bright green, red, blue and yellow—beautiful!

Saturday, October 31, 1992

After breakfast at the apartment, we went to the harbor to board a Quicksilver Catamaran to go to the Great Barrier Reef. It's a very large ship and it was a great trip! After about an hour and a half, we reached an area where they had a large pontoon float/raft, and several specialty boats anchored. Dick and Jeff went scuba diving. Kern, Sandy, and I went into a "semi-submersible" underwater-viewing boat—absolutely amazing views of the coral—so many different shapes, colors, etc. The tropical fish were also great.

There was a lavish lunch on board and a chance to see a video of Dick and Jeff's scuba-ing. We came back by some other sections of the reef. After cleaning up and happy hour, we had dinner on the Wharf at an Italian place and had delicious pasta dishes.

Sunday, November 1

After breakfast and a swim, we started a day of sightseeing in the mountains and rainforest northwest of Port Douglas. We "hiked" a trail in the Mossman River Gorge, then headed toward the Daintree River Rainforest area. We had a delightful lunch at a tea room—open-air type—near where our boat docked. We were on a small boat with only two other people and it was very enjoyable. Our guide was knowledgeable and friendly and

---

23. Alma Smith was Kaye's administrative assistant at work; Jean Morehead, a piano teacher, was a close family friend. (The others are identified in the front matter, pp. ix–xi.)

showed us the features of the rainforest. After a walk on the beach and happy hour, we ate outside at the Coconut Grove restaurant—fine.

The weather here in North Queensland has been quite comfortable. It is warm and breezy—the apartment is open-air all the time. It will get much hotter here in the next couple of months. There is off-and-on rain, some quite heavy, but we have not had a "rainy" day.

Monday, November 2, 1992

We checked out of the apartment after breakfast and drove into the mountains and rainforests around Kuranda. Again, we took a boat on the Barron River and had the boat and guide to ourselves. We saw a crocodile, numerous birds and vegetation, turtles and a water snake. The guide was very knowledgeable as before, and seemed to enjoy the rainforest area and its characteristics.

We had a very good informal lunch—souvlaki and burgers—and mango and macadamia ice cream.

The train station is located above the river on a steep hillside. Sandy drove to Kuranda and the rest of us took a most interesting train ride—15 tunnels and lots of amazing gorges—to Cairns.

We checked into an apartment hotel for the night—more compact than our other apartment, of course, but quite satisfactory. Two new features: a sliding door on the bathroom and a slot for your room key which had to be in place for the electricity to come on in the room. (Jeff says they had this in Hawaii.)

Dick located the Cairns Game Fishing Club, which was having a "Calcutta BarBQ" and racing "lottery" on the eve of the Melbourne Cup races. We had a good meal, and Dick participated in the "horse-trading." He came out a few dollars to the good. There was champagne and a good party atmosphere.

Tuesday, November 3, 1992

We checked out and went to the airport, turned in the car and flew from Cairns to Brisbane and on to Sydney. We got home in the mid-afternoon. Dick had a dinner engagement and Sandy a class, so Jeff, Kern and I had a pizza supper. (The first "sleep-less" night—probably too much caffeine in flight.)

Wednesday, November 4, 1992

We went in with Dick and had a sightseeing day. We took a great cruise all around Sydney harbor and into the river areas. So many bays and coves and hills!! The harbor is a beautiful area—one of the best in the world, we understand.

After the cruise we went to the Park Lane Hotel on Hyde Park for a simply lovely lunch. It is a very subdued, elegant place—meant to be like a London Hyde Park hotel. We had a spaghetti entree with a spicy fresh tomato sauce and *lots* of shellfish. Very unusual but good and we were glad to have had it.

Sandy met us at the Balmoral Harbor for a drink and went to a meeting afterward. Dick stayed in town for a client dinner. Sandy had fixed a very nice roastbeef dinner for Kern, Jeff, and me. We watched TV 'til bedtime. There were only exit poll results in the US elections today.

Thursday, November 5, 1992

We went in early with Dick so we could go on a one-day trip to the Blue Mountains. It was a day of beautiful sightseeing. The mountains get their blue color from the eucalyptus trees' oil in the air. These trees dominate the mountains.

Our first stop was at Featherdale Wildlife Park. Lots of koalas and kangaroos roaming about. Good picture-taking area.

We stopped for lunch at a place which had a revolving restaurant, an aerial cable car out over the canyon and the steepest railroad in the world—believe me! We did everything there and saw the rock formation called the Three Sisters, among other very spectacular views. We returned to Sydney by a very nice express train to Central Terminal, then by subway to Central Quay and ferry to Mosman.

The outstanding feature of this trip, along with the mountain scenery, was the flowers—particularly those planted in peoples' flower gardens. There were traditional flowers such as hollyhocks, foxgloves, sweet pea, pansies, etc., as well as bird of paradise, etc. It is late spring here and the flowering trees are also amazing. The purple jacarandas are just beginning to bloom and are spectacular.

We had happy hour at home and a great steak dinner which Dick grilled. We heard the presidential results today and Terry Sanford's loss but not much else. Dick says Jim Hunt won.[24]

Friday, November 6, 1992

We had a rainy morning. Dick stayed home to do some telephoning and we all drove into the city in the late morning. Kern, Sandy and I went to the Powerhouse Museum—very interesting—science, industry, life styles, etc. Had a nice lunch there and the weather had cleared completely by then. We went to the Chinese Garden, a very lovely place with waterfalls, rock formations, tea houses, and a good variety of plants. We went to the Ansett office to pick up our airplane tickets for internal flights in New Zealand—then home by the ferry. Good beef pie dinner.

Australian words and phrases:
> give way = yield (right of way)
> smash = car accident damage
> removalist = mover
> Eucalypt (no "us")
> panel beaters = auto body repairers
> takeaway = take out (food)
> "ta" = thanks
> double 2 = 22
> triple 3 = 333
> NZ = N Zed

Saturday, November 7, 1992

A beautiful day—sunny and cool to hot. Sandy, Kern and I went by ferry from the zoo to Watson's Bay at the entrance into Sydney from the Pacific Ocean. Dramatic rocks on the ocean side. (Jeff had a basketball game, so Dick picked him up in the car and they joined us at Watson's Bay.) Lots and lots of sail boats, more on the ocean than usual, according to Dick, because of the wind direction. We had lunch outside on the bay—seafood salads, etc.

---

24. Terry Sanford, former governor of North Carolina and former president of Duke University, was defeated in his run for a second term as United States Senator. Jim Hunt won a non-consecutive third term as governor (and then a fourth).

We drove back in by Vaucluse, a house from the mid 1800's, which is now a public park with a nice garden. The house has been furnished with some family heirlooms and other pieces of the period. We had a nice tea at the tea shop there.

Coming back into Sydney, Dick spotted a large freighter coming into the harbor, so we "detoured" down to the harbor level and watched it come in. It was a large Chinese container freighter.

Back home to a spaghetti supper and bed.

This is also the day that Kern was able to get additional Mini-press [a prescription medication] from a pharmacist here.

Sunday, November 8, 1992

We got up early and drove in with Dick who was going to work today. We went to the Opera House and did the Backstage Tour. It was great! Our guide was both knowledgeable and articulate, and we covered the entire complex. The tour lasted 2 hours.

We walked up to the Botanical Gardens area and had lunch in the NSW Art Museum—very pleasant. We looked at several of the galleries of 19th- and 20th-century European and Australian art. We then walked back through the gardens, which are more botanical than decorative. We went on out to the end of the land to Mrs. Macquarie's Chair and walked back to get the ferry at Circular Quay. There was a minor problem with the bus but Dick picked us up. Then home, dinner, and bed. As I was flossing my teeth, a big filling fell out that will have to be dealt with, I'm afraid.

Monday, November 9, 1992

Sandy called and made a dental appointment with her dentist, Dr. Bill O'Reilly. He was very nice and considerate and put in a temporary filling on the badly broken tooth.

We drove over to Manly, early, which is across the bay from the house. It is a beautiful area, partly resort but mostly a local surfing and swimming beach.

After the dentist, we went into the city by bus, took the monorail to Darlington Harbor and had an informal lunch there. We took a little train around the harbor which is the Convention Center for Sydney. (It is also where the Chinese Garden is.) We saw the Maritime Museum and Aquarium buildings and other harbor features.

We took the monorail into the downtown shopping area to go to the QVB [Queen Victoria Building]. Kern got some little koalas and a souvenir spoon. We came back to Mosman by bus, picked up the car and came home to dress for dinner.

We got a cab, picked up Jeff at school and met Dick at the Wharf for a most enjoyable evening. The Wharf is theater-oriented, and the restaurant at the end looks out over the harbor with lots of lights and boats.

We walked around to the very elegant Hotel Park Hyatt for coffee—then home by cab.

Tuesday, November 10, 1992

I paid Dr. O'Reilly $75—MC.

Sandy took us to Manly to get the Jet Cat to the city—nice ride. We went back to the Rocks, the oldest part of Sydney, for looking around. We ate a big buffet lunch at the Lowenbrau, part of the restored area.

We walked over to the Opera House to do some shopping for Sandy as well as for us. We got the 1993 Wine Calendar for Dick and Sandy, two Christmas koalas for Allie and Francis, two pin cushions for Debbie and Connie.

Sandy met us at the Mosman ferry and we went walking on the rocks and beach below their house. Chinaman Beach is a nice beach area which the community uses and the rocks are great to climb around on.

Dick came in from a cocktail party at the American Consulate. He went over all the New Zealand plans and has done a super job.

Wednesday, November 11, 1992

Dick and Sandy had plans to take care of Norris Little's business friends and family, so they bid us goodbye in the morning early. We packed and went by cab to the airport for the flight to Auckland, NZ. There was some delay in processing, but we got everything checked, etc. Most of the flight is over water, but we were able to see some coastline of New Zealand. We checked into our hotel and went to bed early.

We thoroughly enjoyed our stay with Dick's family. Jeff has grown a lot and is active in school. He seemed to enjoy being a part of all of our activities which he could make. Dick stays very busy. There are several unanswered questions about staying in Sydney or going to another post, and it is unsettling to the family. They hope to know soon.

Sandy was so nice to us as we did our sightseeing. She drives a lot for the family, and still likes to take classes and to get involved in various activities. They got word that Mark had mono, and we're glad Dick is leaving Friday for N.C. and will see Mark Saturday and Sunday before going to Orlando on business.

Thursday, November 12, 1992

We were up early for a flight from Auckland to Dunedin. (We lost two hours between Australia and New Zealand.) We flew Ansett NZ and had a very nice flight. New Zealand is very mountainous, and as we flew I could see big blotches of color on the mountainside. It turned out to be masses of gold-colored flowers—Scotch broom and several other deep yellow flowers—in great profusion on the mountains. The flowers here are absolutely gorgeous—beautiful colors and lots of variety. It is spring here and there are rhododendrons everywhere—many larger than our dogwood trees.

We were too early to check in at the motel—Quality Inn—but put our bags in the room and started walking in downtown Dunedin. There's a lot of Scotch Presbyterian involvement in their history here.

We drove out the peninsula which makes the harbor here and visited one of the "historic" houses which is being restored privately—Larnach Castle. We had tea there. The end of the peninsula is a preserve for the Royal Albatross—it's not open now because of nesting season. It was a beautiful drive. This is the Otago area and the Otago peninsula. We had dinner at a local "semi-pub" type restaurant—too much food.

Friday, November 13, 1992

We checked out and headed for Te Anau. It was a long drive but went well. The area is sparsely populated, and there is almost no traffic. Te Anau is on a beautiful lake of the same name with magnificent mountains all around. This area is Fiordland, including the largest National Park, and encompassing all of the Southwest corner of South Island. We checked in at our motel—the Anchorage—got a pick-up lunch and went to the glow-worm caves. They were fascinating—first, there was a short boat ride over the rapidly rushing river, then a walk and a longer boat ride with the glow worms.

Kern does not feel well. He has an intestinal upset. We went to an Italian restaurant for supper where I had spaghetti and he had soup.

Our motel has a kitchen so we got some breakfast items.

SATURDAY, NOVEMBER 14, 1992

We had a short drive to Lake Manapouri to go on a day-long trip to Doubtful Sound. The trip involved a boat ride across Lake Manapouri, then a bus trip which included visiting the West Arm underground power plant. This was unexpected and quite exciting because of the tunnel which was cut through the solid rock for 700 feet *down* to the power station on the bus.

The bus went on to the boat dock on Doubtful Sound. It had been raining and cloudy earlier, but it began to clear as we approached the sound and became a beautiful day. We went over the Wimlot Pass to Deep Cove to get to the boat. The trip was breathtaking, with countless waterfalls caused by the rainy weather. Doubtful Sound is really a fjord. We had a picnic lunch on board. Kern is still not feeling good. Took 2 Imodium caps.

We saw small penguins swimming and one medium-size, traditional-looking one on the shore.

We brought in Chinese for supper (fair) and watched "The Sound of Music" on TV.

SUNDAY, NOVEMBER 15, 1992

We got up early to drive to Milford Sound. The route is very scenic, but it was raining and overcast. It took a little over 2 hours without sightseeing stops. We were changed to a larger boat for the Milford Sound cruise. Although the weather was not good, it was a beautiful trip. Once again we saw 2 penguins quite close by and seals on the rocks. On both trips, the guide/pilots were very good. We had screwdrivers and our picnic lunches. We got back about 2:00 p.m. and re-drove most of the Milford highway, then on to Queenstown. As we changed directions, the weather improved, and we enjoyed the views as we approached Queenstown and Lake Wakatipu.

We checked into our motel, the Blue Peaks. We had a kitchen/room which we did not ask for and was given without additional charge. We drove around the town, checked with the Shotover Jet people and found that they had had to cancel for the past 2 days because of high water (rain!). We are to check in the a.m.

Sunday is not a business day in NZ and many restaurants were closed. We opted for McDonalds in a downtown mall. We wrote postcards before bed, having gotten sweet rolls, juice etc. for breakfast.

Monday, November 16, 1992

We had breakfast in our room and called to find the Jets had been cancelled til noon (later all day). Since we were to go to the sheep station at 2:00, we made a jet booking(!) for tomorrow morning.

We drove out from town and visited Arrowtown, a restored gold mining town. Their newest undertaking is the restoration of the Chinese Village—they were laborers during the gold rush. We came back to town and went up to the mountain "top" on the gondolas. It is the steepest such ride in the world. It was beautiful to see the lake in the mountains. We had an early lunch at the top.

We went on the steamer *TSS Earnslaw* for a ride across the lake to a sheep station. We saw demonstrations of sheep dogs and sheep shearing, had tea at one of the houses there, and shopped in the gift shop. I got neckties—New Zealand wool—for Kern and the boys and a wool scarf for Connie. (Kern got his NZ spoon at the gondola gift shop.) We have had to live with mixed weather for several days now and today was no exception. The morning was fine, but the cruise was done in the rain. The worst part is the decreased visibility of the scenery.

We had dinner at a family restaurant, bought o.j. and sweet rolls and returned home. Although Kern is feeling better, he had a bout of indigestion.

Tuesday, November 17, 1992

We checked out and found that the jets would not be operating in the morning, so we got our MC credit and left for Mt. Cook. Once again we have had a rainy day which has limited visibility but the mountains are tremendous. The lupine has been especially pretty along with other wild flowers. We drove through very thinly populated countryside with almost *no* commerce. There were orchards and vineyards early but nothing further on. We ate lunch at a self-serve cafe—the other real restaurant was expecting 172 tour people within ½ hour! (The only roulette wheel within miles!!)

The hotel, the Hermitage at Mt. Cook, is very nice. It is reminiscent of similar national park facilities. It has rained a lot and we had a sleet shower while we were driving around. It is too "foggy" to do much sightseeing, such as a helicopter ride. We drove out a road which leads to the Tasman Glacier and hope the weather will permit returning there for a walk tomorrow.

We had a lovely buffet dinner at the adjacent Wakefield Restaurant, then home and to bed.

Wednesday, November 18, 1992

We had breakfast in the hotel and checked out. The car battery was dead but the hotel helped start it. We decided the weather did not permit a 'copter flight. We drove out to the walking area and started one of the trails. I decided not to go all the way but Kern did. The weather was basically clear but quite cold. We left to go to Lake Tekapo. Driving by the lakes with all types of mountains was very beautiful. The road was desolate. We had lunch after we got to Lake Tekapo, then checked into the Alpine Motel—very nice room with great view. We drove the scenic drive, visited the Church of the Good Shepherd which has the window behind the altar, and checked at the airport about a flight over the glaciers—the weather may be OK tomorrow—we'll check then. The weather today has been clear but still off-and-on rain. It is quite cold and windy.

(I had a nose-bleed at lunch time—complete mystery!)

We had dinner at the motel dining room—good buffet. We went for a walk—the sunset was beautiful. Kern wrote cards to the Beales, Davis's, Lewis's and church staff. He still does not feel too good.

Thursday, November 19, 1992

We had breakfast at the motel dining room and checked out. The airline was flying so we signed on for the flight. It was simply marvelous. We saw Mt. Cook, many glaciers and so many snow-covered mountains. A great trip.

We drove from Lake Tekapo to Christchurch through beautiful mountains, etc. We came into the city and checked into the Quality Inn in the late afternoon.

We went into the "downtown" area and walked around. Christchurch is the largest city on South Island—about the size of Raleigh. The Avon River winds all through the city, not extremely large but very pretty.

We had a nice dinner in the hotel dining room. Kern still not too hungry.

Friday, November 20, 1992

We had breakfast at the cafe in the Arts Center, former college buildings, very Gothic. We then ran errands, including info from the visitors center, checking with Hertz about turning in the car (it can be left at the train station), and picking up the train and ferry tickets for tomorrow. We can check our bags thru to Wellington!

We drove out the peninsula, which is quite mountainous. The views from the Summit Drive were spectacular. It has been a clear day (but cold), and the Southern Alps with their new snow were beautiful, as was a panoramic view of Christchurch, the harbor villages, the ocean, etc.

We parked back in town and after a slow lunch, did a walking tour of the downtown area. We went punting on the Avon. Our boatman was a college student, very pleasant and conversational—a nice trip.

We went to get the car and realized the key was lost. Fortunately, the person who found it turned it into the Hertz office and they brought it right to us. We were *very* lucky. We went out from town to buy gas, came back to the motel, and eventually decided against dinner. We went to the dining room for dessert, coffee, and liqueur, did the preliminary packing, and turned in.

Saturday, November 21, 1992

We got up early, checked out and went to the train station where we left the car and got the train to Picton. We sat at a table with a young NZ woman and her son and enjoyed talking with her. Picton is a small, pretty resort town. We had a "Devonshire tea" for breakfast. There are a lot of hills and mountains between Christchurch and Picton—the train went through 21 tunnels and pulled some sharp steep grades. We arrived in the early afternoon with a direct connection to the ferry.

The ferry boat ride was also interesting—quite cool and windy. We had a cheese crackers and fruit lunch, while up on deck. They carry train cars as well as autos, etc.

The Wellington harbor is very beautiful—lots of ins and outs. We check into the Quality Inn - Rocksburg St. and after a short stroll had dinner at the hotel.

Sunday, November 22, 1992

We booked on a city tour of Wellington and enjoyed it very much. Wellington is the capital of New Zealand and as such has a lot of public buildings, some going back ± 100 years, others, such as the Beehive, are quite modern. Wellington sits on a fault and has had serious earthquakes. Being very steep and hilly, it reminds you of San Francisco. It was especially nice to have an extended portion of the trip around and above the bay area.

After the tour, we took the cable car up to the top and had a nice lunch at the restaurant there. We then walked down thru the Botanic Gardens, cabbed back to the motel, cabbed to the airport to go to Auckland.

At Auckland, we cleared immigration, etc., walked with luggage to the International Terminal and processed there. Kern got some duty-free liquor, and I called and talked to Jeff. Dick is not back yet, and Sandy wasn't in.

The flight was okay. We took a sleeping pill each, but I had knee pains and slept only so-so.

We arrived in Honolulu very early and this is the day we gain back—2 Sundays!

We were able to check in at the Coral Reef about 7:00 am. We took a nap, and after dressing went out to walk around. It was raining and we went to the Sheraton Waikiki outdoor lounge and had chi-chis. As we were leaving, we realized the camera was missing and we checked back to the few places we'd been and notified the hotel, which suggested we call back later.

We bought some coffee and macadamia candy as well as books for Kate and Michael.

Monday, November 23, 1992

After breakfast at Jack in the Box, we arranged for the shuttle to the airport, etc. I called the Sheraton lost & found, and they indicated they had a camera that that fitted my description—I went to the hotel and it was ours!

We had an uneventful flight to San Francisco. We picked up a Ford Mustang from Budget—a little short on luggage space—and checked in at the Quality Hotel. The room was nice, and the view was great. We think the Leisure Ministries group will enjoy it.

Tuesday, November 24, 1992

We made some Leisure Ministries calls, had breakfast at IHOP and did a grocery shopping at the Presidio commissary.

We then drove to Napa to check out LM possibilities—there weren't many! We ate late at Wendy's and then drove to Irish Beach. It was a very overcast day with a little scattered rain. It was dark most of the way.

We got into Windhaven without difficulty. It's always good to be here. After bringing everything in, we had happy hour and a spaghetti supper. We called Chris and Connie and David and Debbie—all OK. Mike called to be sure we were in.

November 25–29, 1992 — Windhaven

Kevin came in mid-day and Kern's family in the evening on Wednesday. Thanksgiving Day featured good food with contributions from everybody.

The overall atmosphere was one of relaxation, which was great. Mike worked on his computer project which he hopes to complete very soon in order to get it on the market ahead of the others in the making.

While we were there, we went to the beach several times. The tides were extreme both high and low, and the ocean was beautiful.

On Saturday, Kern and I drove to Mendocino and Ft. Bragg, the latter to get steak for Saturday night. Mendocino was crowded but pleasant as always. We ate at a bakery-deli—crab salad croissants.

Everyone left early on Sunday.

Kern and I drove to Sonoma where we began checking the remaining Leisure Ministries needs. We stayed at the El Pueblo Motel and had supper both nights at Carrows, a family-style restaurant. Kern's cold is quite bothersome.

We spent Monday checking in Napa, Calistoga, and Sonoma. Most everything is working out.

We were up quite early Tuesday to drive to the SF Airport. The traffic was slow at times but mostly quite good—it took 2 hours to drive. Our flight home was relatively uneventful—some delay in DFW. We bought sourdough bread, cheese and a bread bag for David and Debbie. They met us at RDU, came back and visited awhile before going home. It's good to be back and everything seems to have remained the same, except for the arrival of winter and below freezing weather.

It was a stupendous trip—the new places, the scenery, and especially seeing the families.

We were fortunate that our health problems were pesky but not serious.

We agree that six-week trips are too long but we are grateful to have had this opportunity.

SCOTLAND

JUNE 17 – JULY 1, 1994

KAYE & KERN HOLOMAN

SOURCE: Diary 5 (1992, 1994, 1997). Brown leather album with gold tooling, roughly 5½ x 8½ inches. (Almost identical to blue album from 1994.) Entirely in Kaye's hand. Inscribed on flyleaf:

Travels — Oct. 18 – Dec. 1, 1992
[added:] *June 17 – July 1, 1994*
Katherine H. Holoman

Begun as the Australia diary, continues with Scotland (1994) and Asia (1997). All three sections in Kaye's hand.

Scotland

June 17 – July 1, 1994

Kaye & Kern Holoman

Friday, June 17 – Saturday, June 18, 1994

We left RDU in the evening (7:30 p.m.) for a non-stop flight to Gatwick (London). Arr. Saturday a.m. This is a new flight for American Airlines and it was full. The flight was nice but uneventful. We transferred from Gatwick to Heathrow by bus without much extra time. From Heathrow we flew British Midland to Glasgow. Our bags did not arrive but the tour guide persisted and they were in the hotel by bedtime. The Hospitality Inn is very nice in downtown Glasgow. We had a welcoming drink and dinner plus breakfast the next morning in a private dining room. We visited the Burrell Collection of artistic and historic items in the afternoon—very interesting—unusual.

We were very tired as were most of the group and we retired early.

Sunday, June 19, 1994

Our first full day of sightseeing. Our guide is Gavin Cruickshank, a native of Edinburgh, and our driver, Tom, is Irish.

We left Glasgow going south and visited Robert Burns's birth-place and museum. It has just been completely renovated and upgraded and was officially opened on Saturday by Princess Margaret. Good exhibits and audio/visuals. Our lunch break was at a woolen center in Moffat. Pea soup lunch and a nice walk in the town park and gardens. On to Gretna Green, a traditional place for marriages by the blacksmith. The ceremony enacted by people from our tour—Kern was the bride's father. Group picture taken. We went into England and toured Carlisle Castle—a border castle since the 11th century and associated with Mary Queen of Scots. Our hotel was lovely—not a "chain type," more an inn (the Crown Hotel). Our room was small but pretty. Kern signed us up for all four optional side trips. After a lovely dinner in the "garden dining room," we walked down beside the train track and on the viaduct over the Eden River—nice view of "dooryard gardens." The flowers are very beautiful—early spring types—peonies, rhododendron, oriental poppies, foxgloves and gorgeous lupines. The town is Wetheral.

Monday, June 20, 1994

We continued in England to ride by and on the remaining bits of Hadrian's Wall, dating from Roman times in the [2nd] century. The remains of the square towers placed every mile in the wall were especially interesting. We had a short coffee break and lunch in Jedburgh, Scotland—fresh vegetable soup at another woolen center. These places are indispensable to the tour planners—flexible lunch opportunities and large, clean restrooms, along with the merchandise, etc.

Our afternoon feature was a visit to Abbotsford House, the home of Sir Walter Scott. It is very large and filled with his collections, books, etc. The grounds are also beautifully designed and maintained.

The ride to Edinburgh was beautiful—very hilly and rural—sheep, cattle, Scotch broom, etc. We stopped for a break at a woolen center(!) so that our bags could be taken to our hotel rooms. We then drove around Edinburgh for a short while and to our downtown hotel, the Mount Royal. We found an ATM and got Scotch money and "a camera."[25]

The optional evening included sightseeing in the suburbs of Edinburgh including the rail and road bridges over the Firth of Forth. We then came to a great pub, the Hunter's Tryst, where we had delicious dinners and drinks. I got T-shirts for the boys—Six-Foot Club.

We are beginning to learn the other members of the tour group. They are from Australia, New Zealand, Canada and USA. Some have

---

25. The travelers appear to have forgotten their slide camera and replaced it with what they call a "snapshot" camera, probably a disposable purchased in a drugstore. But there are no "snapshots" of this trip to Scotland in their archive.

"starting points," such as military background, similar travel experiences, etc. A very mixed group, but no one is a problem, it would seem.

Tuesday, June 21, 1994

This was a "city day," in Edinburgh. We had a very good "step-on" guide for the morning. After chasing down the American Express office and cashing some travelers checks, we had a pub lunch at Brock's of Rose Street and started out on our walking tour of the Royal Mile from the Castle to Holyrood House Palace. We know now about closes and wynds and the many well-known people who lived on the Mile.

As we started out we went to a Raphael exhibit in one of the art museums.

The Scottish Cabaret dinner and show was excellent—the best "traditional" or "folklore" show we have seen—good dancers and musicians.

Wednesday, June 22, 1994

Our 51st wedding anniversary. Our first stop this morning was at Saint Andrews. The wind was blowing amazingly hard—but only moderately cold. We walked about, had coffee and bought some souvenirs.

We were at Glamis Castle in the middle of the day. This is the home of the Queen Mother Elizabeth who is 94. We toured the castle and saw many family possessions, etc. The Bowes-Lyon family still owns the castle and lives there (part-time). We had a bite of lunch before leaving and came along the edge of the North Sea to Aberdeen. We had an hour and a half on our own to see the museums, gardens, etc. before coming to our modern motel in the suburbs, named the Skean Dhu. Our dinner was very nice. We wrote a *lot* of postcards.

Thursday, June 23, 1994

This was a beautiful scenery day—some clouds and sun, etc. We went to Balmoral Castle, Queen Elizabeth's home—not government property. The Royal Family is here in August. Lovely gardens, although we are early for summer color here. We had lunch at Braemar, where they hold Highland Games. In the afternoon we visited the Glenlivet Distillery for a tour and a taste. We stayed in Aviemore, a ski resort. Our hotels are nice—each is different of course. The hot- and cold-water faucets that do not mix are *not* our favorites. Finding the right switch for the TV is also interesting. More cards.

Friday, June 24, 1994

We drove through mountain country to Culloden Battle site. Our Scotch history is getting a little better. The castle at Dunrobin was very interesting because of the insights we got into Scotch "lords" and their dominating roles in social history. We went to a glass factory and checked into our hotel in Wick—not our greatest, but dinner was very good. There were two weddings here. We had an optional pub visit in Lybster—music, dancing—very "cheery."

Saturday, June 25, 1994

This was our day to go to the Orkney Islands and it was a great day. We went to Dunnet Head, the northernmost point on the British mainland. We have been to Land's End in the south and Dunnet Head in the north.

We sailed from John O'Groats on a ferry for a beautiful ride to South Ronaldsay. We had a different coach for the islands. We went to the Italian chapel made by prisoners in World War II. We crossed the Churchill Barriers between the islands, built in WW II when a German sub got into the Scapa Flow, the very large body of water used for naval anchorage, service, etc. (à la Pearl Harbor). We had a soup and sandwich lunch arranged by Globus.

We saw many evidences of 5,000-year-old constructions including the Ring of Brodgar, similar to Stonehenge; and Skara Brae, the village that has been excavated and prepared as a historic exhibit. All the island scenery was spectacular, both in rain and sunshine.

We stopped in Kirkwall, the island capital, and saw a red sandstone cathedral modeled on Salisbury Cathedral. There is a Viking element in the islands. Back by ferry for dinner—nice.

Sunday, June 26, 1994

This was a driving day in magnificent mountain country. We came west along the "top" of Britain to the northwesternmost point, then south through the mountain, lock and coastal areas—all very special. We had a pre-arranged lunch along the way and then into Ullapool and a boat trip on Loch Broom.

The weather has been the usual mixture—quite typical. These were very narrow, single roads but everyone is courteous, and on a Sunday it wasn't a problem.

Monday, June 27, 1994

We continued our beautiful drive in the mountain and loch regions, visiting a lovely garden, Inverewe, which enjoys the moderating effects of the Gulf Stream. The shrubs such as rhododendron and azaleas as well as lots of flowers were beautiful in spite of "Scotch Mist."

We had both mist and sun as we drove to Oban, a large resort on a large body of water. These have been the areas which we had looked forward to with good reason.

Tuesday, June 28, 1994

We were up early to get the large ferry to the Island of Mull. It was about an hour and a half across the island in our coach, and it was beautiful, quite rugged, etc. A short ferry took us to the island of Iona, small but very interesting. It was an early Celtic Christian settlement of St. Columba. We took bag lunches from the hotel and "picnicked" with Willadee and John before visiting the abbey, ruins, etc. The ferry rides were quite enjoyable. Fingal's Cave is on tiny, nearby Staffa Island.

After dinner we had a chance for a short walk beside the water.

Throughout our entire stay we have had little or no complete darkness at night. We are "up north" and it is "mid-summer," quote with the shortest night of the year having been last week. At 3:00 a.m., it is already beginning to be light.

Wednesday, June 29, 1994

This morning we came south to Glasgow. It was quite rainy and this provided numerous waterfalls from the mountaintops—reminiscent of Norway. This is "Loch Lomond" country.

We had a driving tour of Glasgow before checking into the hotel—the same that we started in. We had very good fish and chips nearby and then started a walking sightseeing tour. We went to the main city square,

George Square, and then to the Cathedral area. The Cathedral is very black and was being renovated. The Art Museum nearby had a Dali painting of Christ on the Cross and other religious exhibits. We had a fairly long walk back to the hotel, h[appy] h[our], dinner etc.

Thursday, June 30, 1994

We filled in our Scotch history this morning with the importance of Stirling Castle and the battle of Bannockburn. We saw exhibits and audio-visual presentations at a very nice Visitors Heritage Center. We picked up several souvenir items here.

We then went to Aberfoyle to the Scottish Wool Center where we saw an interesting presentation on sheep in Scotland—and there are plenty, though not quite like New Zealand.

Our driving was through an entirely different type of scenery— lower, rolling hills, highly cultivated, with lots of trees along the roadsides. This is Trossachs area.

We returned in early afternoon to Glasgow and returned to the fish and chips place, as did several others on the trip! After this, we went sightseeing in a different area of Glasgow, visiting the Art Museum. We actually took the bus back and got off at the right place!

There was a farewell dinner at the hotel—very nice with special good-byes to Gavin, Tom, etc. We were given an address list of the group. Packing took care of the remainder of the evening.

Friday, July 1, 1994

We were up at 5:00 a.m. to get our bags out, etc. by 6:00 a.m. We had breakfast in our room, then went to the airport to head home. All went well in the transfers but the flight seems long on a day flight. Louise met us and reported that all is well.

This was a beautiful trip—enjoyable in every way. Our guide was exceptional and Globus had planned well.

Because of our "camera problem," we have no slides but we bought a large quantity of postcards and hope our snapshots turn out well.

The American West

August 29 – October 3, 1994

Kaye & Kern Holoman

Yellowstone National Park

SOURCE: Diary 6 (1994–96). Blue leather album with gold tooling, roughly 5½ x 8½ inches. (Almost identical to brown album from 1992.) Inscribed on flyleaf:

Motor trip to the West
Aug. 29 – Oct. 3, 1994

California — Kern's Award
May 3–13, 1995

Méricourt
Aug. 17 – Sept. 7, 1995

Nova Scotia, etc.
May 14 – June 2, 1996

All four sections in Kaye's hand.

Our Motoring Trip to the West

August 29 – October 3, 1994

Kaye & Kern Holoman

The 1994 "Western Loop" of thirty-six days in the family car was Kaye and Kern's most substantial domestic journey. They began by driving north to visit Chris and Connie in Buffalo, then to Dick and Sandy in Chicago, then on west through the national parks, south through Utah to Arizona, then eastward toward home again via Texas.

Monday, August 29, 1994

We left Raleigh shortly after 9:00 a.m. We chose to go north on US-15 from Creedmoor. It is not a very good road to drive—crowded, etc.

We stayed at Carlisle Barracks [PA] for the night—very nice suite in old building, Washington Hall. Had dinner at Hoss's—a steak/buffet place. Very nice.

387 miles.

Tuesday, August 30, 1994

We drove through the mountains of Pennsylvania and New York on "back roads"—very beautiful scenery, flowers, etc. but a slow route, time-wise.

We enjoyed lunch at a small restaurant, the Royal Drive-In in Ridgeway, PA where the "locals" were great!

We got to Chris and Connie's [Buffalo, NY] around 5:00 p.m. and had dinner. We watched the first part of "The Sound of Music." 704 miles.

Wednesday, August 31, 1994

Chris and Connie were both involved with a big Volunteer Day project in the morning and other activities in the afternoon. After a quiet morning including a walk in the neighborhood, we went shopping and then spent the afternoon at the zoo. It's a very nice zoo and we enjoyed it.

After HH [happy hour] at home we had dinner at the original house of Buffalo Wings, the Anchor Bar. Our dinner was primarily Italian with Wings.

Thursday, September 1, 1994

After a leisurely morning we went by Wegman's and got subs, chips and drinks and set out for Niagara Falls.

We picnicked on Goat Island, then took the tram to all the sights. The girls had an active good time.

The high spot was "The Maid of the Mist" ride. We all had a great time.

We met Chris and Connie for dinner at a Chinese restaurant in Fort Erie, on the Canadian side—excellent, above-the-usual meal.

About 100 miles while in Buffalo.

Friday, September 2, 1994

We got up early to leave for Chicago. Chris was also leaving for New York City for his professional association meeting. We had breakfast at a local restaurant before heading for Niagara, Canada, Detroit, etc. on the way to Winnetka.

It was a long driving day—many construction delays, etc. Soup and sandwich lunch at [Tim Hortons] in Canada. Left the interstate (94) to see the Indiana Sand Dunes [Indiana Dunes State Park]—very surprising in their height!

Got to Dick and Sandy's just before 8:00 p.m. CDT. Dick got in a few minutes later. Nice dinner and conversation before "crashing." Jeff is fine—driving now.

611 miles from Buffalo to Winnetka!!

Saturday, September 3, 1994

After a leisurely early morning, we drove into the city for lunch at Berghoff's—great, as usual. After strolling along downtown, we went on a 1½-hour cruise on the river and lake. It was very enjoyable—good commentary about the architecture, etc. We went through the lock into the lake and back. We drove home—traffic was heavy going into Chicago because of a night football game.

Sandy ordered a pizza, which was more than enough after our heavy German lunch.

Sandy is scheduled to have surgery on next Wednesday, Sept. 7, and she has understandably mixed feelings about it.

Sunday, September 4, 1994

Dick and Sandy went to church at St. Luke's. We went to Skokie for lunch with Morris Springer. We went to the King Solomon restaurant. Morris told us about his activities, family, etc.

We took a walk down to the lakefront—cloudy and slightly drizzly. This area has nice houses and yards with flowers. Sandy cooked a delicious meal for all of us.

Mike called to say he will be going through Dallas–Fort Worth on Tuesday.

Monday, September 5, 1994 – Labor Day

We spent a great middle-of-the-day at the Chicago Botanic Garden, in Glencoe, not far from Winnetka.

The day was cool and the gardens exceptionally interesting. We had lunch in the museum restaurant, interesting grilled vegetable sandwiches.

After some errand running and laundry, Kern talked to David who had called while we were out. He said Dallas was in the hospital with gallstones. I talked to Louise who said she would look into it.

We had dinner at an upscale Italian restaurant near Winnetka.

Back to pack up for tomorrow.

Tuesday, September 6, 1994

We all got up early—us to get underway—Dick for an early appointment. After getting underway, we had breakfast at McDonalds on an "oasis" *over* the interstate.

We came across upper Illinois to Wisconsin. This was to be our "long" driving day—and was. We drove around the State Park area, Devil's Lake—and a *little* free ferry.

We "did" Wisconsin Dells. Very surprised that it was so "honky-tonk" in its development—à la Gatlinburg, etc. We picnicked at a public picnic area and then had a good boat trip on the river to see the rock formations that are the reason for the whole thing!

We drove through Eau Claire and into the wilderness!! There was nothing in the way of commerce. We finally arrived at Bloomer, Wisc., which had a good truck stop with motel and restaurant.

Wisconsin has been very lovely to drive through—lots of rolling hills, corn and wildflowers.

I talked to Sandy about her day of testing at the hospital. It had been slow and messy. I also talked with Carolyn about Dallas and found he had a great deal of infection in his gall bladder and pancreas which will have to be controlled before surgery. Also talked to Louise and Connie.

Wednesday, September 7, 1994

Our first stop was at the National Freshwater Fishing Hall of Fame in Hayward, Wisc. It was quite interesting, with large "statue" replicas of lots of popular fish, the largest a muskie 5 stories high and a half-block long. Good "museum" collections.

We picnicked at a state park, Anmicon Falls, beside the falls (more like cascades) of quite brown water.

We stayed in Bimidji, center of Paul Bunyan lore, with a large statue of Paul and his ox, Babe. Bimidji is called "the first city on the Mississippi River," and we crossed "headwater" streams, etc.

Talked to Connie and Carolyn.

Sandy has her surgery today but we were not able to talk with Dick. We stayed at a lakeside motel with HH by the lake. The trees are turning a little and are beautiful—early "little red" maples and sumac.

Thursday, September 8, 1994

Dick called early to say Sandy had come through her surgery well and is in intensive care, as anticipated.

We went from Minnesota to North Dakota today. The presence of water is everywhere in Minn.—their 10,000 lakes are for real—and all with little black ducks!!

We have seen more fields of sunflowers than we knew existed. There must be a good market for sunflower seeds/oil—miles and miles of fields.

(Dallas is to have surgery on Friday. Kern talked to him.)

We picnicked beside another Devil's Lake and visited the geographic center of North America in Rugby, N.D.

It is wheat harvesting time, and the great sweep of wheat fields and equipment is "awesome."

We stayed at Minot Air Force Base—a nice suite—with Mongolian stir-fry fry at the club.

This is Mike's birthday and we called to welcome him home. He fell in France and one scraped place is infected.

Debbie is "OK" and took the messages about everyone.

Friday, September 9, 1994

We drove from North Dakota into Montana—still a very desolate state. Kern says desolate is wrong—very uninspiring but with lots of grain elevators, etc. to show the industry here. Nevertheless, it was an uneventful day.

When I called to check on Sandy, Sandra B. said "I brought her home today." I talked to Sandy and she was in good spirits (and a brace)—amazing.

Kern talked to a neighbor who said Dal also got along okay with his surgery.

We stayed in Havre (Have-er) with a Chinese dinner.

Talked to David and ask him to send flowers to Sandy.

Saturday, September 10, 1994

We continued across Montana. There are a lot of Indian communities here—not very well kept, etc.

We picnicked at Sun Point in Glacier Park—St. Mary Lake.

We got to Glacier National Park in the early afternoon and made reservations for Saturday and Sunday at hotels in the park. After this, we did the Canadian section of the park—Waterton [Waterton Lakes National Park, Canada], and came back to Many Glacier Lodge for the night. Swiss décor and rustic setting. Beautiful view on all sides.

Talked to Chris. Kern talked to Dallas, who is getting along OK from his surgery.

Sunday, September 11, 1994

We took the outstanding route in the park—the Highway to the Sun [Going-to-the-Sun Road]. It was absolutely fabulous—rugged, different, all you can imagine. We picnicked beside a stream with a tiny chipmunk. We have seen a wolf, a bear, deer, elks and chipmunks on this trip.

We are staying at the Glacier Park Inn—very nice and more up-to-date than the others associated with the park. We had a barbecue dinner here.

I talked to Louise and Louis and all seems well. We wrote postcards tonight.

Monday, September 12, 1994

We left the park and headed south through Montana. We visited several places at Grand Falls—the Charles M. Russell Museum, the Great Falls of the Missouri, and the Giant Spring—very interesting.

We also drove around a Wildlife Refuge but we were early for snow geese and swans, according to the Ranger there.

Our afternoon route was a quiet road, and the Rocky Mountains were great as they grew from the distance.

We stayed in Livingston, one of the main entryways to Yellowstone.

Tuesday, September 13, 1994

We had decided that we wanted to drive the entire Beartooth Highway (Rt. 212) and we "elbowed" back to its start and it was well worth it—a lot of high mountains—beautiful scenery including aspens in full yellow leaf.

We saw two cowboys herding cattle along the highway with the help of two dogs.

We found that everything in Yellowstone was full and drove through the park to West Yellowstone, Montana—also "sold out," so we kept going down the only highway to a place called Mack's Inn. We had a resort "suite" which was quite satisfactory. Unfortunately, we left our freezer packs in the freezer!

Talked to Louis. No special news. Dallas should be home.

Wednesday, September 14, 1994

We came back through Mack's Inn to West Yellowstone for breakfast and got a reservation for the night at the Ho Hum Motel!

We spent the day in Yellowstone doing everything we wanted to—the Great Canyon of the Yellowstone River, the various geysers and other steaming basins and lots of wildlife, especially buffalo. The burned evidence of the 1988 forest fires is everywhere.

Talked to David—all okay.

Wildlife on this Trip

Glacier — wolf, black bear, deer, ducks (everywhere), hawks, mountain goats
Yellowstone — elk, buffalo, geese, swans, marmot (Beartooth), coyote
Tetons — moose with calf, bald eagle, bluebird, pronghorn (antelope)
Wyoming, Utah, etc. — prairie dogs, osprey
Colorado — Steller's jay, Clarke's nutcrackers, maybe ptarmigans
Arizona — a roadrunner (beep-beep)

Thursday, September 15, 1994

We did the southern area of Yellowstone as we headed for the southern gateway between Yellowstone and the Tetons. We had lunch at a small but good campsite restaurant, then thoroughly enjoyed the magnificent Tetons.

We found Jackson "sold out" also and came south to a small town, Pinedale, which had acceptable accommodations. For the second night we had cereal in our room for supper.

Talked to Chris—no special news.

The scenery, including a drive to Teton Pass, is spectacular.

Weather

We are at the approximate halfway point on our trip, and our weather has been most cooperative. We have had some light rain from time to time, but not enough to cause us to get out our umbrellas, raincoats or Niagara ponchos!

As we moved through the Northeast, it was mostly warm daytime weather with cooler evenings.

Coming into the plains states was about the same.

We had chilly winds in the mountains around Yellowstone, etc. and frost in Wyoming.

There was a special weather phenomenon in Colorado—mountain thunderstorms. The dark clouds would gather with wispy tails toward the ground but there is little rain that reaches the ground. There was a little snow from such a pattern at the top of the Rocky Mountain Park.

We also had a little sleet on Grand Mesa.

The weather warmed up in the daytime as we went south but the mountains kept evening temperatures low. It was in the 90s in Arizona by the time we left that area. Still no real rain.

Hot days have been the rule in Texas—record-breaking mid 90s. The evenings are fine, however. Still no real rain.

Friday, September 16, 1994

Our first stop was at the Mountain Man Museum in Pinedale—a good local museum.

Most of the day involved driving in Wyoming, which has a lot of sagebrush-covered land!! We went up and around Fremont Lake and thoroughly enjoyed Flaming River Gorge [Flaming Gorge–Green River] (west side). Late in afternoon, we walked around the Rim Rock Trail at Red Canyon—great.

The road involved 10 switchbacks.

We stayed in Vernal, Utah, and talked to Dal and David. Dal is having prostate trouble.

Vernal is near the Colorado border—we will return to Utah later.

Saturday, September 17, 1994

We made a return visit to Dinosaur National Park—still mind-boggling.

The drive through Colorado has been beyond words. I have wanted for so long to see the yellow aspen and they have been very much in evidence as we came across to Steamboat Springs and then to Granby.

We stopped a little early and did a load of clothes.

Talked to Mike—his leg has been a bother but should be getting better. Totally immersed in starting school and inaugurating a new chancellor.

SUNDAY, SEPTEMBER 18, 1994

We spent today in the Rocky Mountains, which in addition to their size and presence, are splashed with yellow, gold, orange, etc. aspen groves. There aren't enough words to describe them (as I said before).

The driving was maximum mountain-driving—good roads but lots of ups, downs and curves.

We picnicked in a county park near Estes Park beside the Big Thompson River.

We avoided Denver, came around it to Red Rock Park, a very interesting formation.

Once on I-70 we came across to Silverthorne–Dillon at a good clip, including the Eisenhower Tunnel.

We were *extremely* lucky that we were not involved in a 50+-mile slow-down in the east-bound side of the interstate (returning from Vail concert or event—[later:] bike rally, we were told).

Talked to David—he and Debbie had heard the baby's heartbeat!![26]

MONDAY, SEPTEMBER 19, 1994

We headed west and drove through Glenwood Canyon—very impressive, steep and colorful. We drove up to the top of Grand Mesa, not quite the same without wildflowers, but the aspens continue amazing.

After a nice lunch on the way down at Mesa, we came around to Colorado National Monument Park—the canyon rim drive was as breathtaking as ever.

We drove to Moab, Utah, which was full of tourists. We had a large room in a house-keeping unit—shared bath, etc.—which turned out very well.

Talked to Louise who had foot surgery earlier in the day.

TUESDAY, SEPTEMBER 20, 1994

This was a day filled with "awesome" scenery. We visited Dead Horse

---

26. Jordan Belle Holoman was born the following March.

Point State Park plus Arches and Canyonland National Park. The variations in color, shape and erosion factors are endless and spectacular.

We picnicked among the chipmunks and ground squirrels. We continue to be extremely lucky with the weather. We can see heavy storms in other sections.

We checked in a little early at Green River. Talked to Chris and Dal, whose doctor's appointment is tomorrow.

WEDNESDAY, SEPTEMBER 21, 1994

We drove "backroads" and came to Capitol Reef National Park, including fruit growing area Fruita.

Continued driving in Dixie National Forest, picnicked in a park in Boulder, got to Bryce, and found everything full until we got to Panquitch! Talked to Chris.

THURSDAY, SEPTEMBER 22, 1994

This was a day of unsurpassed scenery—Bryce Canyon in the morning and Zion in the afternoon. It was especially interesting that you view Bryce primarily from the top and Zion from the bottom.

We picnicked at a park and had made a reservation (with luck!) at a very nice Best Western—Driftwood Lodge in Springdale. We had a great Mexican dinner.

Talked to Sandy, who is making progress, and Dick.

FRIDAY, SEPTEMBER 23, 1994

Once again we took less traveled roads and visited a small National Monument, Pipe Springs, which was a Mormon settlement which grew up around the springs which is still there.

Our scenery continues beautiful with colors and shapes et cetera that change continuously. The land is *so* barren.

We came to the Grand Canyon in the afternoon. While no one denies its size, grandeur, etc., we were "turned off" by the crowds and did not linger very long.

Once again we encountered problems with finding a place to stay and drove to Flagstaff. We stayed at the Americana Inn, where they charge for ice!!

Talked to Mike—all are fine. He is going to England at the end of next week for five days.

Saturday, September 24, 1994

We made a special return journey to Oak Creek Canyon and the old copper mining town of Jerome, still perched on the side of a mountain.

We also visited Walnut Canyon and Sunset Crater, all beautiful and scenic, including very old cliff dwellings.

We made the decision to alter our tentative plans by not going to the places in "undeveloped country."

Our experiences with finding motels have not been good.

We did not reach anyone by phone.

Sunday, September 25, 1994

We had a beautiful and interesting morning with our first visit to the Petrified Forest and Painted Desert parks. We "did" most of the places suggested and bought petrified souvenirs for David and ourselves.

We ran late and found no picnic spot so we ate a Mexican meal in a deserted hotel coffee shop in St. Johns.

We began driving route 191 through the Apache National Forest and discovered it is totally non-commercial and totally mountain driving. The views were very magnificent but it took twice as long as expected. We were amazed at a huge copper-mining operations near the end in Morenci (Phelps Dodge).

We stayed in Safford and left the number with David's answering machine. The weather is getting hot in the daytime.

Monday, September 26, 1994

This was the day we accomplished our goal—we arrived in Mexico this afternoon from Douglas, Arizona.

Our special side trip was to Chiricahua where the "stand-up rocks" are so spectacular. We had been there on an earlier trip.

We picnicked in the park and drove down to Mexico (Agua Prieta). It was not at all nice, and we turned around and came back without stopping.

On to Lordsburg, NM (ghost town!) for dinner (Mexican) and the night. Talked to Louise—OK. She had foot surgery.

Tuesday, September 27, 1994

We drove from Lordsburg into Texas. The scenery continues about the same—fewer mountains but still a lot of desert land. We checked out a Rock-Hound Park, but it wasn't for us.

El Paso is large and as complicated as most cities. We decided to stay at Fort Bliss and had a nice house as quarters.

We visited one historical area—missions from the 1600s.

Talked to Sandy—fine.

We went into Mexico again today, crossing from El Paso to Juarez. Again, it was crowded and uninviting and we came right back.

Wednesday, September 28, 1994

We left El Paso on I-10 and turned away to visit a mountain area of western Texas—the Davis range, named for Jefferson Davis, as was Fort Davis, which we visited. The fort had an interesting history during Civil War and post-war times and is continually being restored.

We saw the McDonald Observatory and stayed in Pecos, TX.

Kern called and talked to Laura about Dal's surgery today—he is in pain but doing OK. Also talked to David—all is well.

Thursday, September 29, 1994

We made tracks across Texas today, going on I-20 from Pecos to just outside Fort Worth, with a brief lunch stop. The scenery changed a lot. The most interesting was the oil country around Odessa—lots of "drinking ducks" and other equipment.

We planned to stay at Carswell Air Force Base but after a lot of wild-goose chasing learned that it had been de-activated and will start up soon as a Naval Air Station.

We then continued on I-30, which goes from Ft. Worth / Dallas to Little Rock, Ark. It goes from Fort Worth to Dallas at top speed usually, but we were in a slow-down. We stopped in the east side of Dallas for the night.

Talked to Chris—all OK.

Friday, September 30, 1994

We had the car serviced at Wal-Mart and continued across Texas and into Arkansas. The scenery became more familiar as the day wore on. We stopped for lunch at a very nice cafeteria—a good change.

We got to Hot Springs after riding around a couple of beautiful lakes—one with a nice lodge, etc. Hot Springs has become terribly over-built and "tacky." We walked around and went to the top of the tower.

Kern talked to Dal, who is better. He hopes to go home on Sunday.

I talked to Louise. Heather had an appendectomy and Rachel Harris has serious cancer.

We stayed in Hot Springs.

Saturday, October 1, 1994

After breakfast, we went to the Visitor's Center of Hot Springs National Park, which is in one of the old bath houses.

We drove across the state to Memphis, Tenn. We decided to visit Mud Island and the model of the lower Mississippi River. It was very interesting and enjoyable.

We then drove to Jackson, Tenn. for the night.

I talked to Sandy (and Mark) and they are doing fine, except Dick, who has a fever. Sandy is planning to go to Phoenix for P-W meeting, and Mark and Jeff plan to have dinner with us on Oct. 9th.

Sunday, October 2, 1994

We continued to cross Tennessee on I-40, i.e. truck alley. We stopped for lunch at Cracker Barrel in Crossland—good country dinner—and did a little shopping there.

We decided to go home by Gatlinburg and the Smokies and spent the night in Maryville, TN.

Monday, October 3, 1994

This was the last day of our trip.

After coming through the overwhelming commercialization of Pigeon Forge and Gatlinburg (and later Cherokee) we thoroughly enjoyed the Great Smokies. The fall color has started in the higher elevations and all was beautiful.

We rejoined I-40 and came across the state without incident, eating lunch in Morganton. We got home about 6:00 p.m. We drove 10,286 miles, were in 21 states, were gone 36 days (35 nights), had no severe weather and no car trouble. We saw license plates from all 50 states and most of the Canadian provinces.

CALIFORNIA

May 3–13, 1995
Kaye & Kern Holoman

Robert Arneson: "Yin and Yang," UC Davis

SOURCE: Diary 6 (1994–96). Blue leather album with gold tooling, roughly 5½ x 8½ inches. (Almost identical to brown album from 1992.) Inscribed on flyleaf:

Motor trip to the West
Aug. 29 – Oct. 3, 1994

California — Kern's Award
May 3–13, 1995

Méricourt
Aug. 17 – Sept. 7, 1995

Nova Scotia, etc.
May 14 – June 2, 1996

All four sections in Kaye's hand.

California for Kern's Award

May 3–13, 1995
Kaye & Kern Holoman

Kaye and Kern traveled to California for a gala banquet on Tuesday, May 9, 1995, where I was awarded the UC Davis Prize for teaching and research, at the time the largest such prize in the country.

Owing to its placement in blue diary after the France trip in August–September 1995, it is clear that Kaye retroactively added this account, looking at a page of notes on Best Western University Lodge, Davis, stationery, transcribed below. The diary entry stops on Sunday, May 7, 1995; the page of notes carries through Sunday, May 12, 1995.

Wednesday, May 3, 1995

Arr. San Francisco, rented car and drove to Davis. We had supper with Mike and Michael—Kate is in Ashland and Betty at a PTA meeting. We are staying here tonight.

Thursday, May 4, 1995

Drove to Lake Tahoe. Lots of snow! Staying at Big 6 Motel. Went to Nevada for supper, slots, etc. at Harvey's.

Friday, May 5, 1995

Sightseeing around Lake Tahoe—wintry and beautiful. Back to Nevada and Caesar's for dinner, etc.

Saturday, May 6, 1995

We took an interesting boat trip on the Lake. This is a popular wedding place—on shipboard, that is.

Drove to Davis and met Kate, Michael, and Betty at mall with Nordstrom's. We ate at an Italian buffet for lunch.

Sunday, May 7, 1995

This was the day of the performance of [blank] oratorio with Betty's choral group, soloists and orchestra. We had a quick supper at Lyons during the break between sections of the performance. It was in Sacramento.[27]

> *End of diary. The award banquet for DKH was on Tuesday, 9 May 1995. Other notes on trip, handwritten on Best Western University Lodge, Davis, stationery:*

Wed. [May 3, 1995]

Arr. San Fran.–came to Davis–Supper with Mike and Michael–Kate at Ashland–Betty at PTA–slept w/K&B

Thurs.

To Lake Tahoe–Big 6 Motel–to Nev. for supper, etc. at Harveys

Fri.

Tahoe–supper etc. Caesars

Sat.

Boat trip–to Davis–Univ. Lodge–Met Kate, Michael and Betty at Nordstrom's–ate at Ital. buffet

---

27. J. S. Bach's St. Matthew Passion, performed by the Sacramento Area Bach Festival, in which Betty participated for several years. There was a dinner break between the two halves of the work.

Sun.

Betty's oratorio–in Sac–supper at Lyons

Mon.

Met Mike for lunch (w/ new faculty member) at Chinese "buffet"–dinner at Hunan's w/ friends, whole family

Tues.

Banquet. Edna called re: Luna's death–called David, etc.

Wed.

Drove around lakes, etc. Berryessa, etc.–deli lunch–supper at Mike's w/ family, then to UCD for talk and chamber group concert–talked to Connie

Thurs.

Walked on campus taking pix of "eggs"–lunch in "bakery" by train station. Shopping for anniversary mementos for Michael and Kate — coins, etc. Supper w/ B, K, M, and Lauren–(Kern orch. prac.) at Chevy's near Davis–fun. Called Edna and David.

Fri.

Finished shopping and wrapping–Chinese lunch in town. Had champagne and gave gift plus presents for kids. Great dinner in Sac–Italian rest. [Il Fornaio—became one of Kern's favorites].

France

August 17 – September 7, 1995

Kaye & Kern Holoman

Le Vieux Logis, Méricourt, summer 1995

SOURCE: Diary 6 (1994–96). Blue leather album with gold tooling, roughly 5½ x 8½ inches. (Almost identical to brown album from 1992.) Inscribed on flyleaf:

> *Motor trip to the West*
> *Aug. 29 – Oct. 3, 1994*
>
> *California — Kern's Award*
> *May 3–13, 1995*
>
> *Méricourt*
> *Aug. 17 – Sept. 7, 1995*
>
> *Nova Scotia, etc.*
> *May 14 – June 2, 1996*

All four sections in Kaye's hand.

FRANCE

August 17 – September 7, 1995
Kaye & Kern Holoman

Kaye and Kern were anxious to visit our house in Méricourt, France, despite the fact that the remodeling had barely begun. Betty and Michael met them at the airport and introduced them to the place, then left them to their own devices for the rest of their three-week stay.

Thursday, August 17, 1995

Louise took us to the airport mid-morning for our flight to Newark on Continental. The first leg was uneventful, but the Newark to Paris part had been overbooked and we were late leaving. Our arrival was on time and Betty and Michael met us and helped us with our luggage, etc. (Kern and Kate have returned to Davis.) We came through city-type traffic for awhile, then on to Méricourt. Our arrival reinforced some of our impressions and added to our understanding of the whole project.

Kern and Betty are bringing utilities, appliances, etc. up to current standards while maintaining the old features of the residence and its setting in the hillside caves. They have had their separate and their collective patience tried by the local workmen—it is August annual holiday time, for instance, but with a "camping out" approach, progress is happening.

Our trip moved us from Thursday, Aug. 17 to Friday, Aug. 18 and we retired early to avoid as much jet-lag as possible.

(I was not at all comfortable in the airplane overnight—mostly my left side "pinched nerve" situation with no room to move at all. Hopefully this will change.)

Friday, August 18, 1995

Betty and Michael brought us to Méricourt and the house. The separation of the "bathtub" bath and the toilet is awkward but not earth-shattering. The house is asymmetrical and the various rooms are very distinctive. They have painted a lot and purchased new appliances but still need the plumber and others to come and install the new things they have bought. The setting is beautiful, both in terms of the town and of their street, etc.

We shopped a little and had supper at home before hitting the sack. I didn't sleep too well but feel sure I'll be doing better.

Saturday, August 19, 1995

Betty worked on the kitchen ceiling—masking the beams and painting. After lunch we went into Méricourt [Bonnières] and got some French currency. In the late afternoon Betty drove us around the area, particular the towns, etc. along the Seine. We had a lovely supper of barbecued meats, beside the river at a restaurant [La Mère Biquette] at the bottom of the hill which Méricourt and our house are located on. Mike and Kate called from Davis—all okay.

Sunday, August 20, 1995

After an easy early morning we went out on a multi-mission trip. Michael, Kern and I went sightseeing at chateau La Roche Guyon, which we and Michael had visited earlier, us with Mike—separate visits. In addition to its very early history, it served as Rommel's headquarters during World War II. It is now both a historic site and an arts center. The three of us took a fine boat trip on the river while Betty attended to matters. We had supper at Flunch and called it a great day.

Monday, August 21, 1995

This was the beginning of the end, so to speak. Betty and Michael went to Paris today before leaving for California tomorrow.

With a certain amount of cleaning and disposing, we left around noon to have lunch at "Q" burger (McDonalds [actually Quick] by any other name). It was a special promotion with balloons, etc.— fun.

We took Betty and Michael to Ibis at Orly and got them checked in. They did some sightseeing on their own and we got lost and drove through Paris—the Arc de Triomphe, the Eiffel Tower, etc. etc. until we got on the right road to Méricourt.

We shopped at Auchan (alias Wal-Mart, etc.) for groceries. Betty called about 9:00. She and Michael were in for the night after their sightseeing. We were having a nice al fresco supper on the terrace. (Note: We also spent time at Orly getting French money.)

It is very nice to be here alone. We really enjoy it.

Tuesday, August 22, 1995

This was our "explore and enjoy the Seine" day. This was my first time at driving the leased car and all went well—each driver has to experience the car's idiosyncrasies firsthand. Overall, driving is not stressful in France—lots of signs and traffic circles.

The Seine has many loops and curves and we stayed mainly on the western side. The white chalk outcroppings appear quite often. There is a wide variety of agriculture—a surprising amount of corn. We see lots of sunflower fields which are not attractive because they have gone to seed and are drying out.

Among the places we visited after driving by Giverny and heading north were Les Andelys—chapel, castle, lunch, etc.; Amfreville, where we watched the locks on the Seine in operation—this one operated by a horizontal sliding "door." There was a very long bridge-walkway across the river, locks, etc. and a hydro-electric facility.

We had supper at Flunch, located near Mantes-la-Jolie.

Wednesday, August 23, 1995

We spent the day driving and visiting another Seine loop. We had lunch at a facility on the Autoroute (Interstate) and made our way to the Abbey at Jumièges, a 16th-century ruin [i.e. restored in 1573] which we reached by a very small but typical ferry on the river.

We crossed back at Duclair on a busy, much larger ferry (big trucks, etc.). We drove back and "dined" on cereal and bananas.

Thursday, August 24, 1995

We started out on our most ambitious driving today to go to the English Channel coast. The overall scenery is of rolling hills with *lots* of agriculture and livestock. The wheat and hay are being baled in great quantities. There were more beautiful flowers than I can describe—particularly public plantings in gardens, boxes, designs, etc. Every color is used in masses—mixed together. Almost all were completely familiar impatiens, marigolds, ageratum, nicotania, petunias, etc.

We went first to Beauvais, site of the cathedral whose arch broke while it was being built to be the tallest arch—never rebuilt because of lack of funds. All the churches are in need of repair with not enough money.

We reached the coast in mid-afternoon at Dieppe, familiar from WW II. We visited an old chateau which overlooked the city and the beach. The Canadians made an unsuccessful attempt near here before D-day. It is August—the French vacation time—and we are seeing lots of beach, camping, etc. activities.

We drove along the coast to Fécamp, which is where Benedictine liqueur is made. Crowded and late so we didn't stop. We drove to Étretat, a popular beach resort town, casinos, etc. The beach is rock-covered!! We ate on the terrace of a club/restaurant with a chilly breeze blowing. Very French—entrées of paté and crudités, with steak and French fries as a main course. (Pierced rocks and hang gliders were special attractions.)

We drove to Le Havre. A big port city, joined the Autoroute and hurried home—about 11:30 p.m.!! Long but enjoyable day.

Friday, August 25, 1995

We set the alarm for 6:30 a.m. in order to call Kern and Betty at 9:30 p.m. California time. We wanted them to know about the leak from the bathroom into the study (which they were aware of) and that the electrician had not come. We also asked them to call David or Louise, etc. Mike told me how to get the boombox going — wonderful!

Actually, the electrician came early and his thumps woke me about

9:00 a.m. He installed the power to the stove and exhaust fan, plus some wall sockets and patio lights.

We left rather late for sightseeing since Kern went to the grocery store *before* we ate breakfast! We headed for St-Germain-en-Laye where we visited the chateau, now a museum of ancient archaeology. Not a super museum but we're glad we went. We had a bistro lunch nearby, then drove around and headed home. Traffic is always a consideration—this area is not far from Paris. We came back on different roads—but still had busy late afternoon traffic. Our light supper was "deli" lasagna and salad.

We really don't like driving in or around big cities!!

Saturday, August 26, 1995

After getting a few groceries, we stopped by Giverny, looked in the shops, etc. and decided to do a "real" visit on a weekday.

We went to Vernon where market day was in progress. We wanted to get postcards for everyone. We had French "croque Monsieur" for lunch at a sidewalk cafe. We drove north to Gisors, where there was a chateau and park up on a hill and a church which we saw inside—typical but not special.

We got "lost" several times on the way home and were delighted to have soup and salad for supper. We got all the cards written—19 in all—to be mailed ASAP.

Kern (and Betty) called—they were pleased at the thought that we had heated our croissants in the *oven!* This was Sunday night.

Sunday, August 27, 1995

We left to visit Pacy-sur-Eure with a nostalgic detour back to La Villeneuve on the way. We stopped for lunch in Pacy at a "crêperie" and had galettes—a crêpe with cheese, ham, etc.—and a dessert crêpe with chocolate and nuts. Lovely.

We drove along the Eure and its towns, including Anet, where we saw the very very large chateau of Diane de Poitiers. We had a fine Chinese dinner in Bonnières—The Mandarin.

(This is when Mike called.)

Monday, August 28, 1995

We gave this day over to keeping ourselves going! The confrontation was with the laundromat—the Lavage [the Lavorama]—in a location where everything else was "closed on Monday." To get the right coins for the washer and dryer (as explained to us by French customer) we (1) did a big grocery buy, (2) rode all over looking for banks, and (3) ate lunch(!) at Flunch. We managed it all and enjoyed various side trips before getting us, the groceries and clean clothes home. I explored the garden-terrace behind the house and was really impressed by what it had been and can be again.

P.S. We mailed all the cards.

Tuesday, August 29, 1995

Kern was a little "under the weather" this morning, so I took advantage of our delayed departure to wash my hair—thereby becoming involved in the great bathtub rescue!!

We went to Giverny after lunch at home. The flowers were plentiful but were enough past their prime to be disappointing. We saw *many* familiar flowers—summer garden favorites from our own and our childhood gardens. The day was overcast, and there were a few showers later. When we returned home, we took a walk down to the river where there were a good number of barges, etc. going through the lock. This area has a lot of riverside activity in sand, gravel, etc. loading.

We had a spaghetti supper at home and a quiet evening.

Wednesday, August 30, 1995

We spent the majority of the day in Paris. We had an early lunch at Q Burger (crowded with families) and drove to Porte Maillot, Paris, where we parked the car. We took the subway into "central Paris" and revisited many of the landmarks as we walked around. There is a renovation project underway at the Louvre and the cleaned buildings are quite beautiful. We took a sightseeing boat for a good hour's view of the areas along the Seine. We did further sightseeing on foot—Notre Dame, etc., took the subway to Étoile and walked to Porte Maillot. We ate at a sidewalk cafe—very pleasant—while waiting for the evening rush hour to subside, which is after 7:30 p.m. Although somewhat slow at construction sites, we got home without incident.

We were impressed by the large number of "gendarmes" in the city—especially around Notre Dame and other "tourist" points. Whether this reflects "bomb scares," we don't know.

Thursday, August 31, 1995

Today we accomplished one of Kern's desires for this trip—a return to Chartres, with time to do it right. For the first time, we had a really rainy day as we drove down, but about as soon as we arrived, the rain stopped and our sightseeing was great. We ate lunch at a typical bar/restaurant near the cathedral named The Alsatian and we had *choucroute garnie*, which we enjoyed. The cathedral is considered among the loveliest and best, and certainly the stained-glass windows are most impressive. We also took a sightseeing trolley that was the hit of the trip! Chartres is an old city with lots of history which is reflected in the "old city" buildings, etc.—all of which we would have missed had it not been for the train ride, with some English commentary.

The line of least resistance led us to Flunch for supper, which was disappointing.

P.S. We bought the second group of postcards in Paris, wrote and mailed them this morning.

Friday, September 1, 1995

We set the alarm again for a call to Mike and Betty, clearing up small details about leaving, no workman, etc.

Our sightseeing for the day was to follow along the Seine on roads we had not taken. The Seine is a remarkable river, both as a means of transportation and as a scenic asset.

We went to an African Animal Park—enjoyable—with animals in open areas, not pens so much. This is a "state park" type and not very sophisticated as parks go, but a nice break on the trip. We had supper at home—a delicious ham and mushroom tart from Auchan, which has an excellent deli section.

Auchan can only be experienced, not adequately described. It has all the features of Wal-Mart, Kroger's, Food Lion, ABC, etc.—plus electric appliances, etc. The one in the town near here is patronized by several foreign groups who live and work in the area—and the *whole* family goes shopping together.

Saturday, September 2, 1995

We chose the Forêt de Lyon for our destination today. It is very gratifying that these public forests exist since so much of the land—mile after mile—is cultivated.

We saw most of the sights in the Forest—St. Catherine's spring, the estates with deer and other animals, the churches, etc. and especially the town of Lyons-la-Forêt. The flowers were beautiful and the buildings—homes, etc.—very interesting. The square in the center of town has an interesting background for its carpentry work. We ate at a typical restaurant—quiche and salad, etc.

We drove back through familiar territory (daisy-petal-ing) and went to the Petite Marmite Restaurant in Bonnières for a fine French dinner.

Sunday, September 3, 1995

We got up a little early for an early start to Rouen. We enjoyed the scenery of this area once again as we went to the castle of Robert [le] Diable, legendary figure associated with William the Conqueror.

On into Rouen, which is a large shipping center. We had a full dinner at a restaurant at the [Vieux] Marché (the Old Market-place) and revisited the Joan of Arc church and other sites we had seen a couple of years ago with Mike. The Cathedral is very gray and not special.

Again the vistas on the drive home were beautiful.

We had supper at home and had a call from Mike checking on some film of his which we had located.

It rained spottedly today and has turned cooler.

Monday, September 4, 1995

This was a "low-key" day. It has continued to be cool with hit-or-miss rain. I checked the house for closing-up purposes and Kern trimmed the vines off the window areas. We had lunch here and then set out to go wandering through the countryside, beginning with La Villeneuve and other rural areas. It is hard to describe the hills of this area—they are not mountains and are widely cultivated. The rural vistas are beautiful.

We saw the river cruiser *Normandie* approaching the locks at Méricourt, so we hurried along to see it go thru. It is a very large, long white river cruiser—not very full. After the locks, we drove ahead to several places along the river and watched the boat go by—finally bidding it farewell at Bonnières.

Before we left, Kern checked in with the car-lease people with help from Mme. Mahaut on dialing the number.

We had supper at home—a spaghetti and salad menu.

Tuesday, September 5, 1995

We began getting the house ready to leave—the last things we will take care of tomorrow. We went to Pacy-[sur]-Eure to go back to the crêperie and again enjoyed the [galettes] and crêpes. We rode around the Eure River country on back roads—the "hills" are even more mountainous there, but still agricultural. We came home about 4:45 in time to call Kern (who was headed for school) to let him know all is well as we leave.

We returned to the Chinese restaurant for a last "local" dinner.

Wednesday, September 6, 1995

We spent the morning in final errands—me at the [Lavorama], washing the towels, sheets, etc., and Kern getting gas, etc. Kern closed the shutters fast. I finished up the disposal of food, etc. and we left for Paris about 2:30 p.m.

We stayed at Ibis hotel, very compact(!) room but convenient. After verifying our responsibilities with the car, we went to Paris where we saw the Luxembourg Gardens which were beautiful. This is the student area of Paris—the Latin Quarter—and we enjoyed being there. There were lots of police around—we assumed because of unrest about the French atomic testing in the South Pacific. We ate at a typical sidewalk restaurant and returned to Orly by the "scenic route," i.e. we took the wrong train and had to double back.

There was no problem with turning in the car. We got up early, had breakfast and checked in at Orly for the flight home.

The truth is that Betty and I had qualms about the parents coming to stay that long. The remodeling, as Kaye says, had fallen considerably behind, and it had been a stressful summer on that front. Moreover I needed to be back at UCD early, as dean, thus reversing our usual end-of-summer practice. It would not have surprised either of us had they bailed out of staying in the house and gone to hotels. But (as was the case in Australia / New Zealand) the number of things they accomplished in their two weeks alone on the hill in Méricourt—before the English-speaking neighbors had moved in—is impressive. And they both talked frequently afterward about their theory of "daisy-petaling" as it had been perfected from the Méricourt house. I think they remembered it fondly—or, if not (and it was pretty primitive at the time)—they never said so to us.

Nova Scotia

May 14 – June 2, 1996

Kaye & Kern Holoman

Peggy's Cove, Nova Scotia

Prince Edward Island

SOURCE: Diary 6 (1994–96). Blue leather album with gold tooling, roughly 5½ x 8½ inches. (Almost identical to brown album from 1992.) Inscribed on flyleaf:

>*Motor trip to the West*
>*Aug. 29 – Oct. 3, 1994*
>
>*California — Kern's Award*
>*May 3–13, 1995*
>
>*Méricourt*
>*Aug. 17 – Sept. 7, 1995*
>
>*Nova Scotia, etc.*
>*May 14 – June 2, 1996*

All four sections in Kaye's hand.

New England
and Nova Scotia

May 14 – June 2, 1996
Kaye & Kern Holoman

Tuesday, May 14, 1996

We left home about 9:30 a.m. and drove via US 1 to I-95 at Henderson. We had lunch at Cracker Barrel at Fredericksburg, joined the NJTP and came to Fort Dix for the night. Very nice suite, but a *quiet* post. Ate at Burger King. Realized I left my red raincoat at home!!

Wednesday, May 15, 1996

We drove from Fort Dix on the NJTP to the Garden State Parkway into New York State and I-95. We had one very long traffic standstill before we crossed the Tappan Zee Bridge and a couple of "slow-downs" as we came through Connecticut, Rhode Island, etc., probably because of springtime road repairs. It is noticeably earlier here as far as flowers, new leaves, etc. It has been mild and pleasant today.

We came to Hampton Beach, N.H. for the night—the Hampton House Inn on the oceanfront. We had lobster salad for supper—great.

(Called Debbie.)

Thursday, May 16, 1996

We drove along the coastline from New Hampshire into Maine. It was delightful. We went to the Nubble Lighthouse—very picturesque—and had a great croissant lobster sandwich lunch at the Lighthouse Restaurant. We continued up the coast. Stopped at Freeport to get me a new raincoat at L. L. Bean. On to the Hodges [Brunswick, ME]— lots of talk and a good dinner.

Friday, May 17, 1996

After a "talky" breakfast, we set out to go up the coast of Maine. It was raining so we did not picnic at Pemaquid, but went to Farnsworth [Art] Museum in [Rockland]. We had a delightful lunch on the water there. After getting back, resting, happy hour etc., we went to dinner at the Stowe House [Inn]. It was very nice.

Saturday, May 18, 1996

We had breakfast and then packed up. It has been a very nice visit. It's been good to see both Dan and Tempy. Dan seems to be beyond his treatment for prostate cancer and Tempy is her usual self. We learned more about Marian's family, etc.

We drove down I-95 to Hanscom Air Base [AFB], with a waterfront lunch in Newburyport, where they were filming Budweiser commercials.

It has been quite frustrating to work out the details of the car and getting into Boston. We've decided to leave the car here and take a cab to the Holiday Inn.

Sunday, May 19, 1996

We got the taxi with no trouble—he was very friendly and may be our ride back. We got to the Holiday Inn before check-in time, so we set out to see something of Boston. We found it nearly impossible to follow the map, but we enjoyed what we saw and ended up at the Quincy Market for a lovely brunch. We later checked in and at 7:00 p.m. met the tour group and our leader, Nancy Coolidge. She is very amiable and knowledgeable. I washed my hair—there was a dryer available!

Monday, May 20, 1996

We were up with bags out early—like a good tour does. We had to plan to be without our big bags since we will be on the "Scotia Prince."

Our tour on the "Duck" was very good—sprightly driver and new experience.

We (the group) went back to the Quincy Market for lunch—soup and lobster rolls. We then drove along the coast road including seeing the Bush estate at Kennebunkport. We had dinner *en route* to the ferry—I had very good scrod.

We boarded the ferry in the usual manner and spent some time on deck as we left, hit the slots briefly and turned in—small room, as usual, but *not* bunks.

Tuesday May 21, 1996

This was the Evangeline Trail day with history of the Acadian people and the various historical sites associated with it.

We disembarked at Yarmouth and went along the "water's edge" of St. Mary's Bay. Very rural—fishing is restricted now, and it has been economically difficult. We had Digby scallops for lunch. We visited the area of Port Royal, the earliest settlement, and Grand-Pré National Historic Site.

We continued our rural driving and came to Halifax for two nights. Our hotel—the Prince George—is very nice. We had a mediocre meal at a nearby tavern.

Wednesday, May 22, 1996

After hotel breakfast, we went through the beautiful municipal gardens—lots of tulips. On to the Citadel, the fortification on top of a very high bluff, which has been active for many years but has never been involved in action.

We then went on a great boat tour of Halifax. It has been a major harbor throughout its existence, with lots of military importance. We had never been aware of the Great Halifax Explosion of Dec. 6, 1917, when a munitions ship, the Mont Blanc, loaded with 8 million pounds of TNT collided with another ship and exploded. It was a terrible disaster. We also saw additional museum features about it at the Maritime Museum of the Atlantic.

We went to Peggy's Cove in the afternoon—very picturesque and the weather cleared while we were there.

We had dinner in the hotel—at Giorgio's [now Gio in the Prince George Hotel]—nice—and packed for the next two days.

Thursday, May 23, 1996

After a hotel breakfast, we left to go to Cape Breton. The countryside was varied—sometimes rocky, other times with grazing and a little farming. We had a nice lunch along the way and came to Baddeck, Cape Breton—a charming town and a lovely hotel-auberge—Gisele's Inn. A representative from the Alexander Graham Bell Museum came and gave us an excellent presentation on Bell and his family who had (and still have) a large summer home here.

After dinner, two young local girls played the bagpipes and danced Scottish dances for us. They are students at the only Gaelic college—St. Anne's—here. We sent 9 cards—the boys, Dal, Louise and Louis, Lynn, and Jay and Ken, also to Hodges.

Friday, May 24, 1996

This was a driving day to see Cape Breton's mountains on the Cabot Trail. There isn't much population in any rural area. The weather early was foggy and rainy but we had some interesting stops.

At a local gift shop, they demonstrated an especially good rug-hooking craft that they specialize in here.

We got a wildflower piece and a couple of other souvenirs. We then went a short distance to a museum featuring the work of Elizabeth Lefort, who has created amazing hooked tapestries—portraits and large specialty pieces—all completely new to us.

We entered the Cape Breton Highlands National Park and enjoyed the mountain scenery even though it was foggy and raining at times. We had a picnic lunch under shelters in the rain—everybody was good humored about it.

When we had crossed to the eastern side of the park, it cleared and made it even nicer. The mountain/ocean views were spectacular.

We had a delicious salmon dinner at the hotel.

Saturday, May 25, 1996

We drove from Baddeck to the ferry (it snowed!!) at Pictou / Caribou by way of a rest stop and lunch stop where I had fish and chips and Kern had scallops.

The ferry took a little over an hour to go to Prince Edward Island—a remote, beautiful island which grows potatoes mostly.

Our hotel is an "old-fashion" one but nicely updated. It is in Charlottetown, the capital, a moderate size city. There were two weddings going on here.

We walked around a bit, visited the "Anne of Green Gables Store," got some cards, etc. Our dinner was a lobster supper at a facility in a nearby town. It was great—lots of steamed mussels in addition to the whole lobster, fixin's and dessert.

[Editorial at the halfway point: the tour group is surprisingly congenial. Many types but all older, educated, etc.

Our director is Nancy Coolidge, smart, pleasant—fun.

The tour has been well planned to present the history, ethnic characteristics, special interests of each area. Items mentioned in the brochure are very special. Our food has been excellent.

We have one "kook"—a lady writer, but the bridge-players love her!]

Sunday, May 26, 1996

We had a local guide to show us around Prince Edward Island. She pointed out historical and other points of interest on the way to several Anne of Green Gables sites.

We visited a farm home belonging to the family devoted to Anne of Green Gables. At the farm we had a carriage ride and tea.

The other museum was the Green Gables House. We also took a walk on the grounds—all this is a State Park in Cavendish.

Our guide took us down to the waterfront and explained "lobstering."

We returned to Charlottetown for a late lunch (Off Broadway Cafe)—free time—wrote cards, etc.

Monday, May 27, 1996

We took a ferry from PEI to New Brunswick. A bridge is being constructed to replace the ferry in a year or so.

We went to Saint John to see the film and the Reversing Falls. We had large ice cream cones at "break time" and lobster rolls at the city market.

We went on to St. Andrews for our stay at the Algonquin—an old "elegant"-type Canadian Pacific hotel.

We walked into town for dinner—we ended up at a "tavern"—Pickled Herring.

The hotel was full of a "client's meeting"—a little messy.

Tuesday, May 28, 1996

This is a quote "free day" at the Algonquin—we went into town with Nancy and had ice cream on a deck overlooking the waterfront. The wharf had a bad fire a year or so ago. Kern checked in the local library re: Roosevelt and Churchill's meeting.

We went to the local Aquarium in the afternoon—small but interesting, especially a week-old seal, isolated with its parents.

We had dinner at the hotel, "with reservations."

Wednesday, May 29, 1996

We drove into the U.S. and to Campobello, the Roosevelt home. Very impressive "cottage" and a nice drive.

After a lunch stop (Helen's) we drove to Mt. Desert and Acadia National Park. The weather was mixed—not much sun—but the views were great.

We stayed at a motel that was at the top of the bluff—very nice—the Atlantic Eyrie.

We went into Bar Harbor for dinner and had a real hands-on lobster meal at Duffy's Quarterdeck. This is our last *real* tour day.

(Peggy Cochran fell—not serious—pesky.)

Tuesday, May 30, 1996

Back to Boston via L. L. Bean. Most notable were the blueberry fields, both current and dormant/burned. These are low-bush type blueberries.

We went to Bean and I found out how to adjust my green raincoat. We got a tea towel there and a blueberry-decorated pitcher at a gift shop—both for David and Debbie. I had already gotten *Blueberries for Sal.*

We ate at an old inn-type place, Jameson Tavern, and had a lovely lunch—very atmospheric. Then on to Boston—city traffic, etc. We had the "love-feast" reception at the Hilton and dessert and coffee in lieu of dinner.

Everyone was in good spirits and agreed that it had been well-planned and executed.

Friday, May 31, 1996

After breakfast, mostly with tour friends, we got a cab to Hanscom, picked up the car without incident, started home. We chose to take I-90 West to avoid the east coast cities and came as far west as Albany before turning south. We stayed near Wilkes-Barre.

Saturday, June 1, 1996

We continued home especially on Rts. 17 and 15 to Fredericksburg, etc. We stayed in Emporia (again)—Holiday Inn—having taken I-295 around Richmond and Petersburg.

Sunday, June 2, 1996

We got back home about 12:30 p.m.—a little overgrown as is usually the case—but everything in good order.

David, Debbie and Jordan came over for a barbecue sandwich supper, so we are almost back to normal.

We feel that this was a very special trip—well planned and well directed. The area (like New Zealand) is underpopulated, and our focus was on the people who had originally settled in the various areas and on the scenery. We are really looking forward to getting our various pictures back.

Asian-Alaskan Cruise

April 9–29, 1997

Kaye & Kern Holoman

SOURCE: Diary 5 (1992, 1994, 1997). Brown leather album with gold tooling, roughly 5½ x 8½ inches. (Almost identical to blue album from 1994.) Entirely in Kaye's hand. Inscribed on flyleaf:

Travels — Oct. 18 – Dec. 1, 1992
[added:] *June 17 – July 1, 1994*
Katherine H. Holoman

Begun as the Australia diary, continues with Scotland (1994) and Asia (1997). All three sections in Kaye's hand.

ASIAN-ALASKAN CRUISE

APRIL 9–29, 1997

KAYE & KERN HOLOMAN

TUESDAY, APRIL 8, 1997
PRE-TRIP

Coming home from dinner at David and Debbie's, I turned my right foot in the driveway area and fell.

After an interminable wait at the Emergency Room of Raleigh Community Hospital, X-rays showed that I had broken the right-hand side of the metatarsal bone on my right foot. I was given a "boot-cast" (shoe) and a 3-legged walker. It was after 1:00 a.m. before I got home.

WEDNESDAY, APRIL 9, 1997

We left on Northwest Airlines for Detroit. David drove our wagon to RDU. We changed in Detroit to a 747 for Osaka, Japan. 13½-hour flight—good service but a *long* flight. We are grateful that neither the broken foot nor our arthritic knees gave us much trouble, but we were very glad to arrive back on the ground. Customs, etc. went medium well, and we were taken by bus to the very nice Nankai South Tower Hotel, welcomed and checked in. We are now in the hands of Princess Cruise Lines. Since we were exhausted (the flight was quite long) we fell into bed, ready to start out bright and early.

Thursday, April 10, 1997

adjust for IDL [International Date Line]

Friday, April 11, 1997

Our morning was free and we went walking around the area in Osaka where we were. This included a big—and very nice—shopping complex sharing the building with the hotel. We also had a stroll around the streets near the hotel. We stopped for coffee at a neighborhood small "bar," ordered coffee and discovered that we got buttered toast and a hard-boiled egg each! We realized that this is standard in these parts.

We also turned our bags over and checked in for the early evening departure and had a nice "tea room" lunch near the hotel.

The "Sky Princess" is very nice. Although we will have to do some exploring, it seems well equipped and up-to-date. Our room is large—formerly with bunks over the 2 beds—with plenty of space for personal stuff.

The passengers are very much like we are—older and a little limited physically. There are several wheelchairs and lots of canes, etc. It makes for a good level of tolerance.

We sailed at 6:00 p.m. for Hiroshima.

In both Osaka and Hiroshima there were welcoming ceremonies for the ship.

Saturday, April 12, 1997
Hiroshima

We have met our Grand Circle personnel—Bruce and Greg—and they are experienced and nice young men.

The cruise into Hiroshima Bay was just beautiful—the mountainous islands were all around. We learned about oyster beds—artificial floating wooden platforms throughout the harbor area for cultivating food oysters—a popular dish here, we were told.

After some time getting loose ends (tickets, etc.) tied up, we had an early lunch at the buffet around the pool (no water yet) and departed on our shore tour of Hiroshima, which we had chosen—a ferry ride to the island, Miyajima, which has an outstanding historical shrine, Itsukushima and Torii gate. We missed seeing them surrounded by water as they are usually photographed—it was low tide!—but we did see many of the buildings—temples, etc. that make up the complex.

It is interesting to us to find how difficult it is to "get into" the variations of history and religion that we have not grown up with. This is the weekend, and everything is crowded—the roads, the shrine park which was full of families, etc. We drove by the (Atomic) Peace Memorial Park as we returned to the ship but saw very little of it.

Our guide was an attractive young Japanese woman who had prepared origami birds, a song sheet, etc. for us.

The Captain's Welcome Party and dinner were tonight—lots of dressed up people. With late dinner (plus our age and infirmities) we can't make it to late show.

Sunday, April 13, 1997

We arrived in Pusan, Korea [now Busan, second largest city in South Korea] around noon, which gave us a good opportunity to watch the shipping/docking activity. Like our other two ports, the harbor area is busy but not beautiful. There are amazing high-rise buildings visible up the mountainsides. Lots of forsythia and other flowers, although the cherry blossoms so far in the trip have been past their prime.

Our destination was a drive through the country to a Buddhist temple: Tongdosa, the largest in Korea.

Here as in Hiroshima, the park was *very* crowded with families. Our buses were allowed to go to the closest entrance so that the walk was not bad. There were many artworks, etc. to see.

On our return to the city, we went to the International Market, which was unbelievable—it was so crowded. It is in the streets between several rows of business buildings and *everything* was being offered for sale—the Koreans are known for making "knock-offs" of good American products.

We found the Korean countryside shabby and sub-standard.

We watched our departure before our late dinner.

Sunday morning we went to the announced church service but there had been a mix-up and there wasn't a minister. A man stepped forward and did a nice job in leading us informally in worship.

Monday, April 14, 1997

This was a cruise day between Pusan and Vladivostok. We enjoyed various activities on board—mostly relaxing.

Grand Circle had a cocktail party before dinner—it is a large group, at least 120. Between this and our late dinner we went to see the movie *Emma*. Mixed reactions.

Thursday, April 15, 1997

This was the day we visited Russia for the first time—that makes three new countries for us. From the start, there was a lot of evidence of government "rules and regulations." Our passports, which stay on file in the Purser's office, had to be returned to us so we could be identified when going on tour, etc. off the ship—then returned to Purser's staff. Slow but orderly.

The port of call is Vladivostok, Siberia, Russia. It was a closed port until 1992, largely because it has long been the home port of the Russian Pacific Fleet.

It is large and crowded—trolleys, trucks, cars, people, etc. on very basic streets and roads. The overall impression is one of shabbiness and dirty streets, etc. The people are dressed in dark, "no-colors," black, gray, etc. (There may have been a "street cleaners" strike we heard.)

We went on a city tour guided by a woman who had been an exchange student in California for her senior year in high school. She spoke English fluently.

We started late, thanks in part to the police activity, but it was also difficult to make time in traffic and we continued to fall behind. What we saw was interesting. This was and is the eastern terminus of the Trans-Siberian Railway, the world's longest railroad, and the station is architecturally important (17th century [?])—cornerstone laid by the last czar Nicholas II.

We saw the monument to three whales, a joint effort by Russian and American vessels to rescue three whales from the ice in 1988; government buildings, an art museum, oceanarium, etc. etc.

Unfortunately, our guide would not cut the tour short even though we were well over an hour late and it was past lunchtime—therefore we missed our afternoon harbor tour. This did give us an opportunity to see the Russian folkloric show in the Show Lounge, and it was very good. We move our watches back-and-forth daily!!

Wednesday, April 16, 1997

This is a day at sea between Russia and Japan. We have had spectacular weather and were able to sit outside. We did not do much out of the ordinary but did enjoy relaxing, playing a quiz game etc.

Thursday, April 17, 1997

We came back to Japan, to the largest and northernmost of the Japanese islands, Hokkaido. It's mountainous and very beautiful. There are many volcanoes on the island—some were smoking from their tops and sides.

We went on a land tour to Lake Toya, a national park and vacation area about an hour from the ship. It is a lake in the crater (caldera) of a volcano. The island's mountains were truly beautiful with typical peaks covered with snow and quite blue.

The principal attraction was Mount Usu, which erupted in 1978 and which has a cable car to the upper area. Many beautiful views. Also of great interest was Mount Showa (Showa Shinzan), Japan's newest volcano. It built up from within a farmer's potato field. It grew 8 inches each day for seven months and finally erupted to form its peak at 1,312 feet. There are many different colors of soil visible. This was in 1945 and there is a lot of steam coming out all the time.

We returned to the ship for lunch and a relaxing afternoon. Kern is enjoying the jacuzzi most afternoons.

We sailed at 6:00 p.m.

Friday and Saturday, April 18 and 19, 1997

These have been "days at sea." It's a leisurely time with lectures by an excellent Alaska specialist on various aspects of viewing Alaskan features such as whales, Northern Lights, etc. We saw "First Wives Club" and did some quiz contests—our team won once today. There has been a little more rolling and some uneasiness, but nothing debilitating.

Sunday and Monday, April 20 and 21, 1997

There will be two April 21st's.

These have been two more leisurely "at sea" days. It is somewhat colder and has been overcast, but no "rough weather."

Brett Nixon, the naturalist, gave talks on "Orca, the Killer Whale" and "Eagles and Puffins." He is very enthusiastic and the audiences like him a lot.

The shows in the Show Lounge are mixed—one especially good one was "USA Music," with excellent costuming as well as singing and dancing by the troupe on board.

We have had our USA passports returned.

~~Tuesday~~ Monday, April 21, 1997 (second day)

Moving across time zones and the International Date Line can be confusing and we just "do as we are told." We put our watches forward one hour each midnight—which robs us of an hour's sleep, and today is the second April 21, which puts us right with the IDL—oh, well.

Today has been like the previous "at sea" days—unstructured and restful. The lounge at the very front of the ship—the Horizon Lounge —is our favorite for reading and snoozing.

~~Wednesday~~ Tuesday, April 22, 1997

I told you it was confusing!

We arrived in Dutch Harbor in the Aleutian Islands about 7:00 am. This area was important in World War II with Japanese attacks on US bases. We docked at the SeaTrain dock.

Our visit to downtown took all the available busses so we waited a bit and all went well. We saw some local sites on the way to downtown. Walking around we visited a very basic Alaskan town, Unalaska—maybe like the Gold Rush days—small café, stores, gift shop, etc. We walked over to an old Orthodox Russian church—very pretty but closed for renovations. Dutch Harbor and Alaska are connected by "the bridge to the other side." Unalaska has a population of about 8,000 and its main industry [is] fish processing.

Wednesday, April 23, 1997

This is a cruise day toward the more familiar areas of Alaska.

Thursday, April 24, 1997

It was raining as we left the ship for our visit into Seward, which we did on our own in the morning and on a tour in the afternoon. There was a drugstore where we were glad to get a couple of things—plus lots of gift shops, etc. The town was just coming out of winter and was somewhat shabby.

In the afternoon, we were in a van (crowded) to go to Exit Glacier. We could not go up the glacier as planned because the road was closed, but did get out and view it. To make up for this, our guide took us on a more extended ride around town with some good views across Resurrection Bay. We saw the orphanage where Benny Benson grew up—he won the design contest for the flag of the *state* of Alaska.

Friday, April 25 – Saturday, April 26, 1997

This was our day to visit College Fjord and Glacier Bay. Both places are valued for the tremendous glaciers on all sides. College Fjord has them named for both men's and women's "Ivy League-type" schools.

There are so many that it isn't necessary to watch constantly, but it is an area distinctive to Alaska and very impressive.

We understand that we are the first cruise ship to arrive in the area this year and that it may possibly be the earliest cruise ship arrival ever!

Saturday, April 26, 1997, cont'd.

The naturalist aboard, Brent Nixon, was joined by National Park Service rangers so that we had a good running commentary on the natural "wonders" of the region. There have been some sightings of "wildlife"—Kern saw a whale, but overall, we seem to be a little early for the large groups of marine life, etc. who summer here. There is no dearth of bald eagles.

Sunday, April 27, 1997

We were late arriving in Ketchikan, largely due to the very icy—pieces of ice—water in Glacier Bay.

The tour busses were waiting for us. Princess has a standing contract here—and we went on a "town and totem pole park" tour with a very perky and knowledgeable young woman as our driver/guide. She took us through half of the town on the way to the park and the remainder as we returned. The totem pole area was woodsy and natural—we saw immense yellow skunk cabbages everywhere. There was a reconstruction of a "clan house" and lots of types of totem poles. They were genealogical "door Posts" and were never worshipped—in spite of the Christian missionaries to the contrary.

> *The cruise concluded on April 29, 1997; there is no summary page as for other journeys. This journal is the only one of their travel diaries that suggests much ambivalence toward places and personnel, and I remember my father giving an overall negative impression by telephone shortly thereafter. Another reason became clear immediately: my mother was very ill, and she died a little over three weeks after getting back to Raleigh: on May 23, 1997. In 2015 David told me "the minute I saw them at the airport, I knew something was wrong."*

The American West

May 5–21, 2001
Kern Holoman & Jackie Harper

SOURCE: Diary 7 (2001). Spiral-bound light-colored cardboard with cover illustration of three brown bears, roughly 5 x 7 inches. In Kern's hand, except for flyleaf inscription in hand of Jackie Harper:

> *Monday, May 7, '01*
> *To Kern:*
> *To record his*
> *memoirs and*
> *impressions of the*
> *trip through the*
> *National Parks*
> *—JH*

Our Grand Circle Tour of the National Parks of the West

May 5–21, 2001

Kern Holoman & Jackie Harper

In March 1998, about a year from Kaye Holoman's death, Kern let it be known that he was "keeping company" with Jackie Harper, a relationship that lasted until her death in May, 2014. Jackie was the essence of charm and intelligence, though her politics lay decidedly to the left of Kern's. Her house was full of things she had collected over a lifetime of wandering the world. Jackie and Kern became steady travel companions, generally seeking organized tours to destinations they had not visited with their deceased spouses. She insisted on, and I suspect paid for, first-class cruise accommodations.

Saturday, May 5, 2001 – Day 1

Departed RDU at 8:20 a.m. [Jackie's daughter] Susan drove us to the airport. We had seats at the very back of the plane. No window, but a vacant seat between.

Minneapolis airport, our first stop, was cold and rainy. Departed at 1:20, arrived at Rapid City [South Dakota] about 3:00 p.m. Also cold and rainy.

Stayed at Radisson Hotel. Nice room with two double beds. Early supper at Murphy's Sports Bar and Grill. Hamburger and salad. Lots of "pub" atmosphere. OK.

Orientation meeting at hotel at 6:30. 41 fellow tourists in our group. Mostly older married couples. Our Tour Director is Gladys Sifter, about 55 years old. Lots of enthusiasm and energy. Very knowledgeable.

Entertainment was a talk, performance and dance by a Native American. Interesting. Docents served us punch, cheese, crackers.

Sunday, May 6, 2001 – Day 2

Departed hotel by bus at 8:30. Our driver is Dick [Sloniker]. Attentive and competent. Weather was chilly but warmed up during the day.

We drove through deserted, rugged Black Hills country to Crazy Horse Memorial project. Tremendously impressive! Great Visitors Center, remarkable progress on creation of stone statue to American Indians.

Drive to Mt. Rushmore. Although the familiar presidential faces were large, they seemed small compared to the visionary Crazy Horse. We walked the Presidential Trail, about .6 mile. Easy descending, but strenuous uphill return. Jackie bought a National Park Passport and had her first stamp put on it.

Drove to nearby Keystone, very touristy village, much like Cherokee, N.C. Had lunch at "Ruby's" [Ruby House], a replica of a 19th-century brothel. Good atmosphere. Lots of pictures on wall, including some provocative nudes.

Drove back to Rapid City. Visited "Journey Museum," a study of the area from the world's beginning until end of 19th century. Mildly interesting. Walked back to hotel, crossing Rapid Creek.

In the evening we drove to the home of hosts Howard and Audrey Shaff. After nice hors d'oeuvres we had a fine dinner built around buffalo steak. Surprisingly good. Nice experience.

In the dark a beautiful full moon came up. Drove back through Keystone to Mt. Rushmore again. Very little going on there, except that presidential faces were illuminated. Very lovely.

Overnight at Radisson Hotel again.

A *very* good day.

Monday, May 7, 2001 – Day 3

Weather was surprisingly warm and beautiful. Departed Rapid City, drove through Black Hills and surrounding areas to Devil's Monument,

Wyoming. Impressive basalt outcropping several hundred feet high. Several climbers were making the ascent. Kern took 1.3 mile walk around the tower. Quite strenuous.

Stopped at a prairie dog village at entrance to the park.

Lunch in downtown Gillette, WY. Mexican lunch at Las Margaritas. Not bad.

Long drive in the afternoon in sight of beautiful, snow-capped Big Horn Mountains. Drove through town of Big Horn to Bradford Brinton Memorial, reproduction of a ranch, furnishings and lifestyle of a progressive Western family. Numerous pictures and gifts from prominent people. Disappointing.

Overnight at Holiday Inn in downtown Sheridan, WY. Typically nice motel room.

Tuesday, May 8, 2001 – Day 4

Left Sheridan via old Cody Hotel, which Bill Cody bought and lived in for some years.

Beautiful, clear, sunny day.

Drove to site of Battle of Little Big Horn where Custer's 7th Cavalry was annihilated. Interesting presentation with diorama, paintings, descriptive map and walking to main monument.

Meadowlarks sang beautifully.

Lunch in downtown Billings, Montana. At Perkins.

In afternoon drove to Cody, WY. Fine visit to Buffalo Bill Museum. Really good sculpture gardens, very comprehensive presentation of the life and times of the Plains Indians, a section devoted to the life of Buffalo Bill Cody and a *truly outstanding* gallery of Western art including Frederick Remington, Chuck Russell, and many others.

Overnight at Holiday Inn. Chuckwagon-type dinner at a nearby building with live guitarist entertainment. Very pleasant. Evening walk on Main Street to Hotel Irma, started by Bill Cody.

Wednesday, May 9, 2001 – Day 5

Left Cody and rode to Yellowstone via beautiful mountain valley. Stopped to view interesting rock formations.

Entered Yellowstone at East entrance. Fishing Bridge at Yellowstone

Lake. Lots of snow on ground. Had picnic lunch at Canyon Village. Good cappuccino.

We are disappointed that so many facilities—here and elsewhere—have not yet opened because of early season.

Drove to Old Faithful area via Norris, Madison, and Firehole River. Saw many animals, mostly buffalo and elk.

Did Yellowstone Falls and Grand Canyon before lunch. Impressive waterfalls, gorgeous colors.

Stopped to see Gibbon Falls. Walked around geyser, mud pit, fumaroles, etc. Very interesting.

Registered for the night at Old Faithful Snow Lodge. New, well decorated, beautiful cut-out light fixtures with animals.

Went to see Old Faithful erupt. It finally did after a long wait. It was its usual impressive self. Wind came up and made it too cold to walk among other geysers.

Dinner at hotel was OK. Long wait, huge portions. Pricey.

Thursday, May 10, 2001 – Day 6

Left Old Faithful area at 8 a.m. Weather quite chilly, but warmed up beautifully during the day.

The South exit to Yellowstone was closed because of snow, so we left by the West exit and proceeded to Jackson on the *west* side of the Teton Mountains.

It was a driving day and an uneventful one. Drove through West Jefferson. Had coffee break at a general store in Ashton.

Arrived old Jackson about 1:30. Stayed at Jackson Lodge, a Best Western motel. Very nice, rustic decor with lots of carved bears on every hand.

Ate lunch in downtown Jackson at a drug store. Did a load of laundry at a nearby laundromat.

Rode a free shuttle bus around the town.

Ate at a Chinese restaurant. OK. Back to the motel for a quiet evening.

Friday, May 11, 2001 – Dallas Birthday! – Day 7

A good day. Had a comprehensive visit to Grand Teton National Park in all its beauty. Weather was warm, sunny and beautiful.

The parks are simply magnificent. There is no better word. We made numerous picture stops and viewing stops: Mt. Moran, Jackson Lake, Transfigured Chapel, Jenny Lake and, of course, the great Teton peaks themselves, still mantled in snow.

Once again, we are disappointed that because the season is early, so many things are not available or not yet open. No Snake River raft trip.

Returned to Jackson. Lunch at the Bunnery. In the afternoon visited the very good Visitors Center.

Jackie remained in town while I returned to the motel.

Nice dinner at Gun Barrel Restaurant. Lots of Western atmosphere. We love the bear décor of our motel.

SATURDAY, MAY 12, 2001 – DAY 8

Left Jackson at 8:00. Really liked our motel: Best Western Jackson Hole, copiously decorated with bears.

Weather warm and beautiful. Got hot outside by the end of the day.

Day was the long drive to Salt Lake City. Stops at a very touristy cheese factory, recreation facility, and buffet lunch at Logan. All were OK, but all had inadequate toilet facilities.

Arrived at Salt Lake City after a stop at "Saltair," rebuilt recreation facility on the lake. *Very* grungy and unpleasant.

Our hotel in SLC is Embassy Suites. Best commercial accommodation I have encountered. Welcome reception with *free* breakfast.

Took free tram to Temple area. Saw film *Legacy*. Very professional and moving.

Everything in the area is very pious, moving, heavily Mormon religious atmosphere. Beautiful plantings and gardens.

After the film we went to the Crossroads Mall and food court. Dined on Greek food.

Returned to hotel by free tram.

SUNDAY, MAY 13, 2001 – MOTHER'S DAY – DAY 9

A *very* good day. Weather overcast, pleasantly warm.

Our group went early to Temple Square. Lots of volunteer "sisters" and ushers to greet us and make us welcome.

Short guided tour of Temple Square. Then a *marvelous* performance by the Mormon Tabernacle Choir. Mother's Day program. Opened with "For the Beauty of the Earth" arranged by John Rutter. Included "A Mother's Eyes Reflect the Love of Heaven," Irving Berlin "Always," and closed with "Battle Hymn of the Republic" with audience participation. We have now sung with the Mormon Tabernacle Choir.

After the concert our bus took us on a city tour of Salt Lake City: Capitol building, University campus and such. Very pretty city.

Returned to hotel for a snack lunch.

After lunch we returned to Temple Square while our group toured the site of the upcoming (2002) Olympic Games.

We strolled along to look at the many statues and commemorative plaques. The Mormons are big on commemorating.

At 2:00 p.m. we returned to the Tabernacle for an organ recital. This one was marvelous, too. Included Bach's "Now Thank We All Our God," Debussy's "Clair de Lune," "Eternal Father Strong to Save," and closed with the Widor "Toccata."

Then we went to the Mormon History Museum for a comprehensive self-guided tour of the history of Mormonism, from the original vision of Joseph Smith through the founding and establishment of "Zion," "Deseret," i.e. Salt Lake City.

Returned by tram to hotel.

Fine dinner at Plum Restaurant in the hotel. Best yet. I had lamb chops, Jackie had filet mignon.

Jackie received Mother's Day messages from Gerry and from Judy, which she appreciated.

The most important Mormon building is the Temple with the statue of the angel Moroni of the top. Only the public can't enter it. It is only open to members of the Church of Jesus Christ of the Latter-Day Saints, in good standing. This includes (among many other requirements) you must be a tither.

MONDAY, MAY 14, 2001 – DAY 10

Left our *excellent* Embassy Suites hotel at 8:00. The morning drive through Western Utah (via I-15) was nothing. Lots of not very inspiring scenery. Morning coffee / rest stop at a general store type place.

Choice of lunch at a commercial crossroad. We ate at Arby's.

In the afternoon we drove to Bryce Canyon. As always incredibly beautiful. Saw a short film at the Visitors Center.

Had picture visit stop at Bryce Point and Inspiration Point. I took the half-mile walk to Sunset Point.

Stayed overnight at Bryce Canyon Lodge. Rustic, old, but very nice. We have a balcony to our room. Were visited by Steller's Jays and ground squirrels.

Big dinner at park restaurant. I had prime rib. Jackie had trout. Portions were *far* too large.

Addressed post cards in evening.

TUESDAY, MAY 15, 2001 – DAY 11

Travelled from Bryce Canyon to Pace, Ariz. by way of Grand Canyon, north rim.

We enjoyed Bryce Lodge. Rustic but nice. Weather was cool in the morning, but warmed up a lot in the day.

Drive to Grand Canyon was long, but very scenic. The north rim was beautiful and not at all crowded. Lunch at lodge dining room overlooking the canyon. Soup and burgers. Good.

After lunch I walked to Bright Angel Point. Very strenuous, but worth it for the spectacular scenery.

Had almost three hours at Grand Canyon.

In the afternoon had several beautiful picture stops including Vermillion Cliffs, cliff dwellers village, Lees Ferry Bridge across the Colorado, and Glen Canyon Dam.

Checked into Wahweap Lodge, a big luxury operation.

Long day.

Late snack dinner of pizza.

WEDNESDAY, MAY 16, 2001 – DAY 12

Weather: hot, sunny and dry.

This Wahweap Lodge is a really nice resort complex.

Lovely buffet breakfast in a fine dining room overlooking the lake. (Lake Powell named after John Wesley Powell, who explored Colorado River.)

Posed for group picture.

Took a 2½-hour boat ride on the lake. Breathtaking beauty in a colorful, barren land.

Lunch at hotel bar and lounge.

Took a guided tour of Glen Canyon Dam. Huge. Marvelous construction. Vision to help tame Colorado River.

Went into town of Pace for shopping.

Visited John Wesley Powell Memorial Museum. Disappointing. Not important.

Dinner at hotel dining room. Nice and romantic.

Thursday, May 17, 2001 – Day 13

Left Wahweap resort at 8:00 after a good buffet breakfast.

Set off for Durango, Col.

Indian woman (Crystal Waters) and her daughter (Little Flower) selling Indian jewelry. Most of our women bought some. I was disenchanted and was glad when it was over.

About lunch time we entered Monument Valley and were deeply impressed with its *magnificent* buttes of bizarre and imaginative shades.

Lunch was Navajo tacos at Goulding's [Lodge], Utah. Different experience in dining room with Indian decoration.

After lunch we drove around Monument Valley and continued our wonder. It is the location of *many* Hollywood western movies.

We drove on to Durango with a rest stop in Cortez.

Our hotel tonight is the Doubletree Inn, another really nice accommodation. Our room has a balcony overlooking the rushing Animas River.

Dinner tonight was very nice. Special prices to our group at the hotel dining room.

Friday, May 18, 2001 – Day 14

Doubletree Inn is a really nice motel and convention center. Elegantly appointed. Our room is nice. We had two breakfasts and two dinners in their dining room.

After breakfast we motored to Mesa Verde for an all-morning visit to the ancient pit houses and cliff dwellings of the ancient Pueblo peoples. Fascinating!

Scenery magnificent.

Lunch at Far View Lodge in the park. Chicken, rice, salad.

Arrived back in Durango about 3:30.

Jackie went shopping.

I took the one-hour "raft" trip down the Animas River. (It was really a large inflated boat.) Very interesting and fun. Not particularity thrilling.

Back to Doubletree for dinner and evening packing.

SATURDAY, MAY 19, 2001 – DAY 15

Departed Doubletree Inn early. Weather was fair and moderate. Rode Durango and Silverton narrow gauge railway to Silverton, a 3½-hour trip. Slow. Through *magnificent* mountain scenery beside Animas River.

Lunch at Bent Elbow Restaurant, formerly a brothel. Buffet lunch. Very mediocre.

Walk around Silverton after lunch. Tourist town. Lots of restaurants and souvenir shops, but picturesque and nice.

During trip weather turned dark, chilly and drizzly. Stayed that way most of the afternoon.

Reboarded bus and drove through snowy mountain scenery. Old mines. Red Mountain, Uncompahgre Plateau. Town of Ouray. Very nice.

Stopped in Montrose for a Russell Stover candy outlet. Fantastically low prices. Jackie and rest of our group bought a lot of candy.

Overnight at Grand Junction at Adams's Mark [Doubletree] motel. Really adequate, but suffers by comparison with others. Hamburger supper at "Good Pastures."

SUNDAY, MAY 20, 2001 – DAY 16

After breakfast departed Grand Junction for Denver. Weather pleasantly warm and sunny. Wonderful rest / picture stop at Grizzly Bear Rest Center in Glenwood Canyon. Great scenery.

Lunch at a nice "taproom" in Vail.

Continued drive to Denver through more magnificent scenery.

General drive around Denver upon our arrival at our hotel (Marriott City Center). Weather turned suddenly severe. Temperature dropped from 72° to 38° in less than an hour. Heavy winds, rain, sleet.

At night had farewell dinner at the hotel. Lots of merry good fellowship, and affectionate farewells to fellow travelers and especially to our guide, Gladys Sifter and driver, Dick Sloniker.

Monday, May 21, 2001 – Day 17 – Last Day of Trip

Departed Marriott Hotel by stretch limo at 7:00.

Departed Denver Airport at 9:15 a.m. Uneventful flight to Minneapolis.

At Minneapolis, because of an oversold flight, we were offered a $400 voucher to accept seats of a later flight. We accepted.

Flew to Cleveland about 1:15. Arrived about 4:30.

Flew from Cleveland about 5:30. Arrived RDU about 7:30. Taxi first to Jackie's, then to my house.

Somewhere along the way I lost my $400 voucher.

Portugal and Spain

May 7–21, 2002

Kern Holoman & Jackie Harper

The Alhambra, Granada, Spain

SOURCE: Diary 8 (2002). Spiral-bound album with plastic outer cover and light green inner cover. Blue leather album with gold tooling, roughly 4 x 6 inches. In Kern's hand, except for cover title added in hand of DKH:

> *WKH Journal*
> *May 2002*
> *Portugal & Spain*
> and on p. 1 (hand of WKH):
> *Journal*
> *Portugal and Spain Trip*
> *May 7–21, 2002*
> *"Pousadas & Paradors"*
> *Odyssey Unlimited Tours*

Portugal and Spain:

"Pousadas & Paradores"

May 7–21, 2002
Kern Holoman & Jackie Harper

Jackie and Kern often spoke of this tour as their favorite of all.

Jackie found this tour in Odysseys Unlimited catalog. We selected it because of the hotels element. Pousadas (Portugal) and paradores (Spain) are government-owned tourist facilities featuring luxury accommodations and meals at restored monasteries, convents, castles, fortresses, etc.

Cost basic $3,171 + US Air cost $150 = $3,321.

May 7, 2002 – Tuesday

Flew to Atlanta about 2:30 p.m. (Delta). Betty Aydlett drove us to the airport. Security arrangements were tight.

Arrived in Atlanta about 7:30 p.m.

Departed at 9:45 p.m. on Air France. Big plane almost full. We had seats D–E. Fairly cozy[?] behind a bulkhead. Plenty of leg room. Food was okay. Main dish was Coq au Vin.

I slept a little. Jackie not at all. 8-hour flight to Paris.

May 8, 2002 – Wednesday

Routine breakfast on plane. Arrived in Paris De Gaulle on time at 11:59. Departed Paris at 1:00 p.m. Air France. 2½-hour flight to Lisbon, Portugal.

Met at the airport by our tour director "Mickey" Michel. Transport by bus to our hotel. Driver is "Antonio."

Our hotel is Sheraton Lisbon. Very good, luxurious. Lots of Portuguese motif in decor with tiles. Tiles are big in Portugal.

Welcome dinner in hotel dining room. Dinner was *very* good. Rack of lamb.

Met fellow passengers (24). Very nice ladies. 5 Japanese women, 4 Afro-Americans, rest Anglo-Saxon.

May 9, 2002 – Thursday

Big buffet breakfast in hotel.

Bus travel along coast. Lisbon is *very* ornate. Not Spanish. To Sintra, a royal resort city in the hills. Very interesting Moorish and Renaissance architecture. Big tour of royal castle. Good walk-around look at Sintra. Pick up lunch.

Return to Lisbon. Tour of monastery of Saint Jerome. Photo visit to Tour of Belim [Belém Tower / Torre de Belém]. Old fortress. Photo visit to monument to Henry the Navigator and other discoverers. Good. Walking tour of Alfama. Slum of Lisbon. Motor tour of rest of city.

Wrote postcards. Cocktails at hotel lounge.

Taxi to restaurant district. Mostly seafood. Dinner at Loma Real. Modernist restaurant with other fellow travelers. Lots of fun. I had asparagus and lamb. Jackie had lobster. Late night port at hotel.

May 10, 2002 – Friday

Departed hotel at 8:45. Motor travel to a *big* factory of painted Portuguese pottery. Jackie bought souvenirs.

Lunch at a *fascinating* old town on a hill named Monsaraz. Lots of medieval ruins. Lunch at restaurant Santiago. Main entree was lamb. Visited *big* winery. Nice wine tasting.

Return to Evora. Big historic walled city. Our first night at a pousada. "Pousada Dos Loios." Restored medieval monastery. *Very* authentic decor. Marvelous marble stairway.

Dinner with our group in hotel restaurant. Main entree was sea bass. Roman temple to Diana, beautifully illuminated at night. A good day.

May 11, 2002 – Saturday

Buffet breakfast at hotel.

Walking tour of Evora. Guide was "Maria." Temple. Cathedral. Other churches. City park and gardens. Most impressive ruin was "Chapel of the Bones," great room with walls lined with human bones. Especially femurs and skulls.

Pastry and coffee outdoors in town square. Leisurely shopping. Back to pousada. I bought Jackie a rooster charm.

Lunch at pousada. Unnecessarily expensive. Leisurely afternoon in room. Pousada rooms are old monk cells. Well decorated but *very* small.

Dinner with group in dining room. Small fowl (squab?).

May 12, 2002 – Sunday

Buffet breakfast at pousada.

Departed Evora at 8:45. Rest stop at Spanish border. Moved watches forward one hour.

Stop at Merida. Explored old Roman ruins. Amphitheater etc. Very large restoration. Visited museum of Roman artifacts. Lunch was tapas. Ham, cheese, sardines, anchovies.

Departed Merida at 2:45 to Carmona via Seville Road.

Our accommodation is a parador, Parador Carmona. Very large. Very impressive. Very luxurious. A restored old fortress. (Alcazar.) With history back to the Romans, Goths, Moors and others. We are pleased to be here.

Dinner was in large dining room. Shrimp appetizer, swordfish steak, dessert buffet. Good.

May 13, 2002 – Monday

A bad day. I had *big* diarrhea all night. Jackie had headache. We finally decided to go through with the Seville day.

Buffet breakfast at hotel. Bus to Seville. Our step-on guide was Maria. Maria Luisa Park. Plaza de España. *Very* ornate. Bus tour of city. Walk to cathedral. World's largest after St. Peter's and St. Paul's. Big, Gothic, many awe-inspiring religious (Catholic) decor.

Walking tour of old city. Jewish quarter. Santa Cruz. Outdoor lunch at [Hosteria del] Laurel (featured in opera *Don Giovanni*). 1-hour boat trip on River Guadalquivir. Very pleasant. Return to parador. Good dinner of Andalusian soup, veal cutlet, flan.

I am still troubled with diarrhea. Took an Imodium pill.

May 14, 2002 – Tuesday

A pretty good day.

My diarrhea gone. Jackie still has headache. Departed Carmona parador. (Very nice experience.) Scenic ride through mountains to Ronda. Great town (but touristy in daytime). Wonderful parador beside gorge.

Walking tour of old city. Our guide was Diego. Bristling mustache. Gorge, museum, church, also bullring.

Could not punch up money on Visa. Did not accept my number. Lunch was assorted tapas. Long nap in room.

Dinner in parador. Eggplant ratatouille, stuffed pork loin. N[ot] g[ood]. Walked to look at gorge after dinner.

May 15, 2002 – Wednesday

Good day.

Breakfast at parador. *Very* scenic trip through mountains to coast.

Coastal drive to Gibraltar. (Customs and Immigration.)

Fine city tour in minibus. Very steep ride up rock. St. Michael's Cave. Barbary apes [macaques]. Other scenic attractions.

Jackie shopped. Nice lunch at good restaurant on beach. Paella–good salad–nice dessert. Retraced route back to Ronda through mountains. Jackie went shopping.

Dinner at parador. Tapas–guinea fowl–parfait. Good. I had bad indigestion after dinner.

May 16, 2002 – Thursday

Good day.

Breakfast at parador. 3-hour trip to Granada.

Stayed at Hotel Alhambra Palace. *Gorgeous* lobby and downstairs. Heavily Moorish design. Lunch on balcony–sandwiches. Very hot, humid day. Lots of uphill walking.

Afternoon conducted tour of Alhambra. Charles V Palace. Court of justice. Living quarters. Fountain system. Court of lions. Court of myrtles. Generalife gardens. Millions of beautiful roses.

Dinner in dining room. Asparagus soup–trout–ice cream.

Our room is substandard. Crowded, hot. Beautiful view of Granada.

May 17, 2002 – Friday

Very good day.

Breakfast in hotel. (Wonderful lobby and public rooms.)

Walking and riding tour of Granada. Crowded minibus rides. Scenic view of city, Alhambra. Fortress, mountains. Visit to tombs of Ferdinand and Isabella. Royal chapel with great artwork including Italian and Flemish masters. Church.

Lunch in Plaza Nuevo. Asparagus hors d'oeuvres. *Very* good.

Departed Granada at 1:30. Scenic drive through olive farms (many). Scenic drive through canyon.

Overnight at parador in Almagro. Wonderful atmosphere. Old cloisters. Extensive gardens–restored.

May 18, 2002 – Saturday

Breakfast at parador. A fine one. Perhaps our favorite.

Motored to Toledo. Great historic town. Very old, well preserved and designed. Government-controlled to keep it old.

Walking tour of city. Churches, museums. Great cathedral. Sacristy has wonderful paintings by El Greco. Disciple portraits [Apostalados]. Other great paintings by others. Good lunch at Bocis.

Motored to Madrid. Our hotel is "Wellington." Very good. We have nice room.

Completely unpacked preparatory to return home.

Unsatisfactory dinner at a sidewalk cafe.

May 19, 2002 – Sunday

Wellington is a 5-star hotel. Breakfast with group at hotel.

Bus tour of Madrid. Stop at Plaza de España. Opera house. Guided tour of royal palace. Past Plaza Mayor. Stop at bullring. Visit to Prado museum. *Very* crowded. Saw only a fraction. Did see Velasquez, Goya, Murillo, Ribera, Zurbaran, others.

For lunch met with 10 of our group at Posada de la Villa. *Great* lunch. Expensive. Tapas. Roast lamb and veggies, dessert, coffee. Julia arranged it. Birthday party for Maria Elena [illegible].

Leisurely p.m. in hotel room. Evening at sidewalk Cafe "Te y Cafe." Had taz chocolate [Chocolate à la taza]. Okay. Not great.

May 20, 2002 – Monday

Last day before departure. Slept late (8:15 a.m.) Breakfast at hotel. Jackie went shopping. I walked in park ([El] Retiro).

Lunch was anchovies and pimento sandwich (bocadillo [bocadillo de anchoas]). I took Jackie a "tosta" of ham and cheese. Spent afternoon in room.

Farewell dinner with group at a *great* antique restaurant "Botin's" [Casa Botín, est. 1725; claims to be the oldest restaurant in the world]. Meal was mediocre. Gazpacho, roast suckling pig, ice cream, dessert. Walked back to bus through Plaza Mayor. Crowded, but beautifully lighted. Bid farewell to group members. Packed at hotel.

South America

December 6, 2002 – January 6, 2003

Kern Holoman & Jackie Harper

Parque del Amor, Miraflores, Peru

Kern after fall on December 21

SOURCE: Diary 9 (2002–03). Glossy blue plasticized cardboard with travel motifs on cover print, roughly 5 x 8½ inches. Inscribed on flyleaf:

> *Kern Holoman*
> *August 10, 2002*
> *from Jackie*
> *(for our South American*
> *cruise Dec. 2002 – Jan. 2003)*

SOUTH AMERICA

December 6, 2002 – January 6, 2003
Kern Holoman & Jackie Harper

This was the longest cruise Jackie and Kern took together, embracing both the Christmas and New Year holidays. It was probably a last-minute deal, as the children didn't know much about it until getting phone calls after the travelers were underway. They were annoyed to lose their top-class balcony room, doubtless an upgrade, halfway into the cruise.

December 4, 2002 – Wednesday

Following weather predictions, the weather began to worsen about mid-afternoon. Sleet, snow and freezing rain.

In the evening accumulation of ice on the trees and electric wires began to cause major power outages.

Jackie lost her power about 11 p.m. Kern lost his about 1 a.m., and we never had electricity before we departed for the cruise.

Houses began to cool down during the night.

December 5, 2002 – Thursday

Woke up to a darkened city. Power outages were almost universal. Duke Power said most outages in its history (90% out). CP&L reported 400,000 without power. *Extreme* damage to trees and limbs. Many branches down. Many electric wires down and dangling. Traffic signals generally not working. Most stores and gas stations closed with no electricity.

Kern went to Jackie's house about 1 p.m. She had a fire going. Also kerosene lantern. Heated soup in fireplace.

Kern contacted David and Debbie. Gave them Christmas stuff today.

[David] invited us to dinner and to spend the night. We readily accepted. He drove his car and our luggage (which we readily accepted). Drinks and nice dinner at D&D's. Overnight in Jordan's room.

December 6, 2002 – Friday

Taxi ordered for 4:30 arrived on time. We rose at 3:45 a.m. and were ready. Our flight to Charlotte had been canceled, but US Airways arranged for us to fly to Miami via Orlando and Atlanta. Security at airport tight.

Arrived in Miami about 1:15 p.m. Met and found [cruise-ship desk]. Passenger accommodations by Norwegian Cruise Line were efficient and well done.

We loaded ship about 2:30. Our cabin (8231) is a top-cost accommodation. It is OK, but a little short of the necessities we have experienced on other cruises. We *do* have a king-size bed. Balcony is good.

Had snack lunches on deck. Unpacked baggage when arrived. Storage space is minimal.

Ate dinner in Four Seasons dining room (open seating). Very good. Typically good cruise fare. (Kern had roast beef; Jackie had scallops.)

Retired early. Jackie got headache. Bed was OK. Slept well.

December 7, 2002 – Saturday

Pearl Harbor Day. Not observed here.

(By 9:30 a.m. we still had not seen a cabin steward. We met him later. He is very nice and cooperative, but likes to do things his own way.)

A good day. We were at sea all day. Nice continental breakfast on our nice balcony. Explored the ship, shops, etc. Sat on open deck and ate fruit.

Luncheon at Terrace Dining Room. (We like the friendly "eat-any time" dining.) Checked out book at library. Returned to cabin for p.m. TV and reading in afternoon.

Attended captain's champagne party in main lounge. OK. *Very* informal.

Dinner at Four Seasons. Formal attire. Lobster entrees. Very good.

So far food on trip is good, at least as good as on most cruise ships.

Kern bought $30 in quarters at casino. Lost quota of $5.00.

December 8, 2002 – Sunday

(*David's day to teach [Sunday School] for me.)
A good day.
Our ship skipped Belize because of late departure from Miami. [Short visit to] Cozumel (7 a.m. to 2 p.m.) where we had been before. A heavily tourist island. Kern bought a hairbrush, tropical hat, and 2 Cuban cigars @ $5.

Had a drink at a local bar (Planter's Punch). Jackie had coffee. Walked back by the shops, with Jackie looking at jewelry. Coconut milk on the pier.

Lunch at the Terrace. Afternoon napping and snoozing. (Day was overcast with some rain.)

Kern attended worship service. Protestant service conducted by Catholic chaplain.

Italian dinner at the Trattoria. Good.

Entertainment was a revue called "Sea Legs at Sea." Not bad for a shipboard presentation.

December 9, 2002 – Monday

Warm, tropical day.

We docked at Roatán, Honduras, which is the largest of the "Bay Islands."

After buffet breakfast we went ashore. It was lined with *many* souvenir shops, selling all sorts of native crafts. There were some *marvelous* values in carved Honduran mahogany. Jackie bought a grand nativity set and several decorative candles. Bought post cards.

It was *very* hot and humid, and after walking a few hundred yards toward the village, we were glad to return to the ship.

After lunch, walked a mile on the Promenade Deck. Jackie rested. Kern read.

Entertainment was a Hispanic vocalist. Medium good.

Dinner was OK. Jackie had salmon. Kern had fettucine and mushrooms.

Casino and bed. We are enjoying our room.

December 10, 2002 – Tuesday

An uneventful day at sea. Sailing between Roatán, Honduras and Puerto Limón, Costa Rica. We wrote and mailed postcards to friends and relatives.

Lunch on deck at Sports Bar & Grill. Walked a mile on Promenade Deck. Jackie read and napped. Kern went to jacuzzi.

Entertainment was a juggler. Very good and talented in his own field.

Dinner in Tavern dining area. I like that one best.

Lost my quota of $5 in the casino.

Bed about 11 p.m. Our room is not the greatest, but we enjoy the king-size bed and the balcony.

December 11, 2002 – Wednesday

In Puerto Limón, Costa Rica.

Ship docked at 8:00 a.m. Departed at 4:30. Many shore excursions. We did not like any.

Dockside was typical mélange of gift shops and stalls.

We walked to the local city park. Fairly well maintained. Saw a small sloth in a tree.

Walked along the various shop-lined streets. Soon tired of the walk and returned to the ship.

After lunch walked our regular mile.

Jackie telephone Gerry at home. Got his answering machine.

Evening's entertainment was a pianist/vocalist. Moderately good entertainment.

The food on board is generally good. Not outstanding.

We enjoy the dine-around features.

December 12, 2002 – Thursday

This is the day we transited the Panama Canal. It is an all-day experience. We entered the locks at 8:50 a.m. Crossed [under] Bridge of the Americas and exited canal at 5:30 p.m.

We had breakfast at Sports Bar and went on deck. Watched as we entered the first two (Gatun) locks. It was hot, and we soon returned to our balcony cabin. More comfortable and we could see plenty, though perhaps not as much as from our deck.

Enjoyed the Gatun Locks and Culebra Cut. Spent most of the afternoon in our cabin.

After dinner entertainment was a ventriloquist. We did not go.

Kern went on deck and smoked a Cuban cigar and had a Drambuie. Beautiful half-moon overhead.

December 13, 2002 – Friday

This was the day our ship crossed the equator. After lunch they had quite a ceremony on deck and the pool, with most of the passengers crowding around. *Very* crowded.

(People who have crossed the equator before are Shellbacks. Those who have not are called Polliwogs.) To get to be a Shellback, Polliwogs must become covered with soap and then be pushed into the pool. Many did; we did not.

Walked our mile.

Uneventful afternoon and evening. Dinner on the terrace was about as good as could be: (1) ham and melon, (2) Caesar salad, (3) filet mignon, (4) black and white mousse, (5) cappuccino.

(This cruise has some shortcomings, but that dinner was one of the good things.)

December 14, 2002 – Saturday

An uneventful day at sea.

Slept late. Continental breakfast in room.

Worked crossword puzzle.

Took mile walk around promenade deck.

Kern to jacuzzi.

After-dinner show in theatre lounge was *42nd Street,* production adapted from Broadway/Hollywood show.

Holiday decorations on ship consist of heavily decorated Christmas trees in all the public rooms, with wreaths and garlands hanging about. Pretty, but gaudy.

December 15, 2002 – Sunday

First day on land in South America. Salaverry, Peru, a small seaport town.

Weather sunny and pleasantly cool. Took our first shore excursion to Trujillo, largest city of the north. Visited Chan-Chan, an amazing pre-Inca city (about 900 AD) with palaces and temples made of adobe.

Very impressive. A good ride around the countryside. Visited seaside resort town. Saw reed fishing. Looks interesting.

Visited Rainbow Temple [Huaca del Dragon / Huaca del Arco Iris], another adobe monument with interesting symbols.

A good morning. We were not disappointed.

Back on ship. Late lunch. Cocktails in Observatory lounge.

Entertainment was flamenco and tango dance couple. Surprisingly good.

Kern won $35 in draw poker machine.

December 16, 2002 – Monday

A *very* good day.

Docked at Callao (Peru). Shore excursion to Lima. Big capital city (7,000,000). Much poverty, but a great city.

Visited cathedral (first Catholic cathedral in S. A.). Founded by Pizarro (who founded much of Peru and overthrew Inca culture).

Visited San Francisco monastery. A very important and significant monument and historical site.

Visited Miraflores, wealthy section of Lima, including Park d'Amore. Pretty resort spot.

Bought souvenirs—llamas and buttons for Jordan's class.

Went shopping after lunch. Much jewelry. Didn't buy anything.

Good folklore show on ship. Local dancers and singers.

Magician after dinner. Fair.

December 17, 2002 – Tuesday

An uneventful day at sea.

We are (pleasantly) surprised at how temperate the weather is, usually in the 60s or 70s in the daytime, although the sun on deck is warm and "tanning."

Jackie felt poor most of the day.

Spent time reading, napping, sunning.

Dinner in the Terrace was good. This is our favorite dining room.

Did not go to evening entertainment.

December 18, 2002 – Wednesday

A *good* day in Arica, northernmost city in Chile. Nice, temperate weather for sightseeing. Kern went into town in a.m. Bought sundries. Nice commercial city with shops, restaurants, vendors, etc.

In p.m. took shore excursion. Good. Went to [El] Morro, large rock overhanging city. Site and monument to battle where Chile defeated Peru for the land. Visited "geoglyph," stone representation of animals by prehistoric people.

Visited good archaeological museum of area. "Mummies" [Chinchorro mummies, oldest known].

Traveled through irrigation in this barren land. Mostly olive trees. Visited handicraft fair, shops and stalls of native handiwork. Fantastically good values in alpaca and other fabrics.

(In a.m., upon arrival we were greeted and entertained by local band and folklore dancers. Very pleasant.)

Entertainment in evening was stand-up comedian. Very funny.

December 19, 2002 – Thursday

Not a very good day.

(We were told definitively that we will have to move to the lower cabin class without balcony. Told that the cabin steward would move us while we are gone on our shore excursion.)

Shore excursion today was not satisfactory. Places visited in Iquique not very interesting. Theater, museum, palace, walk beside shops. Most interesting was a snack stop at a Spanish restaurant which included good paintings, especially of life of Don Quixote.

Back on ship, usual activities. Beer and pizza. Dinner in Terrace. Casino. Early to bed.

December 20, 2002 – Friday

Another uneventful day at sea. (This does not mean the "at sea" days are unpleasant. Just lots of time for reading, dozing, sunning, etc.)

We continue to be surprised at how cool the days are. This one was overcast nearly all day.

Walked our mile on deck (3½ times around the Promenade). Captain's gala farewell dinner with traditional baked Alaska.

Evening's entertainment was a farewell show by the company. Mostly jazz dancing à la Bob Fosse.

December 21, 2002 – Saturday

(Longest day of the year. Sun was high in the sky at 9:30.)

A *medium* good day.

Beautiful sunshine. A little chilly along the shore and on shipboard.

Shore excursion into Coquimbo and La Serena [Chile]. Nice, well-kept streets and parks.

Drove along shore.

Visited *another!* archaeological museum.

Shopped at local handicraft market.

Didn't buy anything. Visited "winery." Tasted "pisco sour." OK.

Visited canyon for a panoramic overview of the two cities.

Both Kern (first) and Jackie (afterward) had a fall. Not serious but painful bruises and abrasions.

Spent evening preparing for our movement into another cabin. No. 6225 has no balcony and we are skeptical about conditions in new facility.

December 22, 2002 – Sunday

This was the day the first half of our cruise ended and the second half began. We were moved from deck 8 to deck 6. Not very happy. We are missing a number of small amenities.

In a.m. took a land excursion tour of Valparaiso and Viña del Mar. Nice ride and scenic trip. City is very hilly and had good view of the harbor.

Visited another archaeological museum.

Nice trip. Overcharge.

Bought alpaca sweater for Jackie.

Bought crib decoration for cabin door.

Bought postal cards.

New passengers came on board.

Many children and young people. Some disciplinary problems.

Usual evening fare of dinner and casino.

Both Jackie and Kern are still sore and hurting from our fall.

December 23, 2002 – Monday

A day at sea south of Valparaiso.

The day was cloudy, and overcast and got worse as the day progressed. Turned cold and windy—too cold to walk our mile on the Promenade. Heavy rain in p.m. and quite heavy seas (never with white-caps).

In the early evening it faired off to be a pretty sunset (at 8:30 it was still partially light).

Wrote post cards, read, and napped.

At bedtime Jackie was nauseated and felt bad for some hours. Her illness got better during the night.

December 24, 2002 – Tuesday

A *very* good day. Our best shore excursion yet.

Ship docked early at Puerto Montt, Chile. Drove through city to picturesque observation point a little above city.

Day was warm and sunny. Moderate temperatures.

Drove through countryside to Puerto Varas, a nice city beside a huge inland lake.

Walked along lake-side and around shops.

Drove through countryside to Frutilar, a German-settled village dedicated to music, also beside the lake. Wonderful outdoor museum with gorgeous formal planting and flowers.

Chocolate and Kuchen at a restaurant beside the lake.

Back on ship Christmas Eve religious service conducted by a preacher from Raleigh. Poorly done.

Italian dinner in Trattoria.

December 25, 2002 – Wednesday
Christmas Day

Another very good day

Anchored at Port [Puerto] Chacabuco. Tenders to shore. Well organized.

The day was cloudy and rainy. But temperature was moderate and we braved the rain. Got mightily[?] wet several times.

Our tour guide was Priscilla, charming 20-year-old English-speaking girl.

Bused through vast lovely valleys with overhanging rocks and cliffs. Many waterfalls. Green and lovely countryside. Took short hike to a wildlife museum, walk to the river, and close-up look at the cliffs.

Port city of Aysén (suspension bridge). Overlook city of Coyhaique. Visit to city museum.

Road back to ship retraced our steps. Snack stop for wine and snacks. Jackie bought wine.

Back on ship. Religious service. Elaborate Christmas dinner and a nice show with most of the staff performing Christmas numbers.

Sailed out of calm water in the fjord into rough water in the open sea.

December 26, 2002 – Thursday

A simply delightful day. All day on the ship.

Slept late. All day long the ship sailed.

The night was *rough* and the moving forward was also quite uneven. Hard to keep our footing.

Sailed in and out into an archipelago of numerous islands. The sides were like Norway. They were called the Patagonian fjords. Huge, impressive cliffs on both sides with numerous big waterfalls dropping into icy passage.

Many spectacular passages.

About 8:30 p.m. we approached and stopped near Eyre glacier. Very large—3rd largest in world. Very beautiful and blue. 3 miles wide, 102 feet high above water. Took pictures. Lots of ice floes from the glacier. "Calving."

In and out of fog and clear seas.

December 27, 2002 – Friday

Another wonderful day on the ship.

We awoke early with the ship again anchored at a glacier (Amalia). All day we sailed in and out of islands, many very tall and forbidding with snowy summits. The country doesn't vary much: it is very lovely and forbidding. Almost completely uninhabited. It is so pleasing to sit at our picture window and watch this wonder world slip by.

At about 7:00 p.m. we rounded a lighthouse installation on an island

and entered the Strait of Magellan—about 200 miles long and connecting the Pacific and Atlantic Ocean. Surprisingly wide. It was used as an alternative route to rounding the cape by the early settlers.

Uneventful evening. Cocktails. Dinner. Casino.

December 28, 2002 – Saturday

Another perfectly delightful day.

Our ship docked at Punta Arenas, Chile's southernmost city. Our shore excursion was to Otway Sound and Penguin Preserve (a 4-hour trip).

As we drove through countryside (not very interesting) we did see the wild rheas (like ostriches) and a couple of foxes.

The Penguin Preserve was a 1-mile walk along paths to where the penguins congregated. Not an overwhelming number, but plenty. And they are interesting little clowns. We enjoyed. Much.

Back on ship we decided *not* to go into town. (May have been a mistake: those who went said it was good.)

Ship sailed at 6:00 p.m., continued in Magellan Strait. Turned into Beagle Channel (of Darwin fame). *Many* more ragged, snow-covered peaks with small waterfalls.

We are overwhelmed with the scenery.

December 29, 2002 – Sunday

Early this morning we sailed into Beagle Channel with glorious glaciers, waterfalls and snow-capped mountains.

Landed early in Ushuaia, Argentina. (We crossed into Argentina from Chile early in the morning.)

Our shore excursion was a trip in Ushuaia Bay in a large catamaran. Sailed closed to several islands including one with thousands of cormorants and another with hundreds of sea lions. We saw other birds, but not in great number.

We disembarked on the island of Tierra del Fuego and took a bus back through the national park. Saw some wild geese. Nice coffee shop break. Park is interesting but not very well maintained.

In the evening Kern and Jackie contracted bad colds. (Kern was worse.) Spent the night catering to our ailments.

December 30, 2002 – Monday

Cape Horn

A really bad day. Jackie's cold got better. Kern's cold got much worse, and we spent most of the time in the cabin resting or napping.

At about 8:00 a.m. the ship rounded Cape Horn. The cape is really to [the] southwest of a small group of islands, all characterized by treacherous water, waves, and navigating perils. Weather today was pretty good. Moderate seas. Cloudy skies, but not rain.

Many of our passengers got up and went on deck for Rounding-the-Horn ceremony characterized by donning a "horny hat" à la Vikings and being anointed with salty water from the sea around. We didn't go, stayed in bed and rested.

In the afternoon Jackie persuaded Kern to call on the ship doctor. She prescribed an antibiotic, Sudafed, and some cough suppressant which was surprisingly effective. Went to bed with Kern feeling better.

December 31, 2002 – Tuesday
New Year's Eve

A (mostly) good day. Kern's medications were effective and he felt well.

Arrived in Stanley, Falkland Islands about 8:00 a.m. After a *very* long wait (not well organized) we arrived onshore by tender at about 2:00 p.m.

Surprisingly tidy little town. Very British. Impressive Church of England cathedral (small) with whale bone arch outside and beautiful lupine flowers. Waterfront is quite commercialized with gift shops.

Walked around town for about an hour. Nothing surprising. The cafe and restaurants closed at 2 p.m. so we couldn't eat.

Back on shipboard, the ship was decorated for a gala New Year's Celebration. Balloons and other decorations everywhere.

A good nightclub-type singer was our entertainment show.

New Year's dinner was OK. Not special.

The celebration was (beginning at 11:00 p.m.) with songs and free champagne in all lounges.

We welcomed in the New Year with champagne and toasts and then went to bed about 12:30.

January 1, 2003 – Wednesday
New Year's Day

An uneventful day at sea. We slept late and went for a late breakfast.

Kern's cold is better, but still present.

Reading, crossword puzzles, and rest.

The evening's entertainment was the magician and the comedian. Both were good.

Early to bed.

Weather is mild and the seas are modest.

January 2, 2003 – Thursday

A day docked at Puerto Madryn, Argentina. Day began cloudy and rainy, but warmed up beautifully as the day went on.

We decided not to take a shore tour, but to make our own arrangements. We were not successful, and ended up taking the ship shuttle bus into town, where there was not really much to do.

Jackie did some shopping. Kern took a long walk along the shore line. Saw an Argentine folklore show, visited a provincial museum [Provincial Museum of Natural Science and Oceanography], then returned to the ship about 1 p.m. Read, napped, and rested in the afternoon.

Dinner at the Four Seasons and early to bed. Neither of us are feeling top-notch. Kern's cold, Jackie's headache, but we cope.

January 3, 2003 – Friday

A very nice uneventful day at sea.

Weather was warm and seas moderate on way to Montevideo.

Usual morning of crosswords, reading and resting. (We have really enjoyed the crossword puzzle book Chris gave me.)

In the afternoon we opened (finally) our gift bottle of champagne from the captain. Entertained in our cabin with our shipboard friends, Michael and Rita Smith. (Pleasant.)

Captain's Farewell Dinner in the Terrace was delightful: mushroom soup, escargots, green salad, lobster tails, ice cream coupe.

Early to bed.

January 4, 2003 – Saturday
Montevideo, Uruguay
Last day of cruise

Tied up at pier about 9:00 a.m.

A beautiful, warm, sunny day.

Took free shuttle bus to leather factory and workshop. Did not find anything interesting to buy. Prices seemed high.

Contracted with an independent guide to drive us and tour (2 hours for $40). A good deal with an English-speaking girl guide.

Saw local craft market, cathedral (good), then a long drive along the beach shore of the Plato River. Beautiful residential homes.

Back in town saw many government buildings and statuary, some of them exceedingly interesting and beautiful.

On shipboard enjoyed a sunny afternoon. Packed for departure. A nice dinner in the Terrace.

Back to cabin to resume packing.

January 5, 2003 – Sunday
End of cruise

Ship docked at Buenos Aires. Left ship and checked luggage on bus. Our tour bus drove us around Buenos Aires for a routine look at public buildings.

Then a *long* drive to a "ranch" in the countryside. A *very* nice experience. (But expensive.)

We were greeted by the owner and served wine and [empanadas] outside. [Souvenir hunting?] as always, then a show on horsemanship by the ranch hands: "gauchos." Afterward a little show of Argentine folk dancing.

Dinner meats—chicken, sausage, and *good* roast beef, all cooked over an open fire. With beer and wine.

Back to the city. Straight to the airport. Altogether a memorable experience. Security is very tight and lines were long and slow moving. We did not have assigned seats, and had to wait until last minute to find if we could get on plane. We did, but could not sit together.

January 6, 2003 – Monday
End of Trip. Back to Raleigh.

Our plane ride was ten hours long and uneventful. Service was minimal.

Back at Dulles Airport in Washington with the usual waits and lines with customs and immigration. (Air travel these days is no fun!)

Caught commuter plane back to Raleigh and arrived at 11:30, more or less as scheduled.

From arrival at Buenos Aires airport to arrival at RDU was about 18 hours.

THE ADRIATIC

March 22 – April 12, 2005

Kern Holoman & Jackie Harper

Dubrovnik, Croatia

SOURCE: Diary 10 (2005). Brown leather with four small windows for photographs, roughly 5½ x 8½ inches. Inscribed on flyleaf:

>*Jackie Harper*
>*&*
>*Kern Holoman*
>*Mar.–April 2005*
>and, page 1:
>*"The Alps, The Adriatic*
>*Dubrovnik and Beyond"*
>*Grand Circle Tour, Mar. 22 – April 12, 05*

The Alps, The Adriatic, Dubrovnik and beyond

March 22 – April 12, 2005

Kern Holoman & Jackie Harper

March 23, 2005 – Wednesday

An unusually satisfying and fulfilling day.

We were impressed and pleasantly surprised.

Left RDU via United Airlines (Express) at 2:45 p.m. Tuesday.

(Plane and all other flights were on time.)

Jackie's son Gerry took us to the airport, for which we were grateful.

Had a snack before takeoff at Pinehurst Brewery. I had hot dog and beer; Jackie had chicken Caesar salad.

Flight to Dulles Airport in Washington was pleasant and uneventful. Plane took off for Munich at 6:00 p.m. (This area of Europe is nine hours ahead of Raleigh.) Booking agent in Raleigh had given us seats together. The plane was crowded, but we were fortunate in having three seats for the two of us.

Alcoholic beverages now cost $5 for spirits, $4 for wine and beer.

Flight to Munich was eight hours but was relatively pleasant because of the extra seat and for good leg room. Dinner was very good, tasty and plentiful. Jackie had lasagna; I had beef. We were served a continental breakfast about an hour before landing (8:00 a.m.).

Temperature in Munich was chilly (50°) and drizzly.

A [one-hour] flight via Slovenia Airlines took us to Ljubljana, the capital city.

Flew over *many* snow-capped mountains, a southern spur of the Alps.

A Grand Circle [agent] met us at the airport and dispatched us by cab to the lake resort town of Bled, about 30 miles away (northwest).

Bled is a really beautiful lakeside town surrounded by over-looking mountains, spectacular castles overhead, [and] a historic church on an island in the middle of the lake.

Really astonishingly beautiful. We are so pleased with our choice.

Our hotel is the Park, best in town—four stars, really first class. Our tour director (named Biba) is a young attractive blond girl. Seems very efficient.

We went to our room (no. 234), unpacked and took a brief nap. (We had not slept the night before.)

Our group met Biba at 2:45 and went on a brief and instructive walking tour of the prosperous little village.

Jackie and I went to an old-town cafe on the lake. Weather was sunny when we arrived, turned cloudy during the afternoon but remained only a little cool.

We had cappuccinos. I had Sacher torte, Jackie ate "cream cake," a specialty of the area. Everything is in the Slovenian language; they seldom translate for you.

March 24, 2005 – Thursday

Had a nice orientation briefing by our tour director. Her name is Biba. She is a tall, pretty blond girl, quite young, but is pleasant and competent.

The buffet breakfast was very good and complete. No one could wish for better.

After breakfast we went on an included bus tour around Lake Bled and later around Lake Bohinj [Slovenia].

Bled is a very complete resort community with lots of hotels, shops, and restaurants. (Also a casino.) The lake is well built up with cottages, condos, and private homes on its slopes. Reminded us a lot of Lake Tahoe in California.

The lake itself has a number of beautiful and interesting landmarks. Principal one is Bled Castle, away up on a cliff dominating its surroundings. It's like those old monasteries in Greece with sides going straight up. It has belonged to the Bishops of Brixen for over a thousand years. Now it is a tourist attraction. Rather difficult to climb the remaining steps, and we decided not to visit it.

In the middle of the lake is a beautiful church called the Chapel of the Ascension. Has a majestic bell with a legend. Also a tourist attraction. You reach the island on a tour boat rowed along by a boatman in groups of ten or more. About half of our group took the trip, but once again we decided to skip.

Directly across the lake from our hotel is another picturesque church with a high spire. (Churches in this country *do* have mostly high spires.) This one dutifully chimes out the time on the quarter hours.

A quarter way around the lake is the villa where Marshal Tito used to vacation. Now it is an upscale restaurant.

(Bled has been the mecca for several distinguished writers including Agatha Christie and others. President Bush and Laura were here last year.)

After circling the lake our bus took us to Lake Bohinj, about 16 miles away. It is larger, but less well-defined as it meanders through mountain valleys. The Julian Alps, looming overhead, are really spectacular, part of them snow-covered the year round. Tallest is Triglav, "three-headed," about 9,000 feet tall. One peak has a cable-car to the top. It's big ski country here. Lots of chalets and lodges. We stopped for a half-hour walk-around.

One of the features of the landscapes here are the antique hay-racks, originally used for drying hay, now used as shelter and tool sheds. Interesting. Different.

After we returned to Bled we went to a lunch at a nearby pub. Disappointing. Food was mediocre and rather expensive.

During the afternoon we rested and wrote post cards.

We attended a lecture in the late afternoon on Slovenia, its customs, history, and habits. Very interesting and enlightening.

For dinner our group all went on an included dinner to a fine, atmospheric restaurant featuring food specialties of Slovenia. A very good, enjoyable time.

We had costumed musicians playing Bavarian / Tyrolean music and singing. First course was a mushroom soup served in sour-dough type "popovers." Next course was a beef roulade, some kind of pinwheel meat wrapped around dough center. Dessert was crepes stuffed with chocolate and jam. All very good. But the festive atmosphere was the best of all. Everybody had a great time.

After dinner Jackie and I had coffee in the hotel lounge.

Upstairs and in bed by 10 p.m.

March 25, 2005 – Friday (Good Friday)

Weather-wise we were not lucky today. Woke up to a mostly-cloudy landscape and a rain that lasted all day, sometimes heavy, usually drizzly. Temperature was chilly.

With no desire to go out in that kind of weather we slept all morning after breakfast. Read magazines, [did] crosswords, and from our balcony mooned over the landscape—mostly heather in the mist.

For lunch we ate at a nearby restaurant. Medium satisfactory. Jackie had mushroom soup again. I had a tuna salad. Both moderately good.

At 2:00 p.m. we left on the first of our optional tours. This one was through the Slovenian countryside to a little town named Škofja Loka. (The map of Slovenia shows the country as shaped like a chicken.) Rain continued unabated. A guide met us at the bus station and led us on a walking tour of the quaint medieval-type town. Very picturesque and interesting. Went by the tourist bureau, which is also a gift shop.

Then we went to a theater and watched a group of natives in costume present a series of folk dances of about the 16th century. Music and costumes were reminiscent of Shakespeare.

Then we proceeded by bus for an extended visit of a hundreds-of-years-old house which had been tastefully preserved and renovated where necessary. One of the owners was our hostess. She said the house had been in her family for over 200 years. Very crowded for our group but informative.

For our dinner we went to a *very* nice restaurant/cellar with wine and a four-course dinner featuring food specialties of the country. Very enjoyable.

After dinner the bus took us back to our hotel for the night. Arrived back home about 8:30 p.m.

A fairly satisfying day despite the rain.

March 26, 2005 – Saturday

Nice, pleasant day.

The fog and mist lifted up during the night and showed the beautiful lakeside scenery and reflections.

Our included trip took us to Ljubljana, the capital city of Slovenia. It is a nice, clean city of about 250,000. (Slovenia is *not* a backward country; it is highly civilized.)

On bus was met by a pretty, knowledgeable young lady who took us on a 1¾-hour walking tour—the usual, public buildings, churches, statuary, shops, etc. All OK. But city tours everywhere are rather same-y and have their limitations.

The architecture is a centuries-old mixture from Roman walls to 20th-century modernism. It includes many quaint and picturesque buildings from many eras—mostly from the Middle Ages to the Habsburgs.

We were escorted through a large, open-air market, full of flowers, food and hand-made crafts. Because it was a Saturday of a holiday weekend, it was quite crowded—but nice.

After our guide dismissed us, we went on on our walking tour, revisiting some of the places she had shown us. The cathedral is St. Jacobs. Impressive brass door and many gorgeous murals inside.

Afterward we had lunch at a fine, atmospheric restaurant called Sokol, which means "hawk" (I think). Very pleasant, good service by costumed waiters. We both had soup and beer. Then we split a large platter of cold cuts and cheeses.

(Although meals are somewhat more expensive than we had anticipated, they are generally very good and a nice adventure.)

Our bus took us back to Bled through the countryside, arriving about 3 p.m.

(During the day the weather had drizzled a little, but was not really bothersome.)

We spent the afternoon resting and reading.

For an early supper we went across the way to a restaurant adjacent beside the lake of our hotel. Jackie had noodles and cheese; I had asparagus. Both were good, but portions in Slovenia are large.

For dessert we both had the famous cream cake called the Kremeshnitt [Cremeschnitte], and coffee.

After dinner we took a short walk on the lakeside and returned to the hotel to prepare for an early departure tomorrow.

March 27, 2005 – Sunday

Easter Sunday. A very strenuous day!

Left Bled by bus early. Journeyed down to the Croatia border (no trouble with passports or visas).

Arrived at the Postogna caves (caverns). Lots of other tour groups besides our own were there.

A train ride took us deep into the mountains (about 2–3 miles). Most everyone (including us) got off the train and took the 1½-hour trail/trip through the caverns. (It seemed longer.)

Started up with a steep uphill climb which left us (me) puffing and exhausted. It was downhill the rest of the way, but still seemed long. The concrete[?] walk and [hand-]rails helped.

Passed by *many* beautiful stalactites, stalagmites, and columns. Really impressive. Like the other caverns I have seen, but a long, long walk.

Long train ride out of the cave.

We had an included lunch at the upscale restaurant next to the entrance. Good German-type meal with big, fat sausages, sauerkraut and hot potato salad. With beer. Dessert was another cream cake, not quite as good as those in Bled. But good.

In the afternoon we bussed down to Opatija, a large resort town on the Adriatic Sea. View should have been gorgeous, but was less so because of clouds and a heavy rain.

Our bus drove us around town for viewing before our arrival at our hotel, Grand Hotel and Floweri, a new hotel very modern and up-to-date.

We got a top-floor room with a good view of the sea—when it clears up.

After a welcome drink Biba took us on a *long* walk in the drizzling rain. A long, scenic promenade skirts the shore for 7½ miles. We also visited the *good* botanical gardens and several other good places along the way. We were very tired at the end.

Walked back to the hotel, arriving at about 4:30. Spent the rest of the afternoon resting and unpacking.

Didn't want to go out for supper. Ate à la carte at the hotel dining room—where most of our other fellow travelers decided to go.

Had spaghetti, salad, and coffee. OK but not spectacular.

Jackie converted money at the hotel desk. I got money at an ATM machine (about $100 each). Up to bath and bed before 10 p.m.

March 28, 2005 – Monday
Easter Monday

All told a very satisfactory day.

Left by bus at 8:30 for an optional tour of the island of Krk. Largest island of Croatia.

Weather started off cloudy, cold and drizzly, but the sun came out in mid-morning and turned to a gorgeous spring day.

We skirted the shore of the bay of the Adriatic. Industrialized, but many pretty views of the blue sea.

We stopped at the resort village of Punat and were taken by boat to a tiny island owned and cared for by four monks. It included a museum, an art gallery, a collection of ancient manuscripts, and a Stations of the Cross. Trip lasted a little over an hour, then boated back to the big island.

We then bussed back to one of many quaint, picturesque villages by the shore in this area.

We went to a "tasting" of three local brandies. Then on to an included lunch of meat appetizer, hand-made pasta, and cheesecake washed down with plenty of wine. The surroundings were nice and the fellowship at our table was pleasant.

After lunch we were led on a brief walking tour of the village, featuring a passage through the "narrowest street in the world."

The bus trip back continued in good weather, with many more scenic vistas of sea and mountains.

Arrived back at the hotel about 4:00 p.m.

Went to a very nice choral concert at the Church of Saint Jacob. (There was a full moon before dark. Very well attended.)

The concert was by about thirty singers, male and female. The program was mostly religious music. They were well-balanced with a good sound. There was a female soloist with lots of presence but not very good, I didn't think.

After the concert was over we did not find a satisfactory place for the evening meal. Wound up back at the hotel lobby for cappuccino coffee and a pastry. Plus a couple of snacks from the hotel mini-bar.

A nice day though, overall.

March 29, 2005 – Tuesday

An only mildly satisfying day.

Started off with an included bus tour of downtown Rijeka. Highly industrialized, not at all interesting. Population about 165,000.

Took a guided tour through the municipal art [gallery] / opera theater [now Croatian National Theatre]. Very ornate, very impressive, very historic. But reminiscent of many European theaters of the 19th century.

Then went to a local Catholic church up on the hill, fabled to be the one-time site where Mary's (Jesus' mother) home was stationed. Late [thirteenth] century. Very Catholic, very ornate. A jewel, but quite small.

For lunch we were given two hours of free time for lunch and shopping in Rijeka. We had soup, hamburger, and drink at a nearby restaurant. Not outstanding.

Jackie did a little shopping. We were back on the bus at 1:45 and back at the hotel at 2:15.

From 4 to 5 Biba held a class for our group on the Croatian language. It was surprisingly good, as some of our group were sincerely interested in learning. We did not try particularly hard.

In the evening we went to an optional $65 dinner and entertainment. We found it quite expensive for what it was. Two singers and a pianist from the local opera company sang a program of opera arias lasting about a half hour (1 baritone, 1 soprano). Adequate voices, and printed programs. Three-course meal was more than adequate.

Then back home by 8:45 for cappuccino in the hotel lounge.

We'll look for better things tomorrow.

March 30, 2005 – Wednesday

A really good day! In many ways the best yet. Weather was great!

We left the hotel by bus at 8:30 for an optional tour of the Istrian Peninsula (south and west of Opatija). A largely rural area, but with a number of nice towns and villages. Joined to the mainland by a tunnel several miles long.

Our first stop was in the coast town of Rovinj, a charming coastal town with lots of winding streets and village vistas.

We made our way up a cobblestone walkway/staircase for a visit to the Catholic Church of St. Euphemia, a martyr sacrificed during Christian persecution times. The church was opened just for our group, and was a typically ornate Baroque church with many paintings, statues, and symbolic contents. The saint is said to be buried in an ancient sarcophagus.

Marvelous view from the hilltop. Afterward we made our way back down the cobbled stair/pathway. There were many interesting shops along the way. Jackie bought a number of small items.

Coffee at a sidewalk cafe.

For lunch we went to a restaurant on a working farm. Lots of fun amid surroundings of goats, turkeys, and cows. Lunch was good (soup, a mixed meat and veggie platter, and fried "beignets" for dessert). (All meals include wine, red or white, but no coffee.)

From there we went to the town of Pula on the Southern tip of the Istrian Peninsula. Our visit there was to the historic Roman arena (Coliseum), the site of many gladiatorial and annual spectacles in the days of empire.

It is a large, well-preserved arena, and a local guide did a fine job of showing us around and explaining about the surroundings.

Our bus took us back to Opatija along the Western coast. Very mountainous above the Adriatic Sea. Reminded me a lot of the Amalfi Drive.

It is spring! One of the things that has been most pleasant is to see the plants, flowers, and trees come into bloom. Each day more and more blossoms seem to open up to delight our eyes.

The drive back into town took us past many fine, aristocratic old villas of the royalty and formerly wealthy.

For dinner we walked to the Kamelija restaurant for "dine-around" dinner included in our tour cost. It was OK, but not great. We had more mushroom soup. Jackie had fish à la Dalmatia. I had a big mixed grill. Ice cream for dessert.

Back to the hotel. Packed up for early departure.

March 31, 2005 – Thursday

A long bus-ride day. Good but *very* long.

Departed Opatija hotel by bus at 8:30. Weather still gorgeous.

Our trip was to skirt the Adriatic coast to the city of Split—largest city in Dalmatia.

For the early hours we re-traced some of the same course we had followed earlier.

Afterward the coastal road wound in and out among the bays and inlets. Many islands. Very blue and beautiful.

The many towns and villages are very uniformly pretty and interesting. Their pattern is to occupy a hill, with houses (dwellings) ascending the top on all sides. Then crowned by a Catholic church with a cross.

A land wind called the "Bura" blew down from the tall mountains inland and made a chilly breeze.

Our lunch stop was at an interesting restaurant featuring tomato rice soup, fried fish, French fries, and tomato juice. Very good.

The afternoon was more of the same driving. Still interesting, still beautiful but we tired [of it] and are glad for the day to end (about 5:45) at the Hotel Split.

Dinner in the hotel dining room was salad, lasagna, and ice cream. The usual white wine with every meal.

This is a one-night stand, so we did not really unpack.

April 1, 2005 – Friday
Split to Dubrovnik

Another superlative day.

After a one-night stay at the Split Hotel we left at 8:30 for a city tour. Big item was a visit and tour of Diocletian's Palace. Diocletian was a Roman emperor just before Constantine. Last emperor to persecute the Christians. (About 296–304 AD.)

His palace, where he chose to live the last years of his life, is a vast complex.

The lower levels / basement have survived in good condition. Much of the upper floors are in ruins. In later years many people have invaded the space and it is honey-combed now with apartments and shops. Over 5,000 people now reside within its walls. The site of Diocletian's tomb, several pagan temples, and of course later Christian churches are still recognizable.

It was a good tour.

After leaving the palace we found the outlying streets filled with outdoor cafes and many people enjoying a mid-morning break. Kind of a holiday atmosphere.

Jackie and I had a cappuccino and pastry.

Our bus met us at 12:30 and we left for the afternoon ride to Dubrovnik some 150 miles away down the coast.

Once again, the scenery was simply indescribably magnificent. To the blue waters of the Adriatic, the *many* islands nearby off the coast, the brooding gray mountains overhead, some of them snow-clad, and the almost infinite number of shore-line villages with red-roofed dwellings and businesses.

Our drive took us for about eight miles through the country of Bosnia and Herzegovina. We stopped for a short visit at an eclectic department store and cafe.

After that we proceeded to Dubrovnik, arriving at about 5:30 at the Palace Hotel, which will be our home for the next eleven nights (since we are taking the one-week extension). The Palace is a genuine five-star hotel, newly built and really state-of-the-art with all its amenities. Our room is very good, with a nice view of the sea.

We were somewhat disappointed that the hotel is not in the center of town, and we will have to take the bus when we want to visit historic and memorable parts. But other than that we are well pleased.

We completely unpacked for our stay here, and went to dinner in the dining room for a *really* lavish buffet. Ate too much.

Now we are ready to sleep and enjoy our first night here.

April 2, 2005 – Saturday

First full day in Dubrovnik.

Another good day. Sort of.

Day began with a bus tour of the old city. We were met by a man guide who took us on a 2½-hour walking tour.

Great old city. Narrow cobblestone streets. Many outstanding views and usual vistas of churches and municipal buildings. Good tour.

At about 11:00 a.m., both the tourists and the locals came out for outdoor morning break of coffee and other drinks. Many full little outdoor tables.

I withdrew 500 kunas from a local ATM machine. (About $86.) Unfortunately I failed to retrieve my Visa card. Spent several visits and phone calls trying to get my card "blocked" against unauthorized purchases. Finally successful (I hope) about 9:00 p.m.

Spent a good part of the afternoon writing another (and final) round of postcards.

[For] dinner we took the bus to a home-hosted dinner at a local farmhouse. It was a "fun" visit at a far out-of-town series of houses (3). Nice, cordial hospitality. Brandy and figs in the smokehouse. Afterward appetizers of prosciutto, olives, several kinds of cheese and pitcher of red wine.

Entree was a mixed grill of meats and boiled potatoes. Dessert was a rich slice of "flan."

A pleasant ride home and preparations for an early departure tomorrow.

April 3, 2005 – Sunday

Another outstandingly good day.
    Today was a full day optional trip to Montenegro.
    Began with departure by bus at 8:00.
    Beautifully perfect weather.
    All scenery throughout was beautiful.
    We crossed the border into Montenegro. A little checking by border personnel. Not troublesome. The scenery was beautiful throughout. Development in Montenegro seemed a little slower than Croatia and a little slow to get started.

One interesting feature of the environment was big, healthy palmetto trees growing in close proximity to many tall cypresses.

Our route took us beside a string of farm lakes that looked like a fjord. Gorgeous blue water with towering mountains above, some snow-capped.

Our first city of destination was the town of Kotor. There we visited a Roman Catholic Church followed by visit to the local Greek Orthodox church. (The two variants of faith exist side-by-side without violence.) Today the Roman Catholics here and worldwide elsewhere are observing the death yesterday of Pope John Paul II.

A ride of about a half hour took us to the town of Budva for a sumptuous five-course lunch at a sea-side restaurant.

After lunch we turned back to Dubrovnik for about 2½ hours including a short ferry ride.

The border crossing was a little troublesome. But only a short delay.

Back at the hotel we decided we didn't want to go downtown for dinner. Stayed at the hotel for cocktails, then à la carte at the dining room, which was expensive and only minimally good.

Back to our room by 9:00. Were interested in watching all the recognition and eulogies of the deceased pope.

April 4, 2005 – Monday

Another good day in Dubrovnik. Weather perfect.

This was the last day for those tour-group members who were not staying for the one-week extension.

A rep from Grand Circle came to the hotel to listen to feedback from the participants. Most of the comments were good—especially in regard to Biba the tour director and Dennis the driver. Major complaint was the music festival option in Opatija, which everyone agreed was a "bummer." Other complaints were mostly personal and minor.

Afterward another Grand Circle agent named Duran(?) [Goran] came and introduced himself. He promised to come back tomorrow at 10:00 to help us make plans for the coming week.

At 10:30 our group broke up, and our part of it went back to the Old City. Our primary tour consisted of walking the walk around the city. Impressive! Steep! Many steps, turns and ups and downs, but impressive view on every front. We made it about ¾ of the way around the city's outer walls and gave up and came down. (Most of the others continued to the end.)

By that time it was afternoon and we had lunch at Prego, a sidewalk cafe. Had pizza and beer.

After lunch we went to a down-town grocery store where I bought about $25 worth of snacks for the room (candy, nuts, chips, cheese and crackers).

The bus took us back to the hotel at 2:30. We spent the rest of the afternoon napping and resting.

At 6:00 p.m. our group gathered in the lobby for a farewell drink of wine. Everyone used that occasion to tip the tour director and driver. (For us $25 for Dennis, $50 for Biba.)

Then our bus took us to a nice restaurant in the Old City for a farewell dinner. Very nice. Champagne, wine, risotto, garden salad, roast chicken and veggies, and flan for dessert. Also expresso coffee for dessert, which is unusual in these parts.

Back at the hotel for emotional farewell partings and exchange of affection and good wishes.

(The departing group will leave early a.m. tomorrow. We can linger in bed for the first time.)

April 5, 2005 – Tuesday

A day of leisure in Dubrovnik.

Most of our group left early for home. We enjoyed the luxury of lingering in bed. Rose at about 8:00 a.m.

Early on we received the information on TV that UNC had won the national basketball championship. I was very pleased with that.

We met with our local Grand Circle agent at 10:00. He went over our options and planned activities for our time here. The overall program seems pretty good, but a number of options and activities are still up in the air.

The day started off warm and sunny, but clouded over by mid-afternoon.

Our GCT agent led us on a long walk downhill into the little suburban village. Pointed out a supermarket and recommended a drug store. We took the (long) walk back up the hill to our hotel. Tired. Rested.

At about 1:00 p.m. we ate a snack lunch in the room.

Rode the elevator down to the beach level. It is out of season now and nothing is going on. Will no doubt be a busy spot during the high season.

Rested and relaxed until about 3:30. Rode the city bus down into the Old City. (Fare is 8 kuna—about $1.50 each way.)

We shopped along the main street looking for ideas of gifts to take home. Found few.

Had a nice dinner near the boat dock. Relatively inexpensive and quite hospitable.

Rode the bus back to the hotel, arriving before 9:00.

April 6, 2005 – Wednesday

Another leisurely day on the trip extension.

Let ourselves sleep late (until 8:00 a.m.) then the usual buffet breakfast at the hotel. (The "continental breakfasts" at all the hotels are very lavish and superior.)

We met our GCT agent (Goran) at 10:00 a.m. He led us on a two-van trip to a spectacular vista of the city. (Very high.) Impressive view of the Old City and its many surroundings. It was the site of an old cable car terminus, now in ruins, the result of heavy bombardment of the city and its surroundings during the war.

Later Goran led us on a walking tour of some parts of the city that we had not seen: an exhibit of old culture—tools, costumes, and work arrangements.

Then a visit to a group of color photographs and a 20-minute movie depicting the violence and tragedy of the war—and its sometime[?] dissent by the Serbians, who felt that the film depicted them unfairly.

With Goran's help we located the spot for our "dine-around" dinner. Named "Maestoso." We plan to go there tomorrow.

Took the bus back to the hotel for a snack lunch in the hotel room.

Spent the afternoon in rest, relaxation and napping.

In the evening took the long walk down the hill to a nice dinner [at a restaurant] called Fellini, recommended by Goran.

Then the long walk uphill back to the hotel, arriving before 10:00 p.m.

April 7, 2005 – Thursday

Another leisurely day on the trip extension.

Weather continues beautiful. Slept late again.

After nice buffet breakfast met with our friends Frank and Dorrie Palledeane (he is an ex-football player from N. C. State).

Bus ride into town with the four of us. Went to the boat dock in the city. Had cappuccino while waiting for the ferry to depart.

Took the 11 a.m. ferry to the island of Locrin (Lokrum). About a 20-minute voyage. The island is a natural park treasure of the government with lots of trails and vistas and interesting spots to visit.

Had a picnic lunch at the shore with a beautiful vista of the blue Adriatic.

After lunch Frank and I hiked the woodland trail to the top of the island and the old fort.

For me this was a mistake! The trail was steep, rocky and long. I got thoroughly exhausted and depended upon Frank's cane to get me back down.

Jackie is quite angry with me for doing this, after I had promised not to do such things again.

Took the ferry back to the city about 3:00. In my exhaustion I sat at an outdoor cafe and nursed along a Coke for nearly a couple of hours.

Jackie went shopping, and found some interesting things.

At 6:00 p.m. we met with Frank and Dorrie for the "dine-around dinner." This one was at Maestoso. Friendly and with a nice atmosphere.

The food was moderately good. Three of us had steak; Jackie had fish.

After dinner we walked through the Old Town and back to the bus stop for the ride home.

Got back about 8:30. (Exhausted.)

April 8, 2005 – Friday

Another really restful, unstructured day in our extended visit to Dubrovnik.

Jackie and I slept really late and made it to the buffet breakfast about 9:30.

After breakfast we lazed in the room for a couple of hours, then took the city bus into the old city.

Had pizza for lunch at Prague. Bought some medication for the two of us. And a couple of pastries for dinner tonight.

Walked around the streets and shops and soon decided to return to our hotel in mid-afternoon.

More relaxing and resting in the light afternoon. Then snack dinner in the room. Now planning to go to the hotel for a cappuccino before bedtime.

(Today the pope was buried. All the news media, shops and elsewhere are filled with his photos, and all flags are at half-staff.)

April 9, 2005 – Saturday

This was a bad day, weatherwise and entertainment-wise.

The perfect weather we had been bragging about finally caught up with us, and it rained dismally all day. Abating a little later in the day.

The Adriatic

The usually serene Adriatic was sullen and rough today with heavy waves crushing roughly on the rocks.

Jackie and I have both contracted heavy colds—along with several others in our group. Sore throats, coughs, aches and the attendant ills. They are going away, but gradually, only gradually.

We had planned to take another boat ride today to some outlying island, but the sea was far too rough and the trip was canceled.

With a GCT agent we took a short walk through an open-air market, and also a mall department store. Both very tame and we soon took the local bus back to the hotel, where we spent the rest of the day.

Nothing special or even very interesting. Newspaper, TV, crossword and the like. Not uplifting,

In the early evening we ordered a small dinner from Room Service. It was different and pleasant, but really quite expensive.

It's 8:30 now, and we will now turn in with hope and expectation of a better day tomorrow.

April 10, 2005 – Sunday

This was our next-to-last night in Dalmatia and in some ways was the most satisfying of all.

All of yesterday's rain cleared up, and today was sunny, warm, and pleasant all day.

We joined up with another Grand Circle group for an included bus ride to several small villages in the southern-most part of Dalmatia.

First stop was at a fascinating old stone grist mill, 400 years or more old. Still in operation and we were given a demonstration of stone-grinding corn on old grind stones. Also a wonderful moss-covered overhead water wheel. They have trout in the mill race and ponds.

Afterward we went to another village and saw a *good* demonstration of folk-lore singing and dancing in authentic old costume.

For lunch we went to the town of Cavtat, which has a lovely waterfront and promenade. Lunch at an outdoor cafe. (I had a tuna fish sandwich and a banana split. Jackie had a ham and cheese sandwich.)

Back at the hotel we rested for about an hour and then took the bus back to the old city.

There was a concert in the Dubrovnik Theatre (smallish, but pretty).

It was a student performance of *The Fairy Queen,* based on Shakespeare's *Midsummer Night's Dream,* with music by Henry Purcell. It was amateurish, but sincere and pretty. We liked it. (Free.)

Then went shopping for souvenirs. Didn't buy much. I bought Jackie a Croatian charm for her bracelet.

For dinner we went to a somewhat upscale restaurant (don't remember the name). It was indoors with white table cloths and a friendly atmosphere. We had a nice salad of marinated anchovies. Jackie had a filet of red snapper. I had spaghetti calamari. (Both were very good.)

At 8:30 we attended a concert performance at the same Dubrovnik theatre. This one was a *very* good presentation with several groups of singers and musicians. All trained and enthusiastically prepared. The theatre was packed (sold out at 40 kn per head). Everyone was pleased with what we had seen.

Then we went to [get] the hotel van at the other end of the city. We had to wait a half hour for the last bus of the day (11:05 p.m.).

Arrived back at the hotel about 11:15.

April 11, 2005 – Monday

This is our last day before departure.

At Goran's suggestion we signed up for an impromptu dinner and visit in a village outside and above Dubrovnik.

The weather was beautiful in the morning, but turned ugly and rainy early on. It was raining hard at the time we departed the hotel at 4:00.

Our transportation, which Goran arranged, was one van and a taxi. Nine of us went along.

Our destination was a village about 20 miles northwest of Dubrovnik. We ascended to the village location by a series of hair-raising switchback turns several thousand feet above the Adriatic and high in the mountains.

The place where we ate was a restaurant complex which we were told was a really special place. Very stone-y, ancient and old fashioned.

We were taken there to experience several regional meat specialties. We had lamb, goat, and wild boar. I tasted all of these but didn't like many. Also roast potatoes and gnocchi. Also prosciutto, several kinds of cheese and local white wine. It was a real dining experience, moderately priced. Jackie ate and drank her share, but I was disappointed.

The ride down was by the same series of turns and descents. Back to the hotel to pack for early tomorrow.

Kern and Jackie continued to travel when they could, despite increasing challenges of mobility. Their last cruise together appears to have been in December 2009, when they sailed from San Diego to Hawaii and back, expecting to stay onboard ship for the entire journey. Before embarking, they had Kate and David Klein to an elegant dinner at the Hotel del Coronado. Dad complained that he couldn't get mint jelly for his lamb chop.

www.ingramcontent.com/pod-product-compliance
Lightning Source LLC
Chambersburg PA
CBHW030255100526
44590CB00012B/404